William Faulkner

The Sound and the Fury
As I Lay Dying

EDITED BY NICOLAS TREDELL

Consultant editor: Nicolas Tredell

D1494294

Published in 1999 by Icon Books Ltd.,
Grange Road, Duxford, Cambridge CB2 4QF
e-mail: icon@mistral.co.uk
www.iconbooks.co.uk

Distributed in the UK, Europe, Canada, South Africa and Asia by the
Penguin Group: Penguin Books Ltd., 27 Wrights Lane, London W8 5TZ

Published in Australia in 1999 by Allen & Unwin Pty. Ltd.,
PO Box 8500, 9 Atchison Street, St. Leonards, NSW 2065

Consultant editor: Nicolas Tredell
Series devised by: Christopher Cox
Cover design: Christos Kondeatis
Typesetting: Wayzgoose

ISBN 1 84046 079 2

Printed and bound in Great Britain by
Cox & Wyman Ltd., Reading

Contents

T. Irwin's compelling study *Doubling and Incest/Repetition and Revenge*, which sees Quentin Compson as Narcissus and fascinatingly relates his obsessions to incest and to miscegenation, the mixing of races.

Division, Death and Desire: Race and Form in Faulkner in the 1980s

Examines crucial rereadings of Faulkner during the transformation of literary studies in the USA and UK in the 1980s. Discusses Eric J. Sundquist's bracing challenge to the critical 'myth' of *The Sound and the Fury*, and his now-classic analysis of *As I Lay Dying* as an example of 'analogous form'. Considers the fertile and wide-ranging interpretation of *The Sound and the Fury*, bringing together issues of structure, style, race and history, in James A. Snead's major study *Figures of Division*.

Mothers, Signifyin(g) Monkeys, and Significant Eyes: *The Sound and the Fury* and *As I Lay Dying* in the 1990s

Discusses exciting accounts of *The Sound and the Fury* and *As I Lay Dying* produced in the critically diverse 1990s. Considers Deborah Clarke's challenging analysis of the significance of mothers in *The Sound and the Fury* and *As I Lay Dying*; examines William Dahill-Baue's provocative essay on race and language in Faulkner and Toni Morrison in relation to the 'Signifyin(g) Monkey'; and explores Candace Waid's insightful and ingenious discussion of art, gender and the pictorial in *As I Lay Dying*.

A NOTE ON REFERENCES AND QUOTATIONS

Cross-references to the extracts in this Guide, and page references to *The Sound and the Fury* and *As I Lay Dying*, are included in the brackets in the text of the Guide. All other references are given in endnotes.

All page references to *The Sound and the Fury* are to the 1995 Vintage UK edition and all page references to *As I Lay Dying* are to the 1996 Vintage UK edition. These are the most recent and most easily available paperback editions in the UK.

In the extracts in this Guide, insertions by the editor are in square brackets and standard type. Definitions of words, where provided in editorial insertions, have been taken from the *Concise Oxford Dictionary*, unless otherwise stated in the endnotes. Insertions in square brackets and bold type in the extracts are by the authors of the extracts themselves.

In any quotation, a row of three dots indicates an editorial ellipsis within a sentence or paragraph, and a row of six dots (that is, two ellipses) indicates an editorial omission of a paragraph break, or of one or more paragraphs.

INTRODUCTION

THE SOUND and the Fury (1929) and As I Lay Dying (1930) are two of
William Faulkner's most powerful novels, and they have often been
felt to have much in common beyond the fact of their consecutive publication. Both are carnivals of language that create a multiplicity of voices;
both are boldly experimental in their structures; both engage unflinch-
ingly with fundamentals – birth, sexuality and death – and both explore
the dreams, nightmares and realities of the American South. Both offer a
rich range of characters, a copious supply of anecdotes, and an overall
narrative, which at first seems difficult to disentangle but which amply
rewards the attentive reader. Modernist and traditional, American and
European, regional and universal, these two novels seem to combine all
the resources available to the writer of fiction in the late 1920s and to
invent new ones. But despite their many similarities, *The Sound and
the Fury* and *As I Lay Dying* also have crucial differences: each holds a key
place in the whole body of Faulkner's work and in the high echelons
of twentieth-century fiction; but each does so in ways that are distinctive. This Guide explores the critical history of both works, sometimes
taking them together, sometimes considering each separately. In this
Introduction *The Sound and the Fury* and *As I Lay Dying* are set in the context of Faulkner's life and work and the criticism offered in the Guide is
outlined.

William Cuthbert Falkner – he would insert the 'u' into his surname
in 1918[1] – was born in New Albany, Mississippi on 25 September 1897,
the first of four sons. His great-grandfather, William C. Falkner, the 'Old
Colonel', had a quasi-mythic status in the family history: he was a
foundling who had raised himself to prosperity and Southern renown by
becoming a lawyer, a soldier in the Mexican War and in the American
Civil War, and a local land speculator, politician and entrepreneur who
founded a railroad. As Joel Williamson points out in *William Faulkner and
Southern History* (1993), 'contrary to popular myth, [Falkner] was never a
great slaveholding planter',[2] but he did own several slaves and, according
to Williamson, may have had a mulatto family, a 'shadow' family to his
white wife and children.[3] The 'Old Colonel' was also, anticipating his
famous great-grandson, a writer of poetry and fiction whose novel *The*

White Rose of Memphis (1881) sold 160,00 copies.[4] But violence marked his life; as well as serving in two wars, he had twice killed men in times of peace: he stabbed Robert Hindman to death in 1849 and fatally shot Erasmus W. Morris in 1850; on each occasion, he was indicted for murder but acquitted. And the 'Old Colonel''s own end was bloody: on 5 November 1889, Richard Thurmond, a former business partner, shot him in the head and he died the next morning. Fa(u)lkner's grandfather, John Wesley Thompson Falkner, was a lawyer, political campaign manager, banker and administrator of the 'Old Colonel''s railroad, but he sold the railroad before his son Murry Cuthbert Falkner, William Fa(u)lkner's father, could inherit it. This was one of the misfortunes that marked Murry's life; his career was undistinguished and he was not a fulfilled man. It would be up to his eldest son to revive the spirit of his ancestors.

By the time William Fa(u)lkner was five, his family had settled in Oxford in Mississippi, which would be Fa(u)lkner's base for most of his life. In 1914, he formed an important friendship with his fellow-townsman Phil Stone, a Yale graduate who influenced his reading, which included the poetry of Keats and Swinburne, the fiction of Joseph Conrad, and the work of the American writers Sherwood Anderson – to whom Faulkner would dedicate his third novel, *Sartoris* (1929) – and Conrad Aiken – whose essay 'William Faulkner: The Novel as Form', an extract from which appears in this Guide (see pp. 46–48), helped to make 1939, as O.B. Emerson says, 'a turning point in Faulkner's career'.[5] In 1916, he began to contribute to student publications of the University of Mississippi. After America entered the First World War in 1917, he tried to enlist in the U.S. Air Corps the following year, but at five feet five-and-a-half inches,[6] he was too short, and underweight.[7] He finally joined the Royal Air Force of Canada and began training in Toronto in July 1918; it was at this stage of his life that he started to spell his surname as 'Faulkner' rather than 'Falkner'. But the war ended before he saw action.

He returned to Oxford, where he continued to contribute to student publications and wrote a play called *The Marionettes*, which he printed and bound by hand, for the University of Mississipi drama group of that name.[8] On 15 December 1924,[9] largely thanks to Phil Stone's efforts, the Four Seas Company of Boston published a collection of Faulkner's poems, *The Marble Faun*, with an introduction by Stone. It did not attract much attention. But Faulkner's first two novels, *Soldiers' Pay* (1927) and *Mosquitoes* (1927) were quite well received; he was seen as a writer of promise. In 1928, he completed *Flags in the Dust*, in which he invented the fictional county of Yoknapatawpha, which was to provide the setting of most of his subsequent novels. He had a three-book contract with Boni and Liveright,[10] who had published his first two novels, but they rejected his third. Further rejections apparently made him feel that he should write what he wanted without worrying about publication: in one of his drafts of an introduction written for a proposed 1933 Modern Library edition of *The Sound and the Fury*, which never appeared, he recalled: 'When I began The Sound and The Fury, I had no plan at all. I wasn't even writing a book . . . I was thinking of books, publication, only in the sense, in saying to myself, I wont have to worry about publishers liking or not liking this at all' [title unitalicised and 'wont' written without apostrophe in original].[11]

Phil Stone later recalled that Faulkner only told him about *The Sound and the Fury* when he had finished it. He remembered that Faulkner then read it aloud to him 'night after night in Bill's little room in the little tower of the old Delta Psi chapter house'.[12] Meanwhile, Faulkner's New York agent and friend, Ben Wasson, had been trying to find a publisher for *Flags in the Dust*, and, in September, Harcourt, Brace agreed to take it provided that it was cut; Wasson undertook this task, as Faulkner refused to have anything to do with it.[13] In September, Faulkner set off to New York, where, according to Wasson, he typed the final version of *The Sound and the Fury*, adding by hand, at the end of the carbon copy: 'New York, N.Y. 1 October 1928'. He then gave the typescript to Wasson, saying: 'Read this, Bud. It's a real sonofabitch'.[14]

Faulkner returned home to Oxford in December 1928 and began to write *Sanctuary* early in 1929. In February 1929, the shortened version of *Flags in the Dust* appeared under the title of *Sartoris*. The new novel sold badly, and the few reviews were lukewarm.[15] It also looked as if *The Sound and the Fury* would be difficult to place: Harcourt, Brace rejected it. But Harrison Smith, a former editor at Harcourt, Brace who had helped to persuade the firm to accept *Sartoris*, had set himself up as a publisher with Jonathan Cape and he was sympathetic to Faulkner's work; he decided his new firm would publish *The Sound and the Fury*. It appeared on 7 October 1929 in an edition of 1789 copies.[16]

Meanwhile, on 20 June 1929, Faulkner had married Estelle Oldham, a divorcee with two small children; they had been close since early adolescence. The marriage put pressure on him to earn money, and in the autumn of 1929 he started to work night shifts at the power plant of the University of Mississippi, not as a 'coal heaver'[17] but as a night supervisor – the physical labour that he claimed to have carried out himself was in fact performed by two male African Americans.[18] On 25 October 1929 – four days before the Wall Street Crash – Faulkner began *As I Lay Dying*,[19] completing the manuscript in 47 days: the finish date on page 107 reads: 'Oxford, Miss./11 December, 1929'.[20] He then typed it up, making some revisions as he went along, and dated the finished typescript 'January 12, 1930'.[21] Cape and Smith brought out *As I Lay Dying* on 6 October 1930 in an edition of 2522 copies.[22]

This Guide traces the critical fortunes of *The Sound and the Fury* and *As*

I Lay Dying from their first appearance to the 1990s. The first chapter provides an extract from Evelyn Scott's pamphlet, which was issued along with *The Sound and the Fury* on its first publication, and discusses and quotes from a range of early reviews of *The Sound and the Fury* and *As I Lay Dying* in the USA and the UK, indicating how the first reviewers raised questions that would continue, in different idioms and with greater or lesser degrees of intellectual sophistication, to preoccupy subsequent generations of critics. The chapter then moves on to consider essays by Conrad Aiken, George Marion O'Donnell, Malcolm Cowley, Robert Penn Warren and Laurence E. Bowling that were crucial in developing Faulkner's reputation from the end of the 1930s to the end of the 1940s. But in 1950, when it was announced that Faulkner had won the 1949 Nobel Prize for Literature, no book on his work had yet appeared and critics had to make up for lost time. Chapter two of this Guide discusses and provides extracts from the analyses of *The Sound and the Fury* and *As I Lay Dying* in four major studies of the 1950s and 1960s, by Irving Howe, Olga W. Vickery, Cleanth Brooks and Michael Millgate. By the 1970s, Faulkner criticism was well-established, but had perhaps tamed the furies of Faulkner's texts too fully. Chapter three of this Guide therefore focuses on two key critics whose soundings began to arouse those furies from the deep. One is André Bleikasten, a leading French Faulkner critic of sound scholarship and profound sensibility who had already been brushed by the great wings of structuralism and post-structuralism and whose important books on *As I Lay Dying* and on *The Sound and the Fury* came out in English translation in the 1970s; and John T. Irwin, whose *Doubling and Incest/Repetition and Revenge: A Speculative Reading of Faulkner* (1975) quickly established itself as a critical classic. In the 1980s, Faulkner's representations of history and of race came under closer scrutiny than ever before, especially in two major studies: Eric Sundquist's *Faulkner: The House Divided* (1983) and James A. Snead's *Figures of Division: William Faulkner's Major Novels* (1988). Chapter four provides extracts from Sundquist's discussion of *The Sound and the Fury* – which, among other things, raises bracing questions about the pre-eminence that novel has often enjoyed – and from his analysis of 'analogous form' in *As I Lay Dying*, which, like Irwin's study, soon came to be regarded as a landmark in Faulkner criticism. This is followed by Snead's lucid, learned and richly provocative analysis of *The Sound and the Fury* as an exploration – and subversion – of racism. The final chapter of this Guide includes extracts from Deborah Clarke's challenging analysis of *The Sound and the Fury* and *As I Lay Dying* in her important feminist study, *Robbing the Mother: Women in Faulkner* (1994); a segment of William Dahill-Baue's controversial essay on race and language in Faulkner and Toni Morrison in which he draws on Henry Louis Gates, Jr's discussion of the 'Signifyin(g) Monkey'; and Candace Waid's keenly perceptive exploration of art, gender and the pictorial in *The Sound and the Fury* and *As I Lay Dying*.

To lose oneself in the labyrinths of *The Sound and the Fury* and *As I Lay Dying*, whether for the first or the fiftieth time, is a disturbing and exhilarating experience. The maps, torches and Ariadne's threads of the best criticism do not seek to rob the reader of that disturbance and exhilaration; indeed, they should, in some ways, deepen her or his perplexity and pleasure. But they can offer provisional routes, momentary illuminations, fragile means of retracing our steps, venturing into obscure corridors, and moving forward. This is what the criticism in this Guide aims to provide: a series of suggestions, insights and indicators that will help us to navigate Faulkner's labyrinths and to emerge with a richly enhanced understanding of the styles, structures and multiple meanings of two of his greatest works.

CHAPTER ONE

Trying to Say: Critical Responses to *The Sound and the Fury* and *As I Lay Dying* 1929–49

IN THE critical debates about *The Sound and the Fury*, Cape and Smith, its New York publishers, cast the first stone. To coincide with the appearance of Faulkner's new work in October 1929, they issued a pamphlet about it by Evelyn Scott in a 'limited' edition of 1,000 copies – a print run that was, in fact, quite close to that of the novel itself, of which 1789 copies were initially produced. The pamphlet developed from a letter Scott had written to Cape and Smith after reading *The Sound and the Fury* in manuscript. At that time Scott, a poet and novelist from Tennessee, was a better-known writer than Faulkner; her novel of the American Civil War, *The Wave* (1929), had been Cape and Smith's first publication and had enjoyed commercial and critical success. Scott's pamphlet provided a means of promoting Faulkner and Scott as novelists, and Cape and Smith as a new publishing house. A note at the front of the pamphlet claimed that *The Wave* had placed Scott 'among the outstanding literary figures of our time' and said that her account of *The Sound and the Fury* was 'being distributed to those who are interested in Miss Scott's work and the writing of William Faulkner. *The Sound and the Fury* should place William Faulkner in company with Evelyn Scott. The publishers believe, in the issuance of this little book, that a valuable and brilliant reflection of the philosophies of two important American authors is presented to those who care for such things'.[1] Scott's pamphlet constitutes the first significant public explication of, and critical response to, *The Sound and the Fury*. As the following extract shows, she makes high claims for the novel's achievement, which rest centrally on her definitions of it as a tragedy and as an affirmation of mankind:

■ ... I want to write something about *The Sound and the Fury* before the fanfare in print can greet even the ears of the author. There will be many, I am sure, who, without this assistance, will make the discovery of the book as an important contribution to the permanent literature of fiction. I shall be pleased, however, if some others, lacking the opportunity for investigating individually the hundred claims to greatness which America makes every year in the name of art, may be led, through these comments, to a perusal of this unique and distinguished novel. The publishers, who are so much to be congratulated for presenting a little known writer with the dignity of recognition which his talent deserves, call this book 'overwhelmingly powerful and even monstrous'. Powerful it is; and it may even be described as 'monstrous' in all its implications of tragedy; but such tragedy has a noble essence.

The question has been put by a contemporary critic, a genuine philosopher reviewing the arts, as to whether there exists for this age of disillusion with religion, dedication to the objective programme of scientific inventiveness and general rejection of the teleology ['teleology' is the view that developments are due to the purpose, design or end that is served by them] which placed man emotionally at the center of the universe, the spirit of which great tragedy is the expression. *The Sound and the Fury* seems to me to offer a reply. Indeed I feel that however sophistical the argument of theology, man remains, in his heart, in that important position. What he seeks now is a fresh justification for the presumption of his emotions; and his present tragedy is in a realization of the futility, up to date, of his search for another, intellectually appropriate embodiment of the god that lives on, however contradicted by 'reason'.

William Faulkner, the author of this tragedy, which has all the spacious proportions of Greek art, may not consider his book in the least expressive of the general dilemma to which I refer, but that quality in his writings which the emotionally timid will call 'morbid', seems to me reflected from the impression, made on a sensitive and normally egoistic nature, of what is in the air. Too proud to solve the human problem evasively through any of the sleight-of-hand of puerile [childish, trivial] surface optimism, he embraces, to represent life, figures that do indeed symbolize a kind of despair; but not the despair that depresses or frustrates. His pessimism as to fact, and his acceptance of all the morally inimical possibilities of human nature, is unwavering. The result is, nonetheless, the reassertion of humanity in defeat that is, in the subjective sense, a triumph. This is no Pyrrhic victory made in debate with those powers of intelligence that may be used to destroy [a Pyrrhic victory is one gained at too great a cost, like that of Pyrrhus, King of Epirus, over the Romans at Asculum in 279 BC²].

It is the conquest of nature by art. Or rather, the refutation, by means of a work of art, of the belittling of the materialists; and the work itself is in that category of facts which popular scientific thinking has made an ultimate. Here is beauty sprung from the perfect *realization* of what a more limiting morality would describe as ugliness. Here is a humanity stripped of most of what was claimed for it by the Victorians, and the spectacle is moving as no sugar-coated drama ever could be. The result for the reader, if he is like myself, is an exaltation of faith in mankind. It is faith without, as yet, an argument; but it is the same faith which has always lived in the most ultimate expression of the human spirit.

The Sound and the Fury is the story of the fall of a house, the collapse of a provincial aristocracy in a final debacle of insanity, recklessness, psychological perversion. The method of presentation is, as far as I know, unique. Book I is a statement of the tragedy as seen through the eyes of a thirty-three-year-old idiot son of the house, Benjy. Benjy is beautiful, as beautiful as one of the helpless angels, and the more so for the slightly repellent earthiness that is his. He is a better idiot than Dostoevsky's [that is, than Prince Myshkin, the central character in Dostoevsky's novel *The Idiot* (1868)] because his simplicity is more convincingly united with the basic animal simplicity of creatures untried by the standards of a conscious and calculating humanity. It is as if, indeed, Blake's Tiger had been framed before us by the same Hand that made the Lamb, and, in opposition to Blake's conception, endowed with the same soul [Scott's reference is to the poem 'The Tyger' by the Romantic poet William Blake (1757–1827); this begins: 'Tyger, Tyger burning bright/In the forests of the night/What immortal hand or eye/Could frame thy fearful symmetry' and asks, in its penultimate stanza: 'Did He who made the lamb make thee?'.[3] Scott's linking of Faulkner with Blake, and her suggestion that Faulkner, in the portrayal of Benjy, fuses what Blake left distinct, could work to enhance Faulkner's status in a later twentieth-century cultural context in which Blake would be revalued as a proto-Modernist poet aware of, and seeking to heal, splits in the human psyche]. Innocence is terrible as well as pathetic – and Benjy is terrible, sometimes terrifying. He is a Christ symbol, yet not, even in the way of the old orthodoxies, Christly. A Jesus asks for a conviction of sin and a confession before redemption. He acknowledges this as in his own history, tempting by the Devil the prelude to his renunciation. In every subtle sense, sin is the desire to sin, the awareness of sin, an assertion in innuendo that, by the very statement of virtue, sin *is*. Benjy is no saint with a wounded ego his own gesture can console. He is not anything – nothing with a name. He is alive. He can suffer. The simplicity of his suffering, the absence, for him, of any compensating sense of drama, leave him as naked of self-flattery as was the first man. Benjy is like Adam, with all he remembers in the garden and one foot in hell on earth. This was where knowledge began, and for Benjy time is too early for any spurious profiting by knowledge. It is a little as if the story of Han[s] Andersen's Little Mermaid had been taken away from the nursery and sentiment and made rather diabolically to grow up. [In the Hans Andersen fairy tale, the Little Mermaid wishes to become human so that she can marry the prince she loves and thus gain an immortal soul; she obtains a potion from a sea-witch that will make her human, but she has to pay for the potion with her voice – the witch cuts out the Little Mermaid's tongue so that, like Benjy, she is dumb. The witch has warned her that if the prince marries someone else, she will never gain an immortal soul and will die the morning after his marriage – but when he does finally marry another woman, the Little Mermaid, because of her spiritual striving, is allowed to join the daughters of the air and given the chance to create an immortal soul for herself by good deeds.[4]] Here is the Little Mermaid on the way to find her soul in an uncouth and incontinent body – but there is no happy ending. Benjy, born male and made neuter, doesn't want a soul. It is being thrust upon him, but only like a horrid bauble which he does not recognize. He holds in his hands – in his heart, exposed to the reader – something frightening, unnamed – *pain*! Benjy lives deeply in the senses. For the remainder of what he sees as life, he lives as crudely as in allegory, vicariously, through uncritical perception of his adored sister (she smells to him like 'leaves' (p.4)) and, in such emotional absolutism, traces for us her broken marriage, her departure forever from an unlovely home, her return by proxy in the person of her illegitimate daughter, Quentin, who, for Benjy, takes the mother's place.

Book II of the novel deals with another – the original Quentin, for whom the baby girl of later events is named. This section, inferior, I think, to the Benjy motive ['motive' is perhaps being used here in the sense of 'motif' to mean a distinctive feature in a literary composition], though fine in part, describes in the terms of free association with which Mr. [James] Joyce is recreating vocabularies, the final day in this life of Quentin, First [as distinct from Quentin, Second, that is, Caddy's illegitimate daughter], who is contemplating suicide. Quentin is a student at Harvard at the time, the last wealth of the family – some property that has been nominally Benjy's having been sold to provide him with an education. Quentin is oversensitive, introvert, pathologically devoted to his sister, and his determination to commit suicide is his protest against her disgrace.

In Book III we see the world in terms of the petty, sadistic lunacy of Jason; Jason, the last son of the family, the stay-at-home, the failure, clerking [working as a shop assistant] in a country store, for whom no

Harvard education was provided. William Faulkner has that general perspective in viewing particular events which lifts the specific incident to the dignity of catholic [in the sense of 'universal'] significance, while all the vividness of an unduplicable personal drama is retained. He senses the characteristic compulsions to action that make a fate. Jason is a devil. Yet, since the author has compelled you to the vision of the gods, he is a devil whom you compassionate [used here as a verb, to mean 'regard with compassion']. Younger than the other brothers, Jason, in his twenties, is tyrannically compensating for the sufferings of jealousy by persecution of his young niece, Caddie's [sic] daughter, Quentin, by petty thievery, by deception practiced against his weak mother, by meanest torment of that marvellously accurately conceived young negro, Luster, keeper, against all his idle, pleasure-loving inclination, of the witless Benjy. Jason is going mad. He knows it – not as an intellectual conclusion, for he holds up all the emotional barriers against reflection and self-investigation. Jason knows madness as Benjy knows the world and the smell of leaves and the leap of the fire in the grate and the sounds of himself, his own howls, when Luster teases him. Madness for Jason is a blank, immediate state of soul, which he feels encroaching on his meager, objectively considered universe. He is in an agony of inexplicable anticipation of disaster for which his cruelties afford him no relief.

The last Book is told in the third person by the author. In its pages we are to see this small world of failure in its relative aspect. Especial privilege, we are allowed to meet face to face, Dilsey, the old colored woman, who provides the beauty of coherence against the background of struggling choice. Dilsey isn't searching for a soul. She *is* the soul. She is the conscious human accepting the limitations of herself, the iron boundaries of circumstance, and still, to the best of her ability, achieving a holy compromise for aspiration.

People seem very frequently to ask of a book a 'moral'. There is no moral statement in *The Sound and the Fury*, but moral conclusions can be drawn from it as surely as from 'life', because, as fine art, it is life organized to make revelation fuller. Jason is, in fair measure, the young South, scornful of outworn tradition, scornful indeed of all tradition, as of the ideal which has betrayed previous generations to the hope of perfection. He, Jason, would tell you, as so many others do today, that he sees things 'as they are'. There is no 'foolishness' about him, no 'bunk'. A spade is a spade, as unsuggestive as things must be in an age which prizes radios and motor cars not as means, but as ends for existence. You have 'got to show him'. Where there is proof in dollars and cents, or what they can buy, there is nothing. Misconceiving even biology, Jason would probably regard individualism of a crass order as according to nature. Jason is a martyr. He is a completely rational being. There is something exquisitely stupid in this degree of commonsense which cannot grasp the fact that ratiocination [logical, formal reasoning] cannot proceed without presumptions made on the emotional acceptance of a state antedating reason. Jason argues, as it were, from nothing to nothing. In this *reductio ad absurdum* [reduction to absurdity] he annihilates himself, even his vanity. And he runs amok, with his conclusion that one gesture is as good as another, that there is only drivelling self-deception to juxtapose to his tin-pot Nietzscheanism – actually the most romantic attitude of all.

But there is Dilsey, without so much as a theory to controvert theory, stoic as some immemorial carving of heroism, going on, doing the best she can, guided only by instinct and affection and the self-respect she will not relinquish – the ideal of herself to which she conforms irrationally, which makes of her life something whole, while her 'white folks' accept their fragmentary state, disintegrate. And she recovers for us the spirit of tragedy which the patter of cynicism has often made seem lost.[5] □

Scott's pamphlet offers several topics that will be significant for reviewers and future critics of *The Sound and the Fury* (whether or not they derive those topics directly from Scott). There is the notion of the novel as a tragedy of ancient Greek proportions; the sense that it is a kind of religious work for a non-religious age; the view of Benjy as resembling to some degree the Dostoevskyan idiot or Blakean innocent but improving on them because of his animality, his terrible and sometimes terrifying quality; the idea of Benjy as a new, unorthodox kind of Christ symbol; the likening of the technique used to represent Quentin's final day to the technique of James Joyce; the interpretation of Jason as sociologically representative of 'the young South' and philosophically representative of complete rationality; the commendation of the accuracy of the representation of Luster; and the elevation of Dilsey to a holy and heroic stature. Scott also provides a clear explication of some of the important but potentially confusing details of *The Sound and the Fury* (for example, that there are two Quentins, the suicidal son and the illegitimate granddaughter).

The issue of such a pamphlet suggests, however, that the publishers of *The Sound and the Fury* were concerned about the reception of Faulkner's fourth novel – Harrison Smith knew, of course, that it had been rejected by the firm for which he had previously worked, Harcourt, Brace. How did the first reviewers of *The Sound and the Fury* respond? Frances Lamont Robbins, in the *Outlook and Independent* of 16 October 1929, offered a balanced appraisal of what is, as she acknowledges, the first of Faulkner's novels that she has read; she thus relates it, not to

Faulkner's earlier work, but, like Evelyn Scott, to the work of James Joyce, contending at the start of her review that, '[j]udging from *The Sound and the Fury*', Faulkner is 'Joyce's most able and most consistent American disciple'. Faulkner and Joyce are linked by the 'discontinuity' of their presentation and by their 'search for a clear way to investigate and express the broken motive patterns of human behaviour'. The American writer is, however, 'by no means a slavish imitator of Joyce's style, and only in the second section of *The Sound and the Fury* does his effort to follow it seem labored and unoriginal'.

Robbins calls *The Sound and the Fury* 'a tragedy of disintegration' and defines this 'disintegration' partly in racial terms. It is a 'spectacle of white disintegration' in which a 'southern family of gentle blood is shown in decay' and contrasted with 'the full-living wholeness of their Negroes' – although Robbins feels this contrast suggests 'a second theme' that is 'too faintly expressed to be clear'. She judges that Faulkner 'has strong creative talent, and is richly sensitive to poetic emotion', and finds *The Sound and the Fury* 'a novel of power and of terrible sincerity'. But Faulkner's work is 'still no more than an exciting promise' and displays three major flaws: an excessive 'juvenile preoccupation with the *melodramatic* aspects of tragedy' (Robbins's italics); too great a 'distrust of familiar values', a distrust that 'characterizes the work of so many writers of the present generation and limits their understanding of life'; and a method of presentation that, because it relies mainly on 'subjective analysis', robs the novel's 'dramatic and potentially moving' theme of 'much of its force and clarity'.[6]

In contrast to Robbins's stress on the subjective element in *The Sound and the Fury*, the anonymous writer in *The New York Times Book Review* found that the novel had an 'objective quality' that 'save[d] it from complete morbidity', despite an 'array of characters, which bids fair to out-Russian the Russians'. Like Scott and Robbins, the reviewer invokes Joyce, recalling the review reception of Faulkner's first novel, *Soldier's Pay*, when critics had felt that here was a writer who was 'undeniably worth watching' but who had 'a rather uncertain style, sometimes original, sometimes imitative of the school of James Joyce'. In subsequent works, Faulkner's style became 'no less promising' but 'no more settled', prompting the question: 'Has he a style or hasn't he?'. *The Sound and the Fury* did not settle the question, because it was a novel in which Faulkner used four styles: nonetheless, these were 'welded together in perfect unity' and helped to achieve the 'objectiv[ity]' of the novel.[7]

In *The Saturday Review of Literature* for 28 December 1928, Basil Davenport judged *The Sound and the Fury* 'original and impressive'. Categorising it as 'a new departure in the stream-of-consciousness school', Davenport finds it has 'a plainer architecture than . . . most books of this kind, a steady progression from fantasy to fact, and a steady movement toward externality and away from emotion'. This produces the sense of a constantly deepening tragedy 'of the kind that has appeared in literature almost within the memory of man, that of frustration, futility, imprisoned monotony'.[8] Davenport sees every character in this novel as affected by a 'mortal stupor' that, in one way or another, prevents each of them 'from really suffering from events':[9]

■ If only one of them could feel sharp pain at anything, there would be hope or at least exaltation; but there is only a dull resentment of the life narrowing and hardening around them. The last incident [in the novel] is trivial but terrifying: Benjy is taken for his usual drive, but because they pass the monument on the right instead of the left, he bellows in wordless rage till they go back and take the unalterable way.[10] □

Davenport highlights Faulkner's 'remarkable knack of opening a vista of horror with a single sentence' and suggests that '[h]is power is shown almost as much by what he does without as what he uses'. He claims, questionably, that Faulkner, for the most part, 'rigorously denies himself humor and tenderness' because 'they would be in his way', but concludes that the novelist is 'a man to watch'.[11]

Henry Nash Smith's account of *The Sound and the Fury* in the *Southwest Review*, under the heading 'Three Southern Novels', engages with the issue of the relationship between the provincial and the universal in Faulkner's work – a question that would clearly become of importance to a mid-twentieth-century literary criticism that required its great writers to be 'universal'. Smith poses two questions: does a provincial setting make a book a provincial piece of writing, and what are the characteristics of a provincial style? In the extract below, Smith first affirms the universal greatness of parts of *The Sound and the Fury*, and he does so, significantly, by comparing Faulkner to one of the great founding fathers of English literature – and a poet – Geoffrey Chaucer (about 1343–1400):

■ No matter how universal the standard, there are certain pages in this novel which are very near great literature. I refer, for instance, to the character of Jason Compson, Senior, in which the typical citizen of a decadent aristocracy is merged with – perhaps grows out of – an intensely individual delineation. They praise Chaucer for taking a stock character like Criseyda and, without losing typical traits, making her a person; for writing that half-allegory, half-comedy, the *Nonne Preestes Tale* [*The Nun's Priest's Tale*, from Chaucer's *The Canterbury Tales* (about 1387)], in which a remarkable verisimilitude alternates with the complete fantasy of the beast fable as colors play back and forth with the shifting light on changeable silk. In both of these respects *The*

Sound and the Fury will easily bear comparison with the verses of the fat customs officer himself.

From another 'universal' standpoint – the traditional definition of tragedy – Faulkner's achievement is also remarkable. Pity and fear are not often more poignantly aroused than they are in the scene where Candace Compson stands cursing her brother for the devil he is. The subject, too, is of an imposing magnitude; for as the story spreads its fragments before the reader there emerges the spectacle of a civilization uprooted and left to die. Scope such as this is not usual in American novels. [By 'the traditional definition of tragedy', Smith means that of the ancient Greek philosopher Aristotle (384–322 BC) in his *Poetics* (date unknown): 'Tragedy . . . is a representation of an action that is worth serious attention, complete in itself, and of some amplitude; in language enriched by a variety of artistic devices appropriate to the several parts of the play; presented in the form of action, not narration; by means of pity and fear bringing about the purgation of such emotions'[12] (that is, tragedy, by arousing pity and fear, drives out pity and fear).]

Faulkner's handling of the tradition of the Old South, nevertheless, is distinctly related to provincialism. He has realized minutely and understandingly a given milieu and a given tradition – to all intents and purposes, the milieu of Oxford, Mississippi, where the author has lived most of his life, and the tradition of the ante-bellum aristocracy ['ante-bellum' means 'occurring or existing before a . . . war', especially – and certainly in the context of Faulkner – the American Civil War of 1861–65]. He has avoided the mere sophistication which sometimes is evident in his earlier novels, and is certainly at the farthest remove from a metropolitan smartness. That he has borrowed the stream-of-consciousness technique from Europe seems to me of minor importance: to say the least, he has modified it to his own use and has refused to be tyrannized by conventions, even the conventions of revolt.

In short, by the only definition that means very much, Mr. Faulkner is a provincial writer. He belongs to the South, if not to the Southwest. Though he is not a folklorist, though he is more concerned with life than with regionalism, his book has shown unguessed possibilities in the treatment of provincial life without loss of universality.[13] □

Smith's review outlines a repertoire of themes that will recur and be elaborated in later twentieth-century criticism of Faulkner. Faulkner's status is mightily raised by Smith's comparison of him to Chaucer and by his suggestion that *The Sound and the Fury* meets Aristotle's criteria for classical tragedy because it deals with a large subject in a way that arouses pity and fear. In view of the Shakespearean echo of the title of Faulkner's novel, the idea that *The Sound and the Fury* is a tragedy could also be taken to imply a comparison between Faulkner and Shakespeare. Faulkner achieves a 'magnitude' and 'scope' unusual in American fiction. His provincialism has not prevented him from being 'universal' but it has distanced him from 'a metropolitan smartness', and his unusualness in the context of the American novel has not involved a slavishness to the practice of the European avant-garde: he may have borrowed the 'stream-of-consciousness' techniques from Europe but he has changed them to suit himself. Faulkner is both provincial and universal; he escapes 'metropolitan smartness' and 'mere sophistication'; he escapes the limitations of much American fiction but is not subservient to Europe; he can deploy avant-garde techniques but remains his own man.

Harry Hansen, in the New York *World* of 9 October 1929, was more sceptical of large claims for Faulkner. Asserting that, for many readers, *The Sound and the Fury* would be 'as incoherent as James Joyce', Hansen welcomes the clarification provided by Evelyn Scott's pamphlet as 'a godsend';[14] he nonetheless questions her estimate of *The Sound and the Fury* as a tragedy with, as he misquotes it, '"all the spaciousness of Greek art"' (p. 13 – Scott in fact wrote 'spacious proportions'), feeling that this is 'a superlative which more routine reviewers might hesitate to apply to a product so unmistakably barbarian'. Hansen also wonders 'just what Miss Scott meant when she says that Faulkner's idiot is better than Dost[oe]vsky's' (p. 14). Despite these reservations, Hansen does affirm that Faulkner is 'a man of mature talent' and that 'the story, if read with patience, turns such a powerful light on reality that it gains a fast grip on the emotions of the reader'.[15]

Hansen's reservations were not shared by Lyle Saxon who, in the *New York Herald Tribune* of 13 October 1929, offered unequivocal praise of *The Sound and the Fury* in terms that resembled, to some extent, those of Henry Nash Smith. Like Smith, Saxon defined the novel as a 'tragedy' that, although it concerned 'a family in a small Mississippi town', was 'universal', 'like all great stories'. In contrast to Smith, however, Saxon did not employ a comparison with Chaucer, but invoked the names of Joyce, Proust, Chekhov and Dostoevsky in a way that partly implied that Faulkner was worthy to stand comparison with them but which also highlighted his difference and his Americanness: to compare Faulkner with these writers 'gets one nowhere, for Faulkner is definitely American'. *The Sound and the Fury* was difficult but compulsive reading, 'a novel of the first rank'.[16] A very different response came from Clifton P. Fadiman in *The Nation*. Fadiman began with a general theoretical proposition, affirming that 'the perfect enjoyment of great literature' had two features: '[t]he reader should make an analysis of the methods employed by the artist to produce a given effect' – an analysis that 'must be almost instantaneous, almost unconscious'; and 'at the same time he should experience a synthetic appreciation of that effect in its emotional totality'. The 'newer literary anarchies' of 'the present-day revolutionary novelist', however, often demand 'an effort of analytical attention so strained that it fatigues and dulls [one's] emotional perception'. This dulling of the synthesising emotional response by analytical effort can be at least partly counteracted – as it is in Joyce – 'if the theme is sufficiently profound, the characters sufficiently extraordinary, [and] the plot sufficiently powerful'; 'the reader is bound to absorb some of all this despite the strain on his attention'. But if, after a long effort of analysis, it turns out that 'the action and characters are miniscular', the reader will be disappointed: '[t]he analysis has taken too long for the synthesis to be worth the trouble'.[17] This is the case with *The Sound and the Fury*; Fadiman acknowledges Faulkner as 'an extremely talented young writer' and recognises the craftsmanship of his latest novel, but feels that it is applied to inadequate material:

■ Mr. Faulkner's work has been magnificently praised by Evelyn Scott and other critics for whose opinions one must have respect. It is in all humility, therefore, that I record the feeling that the theme and the characters are trivial, unworthy of the enormous and complex craftsmanship expended on them. I do not see, for example, that Dilsey is more than a faithful old Negress; she is not, for me at least, 'stoic as some immemorial carving of heroism,' nor does she 'recover [*sic* – 'recovers' in original] for us the spirit of tragedy which the patter of cynicism has often made seem lost'[18] (p. 17). I admit that the idiocy of the thirty-three year old Benjy is admirably grasped by Mr. Faulkner, but one hundred pages of an imbecile's simplified sense perceptions and monosyllabic gibberings, no matter how accurately recorded, are too much of a good thing. Similarly, Quentin and Jason are not sufficiently interesting, not large enough, in a symbolic sense, to make it worth while to follow painfully the ramifications of their minds and memories.

One has the feeling that Mr. Faulkner's experiments in the breaking-up of consciousness, in the abolition of chronology and psychological continuity, are both ingenious and sincere, but they are not absolutely necessary to his story. The fact that his material includes imbecility, incest, paranoia, and sadism does not mean that his tale is therefore complicated or obscure and in need of oblique and bizarre treatment. The relationships between his characters are a trifle unhealthy, one must admit, but must the prose in which they are described therefore be feverish? After one has penetrated the mad, echoing labyrinth of Mr. Faulkner's style one finds a rather banal Poe-esque plot, a set of degenerate whites whose disintegration is irritating rather than appalling, and two or three Negro characters who, if they were reproduced in straight prose, would appear as fairly conventional types. Sound and fury indeed. Signifying (the witticism is cheap, but inevitable) almost nothing.[19] □

Fadiman threw down the gauntlet to those who claimed that *The Sound and the Fury* was a 'great' novel, and he did so in a skilful way, by invoking a criterion that derived from nineteenth-century Romanticism but which would become a central tenet of what later came to be called modernist aesthetics – the criterion that a successful modernist work was one in which form and content were fused. According to Fadiman, *The Sound and the Fury* fell short of this criterion because the interpretative effort its technique demanded prevented the reader from experiencing it as a totality and because of a disproportion between the complexity of its technique and the banality and triviality of its content. It echoed the criticism of Flaubert's *Madame Bovary* (1857) made by one of the founders of modernist aesthetics, Henry James: that for all the novel's technical brilliance, Emma Bovary was 'really too small an affair'.[20]

In contrast to Fadiman, the review in the 'Literature and Less' column of the New Orleans *Times-Picayune* of 29 June 1930 offered a much more positive endorsement of *The Sound and the Fury*. Although the byline names John McClure as the author of the column, Thomas M. Inge identifies the writer as Julia K. W[etherill] Baker,[21] and the name 'Baker' and the feminine pronoun will henceforth be used to refer to her in this Guide. According to a later 'Literature and Less' columnist, Baker was 'a real Southern literary lady of the old school',[22] and this may help to account for her desire to promote a Southern writer and her attitudes towards women and African Americans (see p. 24). But she was also, clearly, a perceptive and informed critic, open to modernist experiment. Her first paragraph affirms Faulkner's achievement in ways that anticipate the grounds upon which that reputation would be elevated after the Second World War: as a great modernist tragic American writer who, without being imitative, rivalled and sometimes surpassed Joyce and who made demands on his readers:

■ William Faulkner['s] *The Sound and the Fury* . . . has more than fulfilled the promise of his first novel, *Soldier's Pay* . . . . . . *The Sound and the Fury* is one of the finest works in the tragic mood yet to appear in America. With it Mr. Faulkner is definitely established as one of the most gifted of contemporary novelists. He is the only American who seems capable of rivalling James Joyce; in parts of this book he seems to have beaten Joyce, hands down, with a simplification of his [that is, Joyce's] own method. Not that the work is imitative. It is highly original. You have not read anything like it. But the style and method of approach – fluid and fragmentary and inconsequent as dream – represent something new in the world of letters that James Joyce more than any other one person brought into it. Yet Faulkner's method is simpler, more direct than Joyce's. *The Sound and the Fury* is a work less bulky than *Ulysses*. It is, in this reviewer's opinion, in some respects a finer work of art. There is more force in it. Indeed, terrific force. There is more economy. There is a truer note of tragedy, not marred by a cynical tone of self-pity. It is a rare book, disturbing as all true tragedy is disturbing, heart-rending, terrible, yet gratifying. It is a difficult book, too, for it requires of its reader an alert intelligence and keen sympathy. It is so rich in substance, so curiously handled, that it will repay many readings.[23] □

Baker also praises – in ways that would certainly be questioned today – Faulkner's 'penetration of the feminine heart', in which '[t]here is something uncanny'; '[a]sk women how true his rendering is. They know it, men can merely sense it'. Baker's praise of the representation of African Americans would also undoubtedly be challenged now; according to Baker, Faulkner's 'negroes are the most skilfully rendered in American fiction'.[24] The way in which Baker expands upon this topic is significant both for its patronising tone, and for the way in which it charges the American North with an incapacity to understand the role of African Americans in the Southern USA in the way in which Faulkner – and, by implication, Baker herself – can:

■ The benevolent tyranny of negroes over any Southern household is charmingly reflected in *The Sound and the Fury*. Faulkner knows and loves the negro. There is the fine inflection of sympathy and truth in his portrayal of Dilsey and her brood. The bossiness of a true Southern negro who lords it over the incompetent white folks in the big house is something that self-conscious Harlem negroes, or their white satellites, can never understand. The Southern negro, on the ante-bellum plantation or in later years, is part of the family. Dilsey tells her grandson, Luster, who looks after Benjy as T. P. did before him: '"you got jes es much Compson devilment in you es any of em"' (p. 276). The Compson negroes are Compsons, too.[25] □

The last paragraph of Baker's review expresses some reservations about *The Sound and the Fury*'s technique, suggesting that possibly 'the novel succeeds in spite of its more Joycean passages rather than because of them'. Benjy's tale is judged '[t]he strongest', and this tale is – perhaps surprisingly – seen as relatively easy to interpret, even 'though the author uses shifting sense and scene with more lightning-like rapidity than elsewhere in the book'. The 'more intricate variation' in Quentin's stream-of-consciousness 'soliloquy' is 'at times remarkably successful, attaining a high degree of poignancy' but '[a]t other times it is difficult if not incomprehensible reading'. The stream-of-consciousness method, 'when carried to an extreme, is not a complete success'. But while '[c]onservative readers will no doubt consider the more involved passages in *The Sound and The Fury* grievous faults', the 'mass effect' of the novel is so 'powerful' that 'it is idle to pick flaws'. For Baker, the work's strengths far outweigh its weaknesses and will contribute to positive innovation: '[o]ut of such experimentation as *Ulysses* and *The Sound and the Fury* will grow fine new impulses in English prose'.[26]

In the *Virginia Quarterly Review*, Walter L. Myers considered *The Sound and the Fury* along with eight other new novels by authors ranging from James Branch Cabell to Frank Swinnerton (who was soon to review *The Sound and the Fury* in England (pp. 30–31)). Myers begins by highlighting the diversity of the novels he has to discuss, and points to the problem of classification that it poses. Once, it 'would have been much easier and the task of the critic simpler'. A novel could be defined with reasonable exactness as 'a story in prose that fills a book'[27] and that chiefly offered 'an abundant and detailed realism and unabashed telling of large truths'.[28] But now novels have decreased in size and grown more concentrated and dependent 'upon inference and overtone and subtle unity of effect'. As a result, '[s]undry novels nowadays are obviously intended to be incomprehensible at first perusal', at least without the help of a summary on the dust jacket of plot and theme. But even such help, Myers suggests, will not enable one fully to understand the first chapter of *The Sound and the Fury*. Rather than complaining of this, however, Myers contends that the first chapter, insofar as it is intended to represent 'the stream of a congenital idiot's consciousness', is not incomprehensible enough and that Faulkner 'has been a bit timorous in its use'. Myers's point is made playfully and subverts the expectations of a reader who might have supposed that the reviewer was about to complain about incomprehensibility; but it is also perceptive insofar as it draws attention to the edited, artificial quality of the representation of Benjy's consciousness: Faulkner, Myers observes, 'has cast Benjy's thinking in the past tense, has made of it recollection, or at any rate has given that effect to it. Thus the reader knows that his idiot has been edited'. But the editing 'produces bewilderment and does not deepen the mood required. Mr. Faulkner missed an opportunity to write more idiotically than ever man has writ and not a critic able to say him nay'.

Myers finds the use of the stream-of-consciousness method – or what he calls the 'expressionistic method' – more satisfactory in the Quentin section of *The Sound and the Fury*. 'The best of the book' is in those 'moments in this section that recall Dost[oe]vsk[y] with their trance-like actuality and their clairvoyant naïveté'. The subsequent chapters 'bring us step by step to a thinning of the dreadful wood and finally to the clear air of conventional narration'. Myers concludes with a more enthusiastic endorsement of the book than his earlier comments might have led one to expect: it is 'impressive' and does not 'signify nothing':

■ It indicates that artists may yet subdue expressionism and make it contribute less to obfuscation than to suggestivity, learn to make it aid in transmuting depression, head-achey shame, the sense of stagnant uncleanness, the odor of dry rot, into wonder and awe and high despair.[29] □

Dudley Fitts, in the journal *Hound and Horn*, did not share Myers's general enthusiasm and saw the Benjy section as 'courageous' but of questionable 'practicability', even if Benjy is the novel's most realised character: '[t]he deliberate obscurity of the opening pages repels rather than invites'. Reviewing the novel along with Thomas Wolfe's *Look Homeward, Angel* (1929), Fitts finds that 'the striking characteristic' of both novels 'is the style'. Both are 'unusually rhetorical';[30] indeed each is 'a rhetorical *tour de force*';[31] they are 'really not novels, but declamations'; their 'effects are emotional, not cerebral'; their authors 'are poets, and they write in the manner of poets'.[32] Fitts then homes in on *The Sound and the Fury*: in the extract below, which begins immediately after his discussion of the Benjy section, Fitts identifies the narrative of the novel in terms of genre as a melodrama; makes observations that implicitly anticipate Faulkner's future work as a Hollywood scriptwriter; attacks Faulkner's characterisation as relying on 'dramatic clichés'; and – for the first time in the reviews of *The Sound and the Fury* that have been considered so far in this Guide – offers an analysis of a specific passage from the novel in order to demonstrate more general features of Faulkner's style:

■ Once [the Benjy] section is traversed . . . the going is easier. There is still considerable incoherence: Mr. Faulkner is fond of the psychological throwback and the technic [technique[33]] perfected in the Gaea episode of *Ulysses* [Gaea, or Ge, is the Greek goddess of the earth, and Fitts perhaps means the last section of *Ulysses*, consisting of Molly Bloom's unpunctuated monologue, which is now more generally known as the 'Penelope' section;[34] Molly can be seen as a kind of earth-mother]; but in spite of these interruptions the story marches on vigorously and intelligibly. By the time he has reached the last pages, the reader is somewhat astonished to discover that he is being held by the force of narrative alone; and even more astonished when he realizes that the narrative is straight from the old school of melodrama – nothing more nor less than the pursuit-on-wheels of eloping lovers. And this after so much agony in stony places! [Fitts is alluding to the line 'After the agony in stony places' from T. S. Eliot's *The Waste Land* (1922; line 324[35]), which first appeared in the same year as *Ulysses*, and which was, like *Ulysses* and *The Sound and the Fury*, to arouse charges of being incomprehensible. *The Waste Land* and *Ulysses* were to become the leading European modernist classics, with *The Sound and the Fury* ranking not far below them as the leading American modernist classic.] Almost what the movie-blurbs would call 'a gripping story'. Especially in the last pages, once the stylistic surface has been penetrated, the scenario atmosphere is unmistakable; and looking back, the reader recovers and reaffirms a suspicion which was always felt: that the men and women of *The Sound and the Fury* are not real men and women at all, but dramatic clichés for all their individuality of vice and action. Only the idiot Benjy is realized;[36] Caddy and Quentin and Dilsey and Miss Caroline [Mrs Compson] and Jason are melodrama types.

The style, then. It is the study of Mr. Faulkner's style, the consideration of the book as a rhetorical exercise, as a declamation, that repays the reader. Joyce is the ultimate source, obviously; but the [J]oycean technic has been pretty thoroughly absorbed, integrated with the author's sensibility. Much of the time the writing is on two or more concurrent planes; and Mr. Faulkner's skill in avoiding the clash, while preserving the identity, of each tone is noteworthy. A typical passage (not, by the way, from the idiot's stream-of-consciousness [but from the Quentin section]) illustrates his method admirably:

'and Gerald's grandfather always picked his own mint before breakfast, while the dew was still on it. He wouldn't ever let old Wilkie touch it do you remember Gerald but always gathered it himself and made his own julep. He was as crotchety about his julep as an old maid, measuring everything by a recipe in his head. There was only one man he ever gave that recipe to; that was' *we did how can you not know it if you'll just wait I'll tell you how it was it was a crime we did a terrible crime it cannot be hid you think it can but wait Poor Quentin you've never done that have you and I'll tell you how it was I'll tell Father then it'll have to be because you love Father then we'll have to go away amid the pointing and the horror the clean flame I'll make you say we did I'm stronger than you I'll make you know we did you thought it was them but it was me listen I fooled you all the time it was me you thought I was in the house where that damn honeysuckle trying not to think the swing the cedars the secret surges the breathing locked drinking the wild breath the yes Yes Yes yes* 'never be got to drink wine himself, but he always said that a hamper what book did you read that in the one where Gerald's rowing suit of wine was a necessary part of any gentlemen's picnic basket' *did you love them Caddy did you love them When they touched me I died* (pp. 147–48)

While this is by no means an original technic, it is nevertheless beautifully employed. The diction [choice of words and phrases] is generally natural (although I suspect a certain stagey cleverness in the interjection of 'what book . . . rowing suit' into the progressing statement 'he always said that a hamper of wine was necessary'; it is improbable that two voices would combine so happily as to result in the amusing 'Gerald's rowing suit of wine'); the expression of the subjective stream is balanced, rhythmic, intense, and at the same time lacking in affectation. The prose owes a great deal to Joyce – possibly too much;[37] but the individual impetus of Mr. Faulkner's sensibility is unmistakable.[38] □

Whatever Fitts's reservations about *The Sound and the Fury*, his close reading of an extract from it set an important precedent: close reading – the detailed scrutiny of the language of a text – was to be central to the development of literary criticism as an academic discipline in the USA and the UK, and would comprise a key strand in the growth of Faulkner studies. The critical emphasis on close reading perhaps emerged partly from the renewed interest in technique and language evident in writers like Joyce, Eliot and Faulkner; in his concluding paragraph, Fitts underlines the significance of this renewed interest, which he attributes primarily to Joyce's influence. Simply having something to say is no longer enough: '[w]e know that in order to say anything, we must first of all learn to write. The instrument is too precious to abuse. And, whether we care to admit it or not, Joyce has been teaching us all over again its uses, old and new'. But, Fitts suggests, Joyce's true heir has not yet quite arrived, even in the shape of Faulkner or Thomas Wolfe. In the last sentence of Fitts's review, the meaning of his title, 'Two Aspects of Telemachus' becomes clear. Telemachus was Ulysses's son, but 'Ulysses' – Joyce's novel and Joyce himself as a writer 'is still looking for a Telemachus'.[39]

As well as this range of American responses to *The Sound and the Fury*, two significant responses came from British reviewers. Both stressed the mixture of power and difficulty in Faulkner's novel. In the *Sunday Referee* of 26 April 1931, Edward Crickmay starts by recalling *Soldier's Pay* – first published in England the previous year, 1930 – and claims that readers of that novel 'will in some measure by prepared for the poignant and bewildering experiences offered by *The Sound and the Fury*'. But this latest work 'is not a book for every novel reader', and Faulkner will be lucky 'if he finds a hundred discerning readers in this country'. Crickmay suggests, however, that Joyce's *Ulysses* 'had considerably fewer genuine appreciators on its first appearance'. He does not want to 'insist too strongly on a parallel between *The Sound and the Fury* and *Ulysses*', but finds the Joycean influence 'so strongly marked on the first hundred pages' that some mention of Joyce is necessary. Crickmay finds *The Sound and the Fury*, however, 'an even tougher proposition for the general novel reader than *Ulysses*' – '[t]o begin with, its outline is less strongly drawn and the emotions in which it deals are not so universal'.[40] But its positive significance remains: Crickmay goes on to declare:

■ . . . Mr. Faulkner's book, however strange and obscure it may appear, is one of the most important experiments in creative form and approach I have read for ten years; I hesitate in saying one of the most important achievements only because – although I have read the book twice – I have not yet completely grasped its inner significance. Laying the book aside for a second time, I feel that I have passed through one of the strangest experiences of my life – an experience which can only be paralleled in actual life by walking through a darkness which is lit fitfully by an electric storm and from which isolated figures emerge for a moment and disappear. That is precisely the effect the first part of the book left upon me. The early introduction to the narrative is made by Benjy, a congenital imbecile of thirty-three who has no time sense and who reacts naïvely to the surging of memory from a timeless flood of experiences. It is, I think, quite impossible to disentangle any clear lines of movement or any consistent action from Benjy's wanderings; but characters now and then stand out with an almost supra-natural power, as, for instance, the sister Candy [*sic*], a superb sketch in idiot chiaroscuro [the term 'chiaroscuro', from the Italian *chiaro*, meaning 'clear', and *oscuro*, meaning 'dark', can refer to the 'treatment of light and shade in painting', 'light and shade effects in nature', and 'the use of contrast in literature'; all three senses of the term are perhaps active in Crickmay's use of it here]. From Benjy we are taken back eighteen years and plunged into the last day of a young Harvard man's life. He commits suicide under the spell of reaction to sexual crime [it is not clear what Crickmay means by 'sexual crime' here; the term almost suggests that Crickmay believes that Quentin has indeed committed incest, when the actual situation is that Quentin claims (or imagines that he claims) to have done so in an attempt to keep the shame of Caddy's deflowering within the family and to avoid acknowledging that it was an outsider, Dalton Ames, who was responsible for the loss of her virginity]; and then the story is in some measure rounded off and completed by a third part. But long before the end is reached the reader has made the fullest contact with the characters. Benjy's confused and distorted images of fog have gained in outline and substance, but they have gained immeasurably in creative significance by being first passed through the corridors of an imbecile mind. It will be interesting to know how the English public receives this strange and disturbing novel. I imagine that the popular public – and its fuglemen [spokesmen], the popular critics – will be indifferent or contemptuous or openly hostile; yet it is my conviction that *The Sound and the Fury* will exert a powerful influence on those handful of readers who can see deeper than the mirror of fashionable and commercial art forms permits. For myself, I hold that *The Sound and the Fury* will outlive most of the works that at present loom so large, for its influence

**will be educative and thus create a wider and wider circle of appreci-
ators for its own authentic creative viewpoint.**[41] □

Crickmay's powerful endorsement was not quite matched by the
response of Frank Swinnerton; nonetheless, Swinnerton, like Crickmay,
acknowledged Faulkner's talent, and his views carried some weight. A
prolific writer of fiction in a traditional realist mode, often set in London
and dealing with lower middle-class life, Swinnerton was also a regular
reviewer for a number of journals and newspapers. On 15 May 1931,
Swinnerton began his regular Friday column for the London *Evening
News* by making a general distinction between contemporary English
and American writers; it was a distinction of a kind that was to recur and
to be amplified in the mid-twentieth century, and which would often
work to Faulkner's advantage. Swinnerton argued that, while England's
'standardised fiction' was 'superior to America's standardised fiction',
'there is an energy, an enterprise, and a daring in American literature of
the best types that we [the British] cannot equal'. In the light of this kind
of distinction, Faulkner's work could be seen to exemplify the energy,
enterprise and daring that his English literary contemporaries lacked.
Swinnerton attributed the difference between English and American
writing to the fact that most young English writers belonged to 'the
genteel class' – and it was their sudden discovery, in manhood, of '"the
facts of life"', which produced, in reaction against gentility, a concern
with 'perversion' and excretory functions and a use of four-letter words.
American writers, in contrast, were free of the curse of gentility. Living
in a 'vast and still largely unsettled continent' that 'offer[ed] an extraordinary variety of experience to an adventurous person', they were able
to gain 'a vigour, a practical knowledge of all classes of society', and what
seemed to be, for Swinnerton, both a failing and a strength – 'a coarse-
ness and indifference to beauty which is outside the range of the typical
young English litt[é]rateur [literary man] who is forced by his timidity
into an ironic aloofness from life'. The American writer, '[w]hatever his
faults, and the faults of his environment, . . . really has rubbed shoulders
with half a world. And his work, if he is any good, shows that this is so'.[42]

After this general discussion, Swinnerton focuses on two specific
new novels – Myron Brinig's *Copper City* and Ivan Beede's *Prairie Women*
– before concluding his review with an account of *The Sound and the Fury*.
Faulkner seems to Swinnerton 'the most powerful and the most enigmatic' of all the 'newer American talents'. Like Crickmay, Swinnerton
recalls *Soldier's Pay*, and observes that it 'made something of a sensation
when it was published [in England] last year' (Faulkner's first novel did
not appear in England until 1930). Swinnerton finds *The Sound and the
Fury* 'more ambitious [and] intricate' than the earlier work and 'often
unintelligible'. He says that he would be 'lying' if he 'were to pretend

that [he] understood' the novel and would 'still exaggerate' if he 'were to say that its obscurity seems to be justifiable'. At the same time he concedes 'the general assumption that a book should be plain at sight is not necessarily valid', while suggesting that life may be too short to spend too much time on rereading. Swinnerton confesses that he is 'not sure' what *The Sound and the Fury* is all about – though perhaps in such a way as to imply a limitation in the novel rather than in himself[43] – and he compares reading it to reading 'a work in a foreign language of which one ha[s] a slight knowledge'.[44] Even so, the power of the book comes through:

■ Every now and then the meaning is brilliantly clear. One is conscious of immense power, a terrific drive of creative invention. Then darkness follows. One can tell that everybody is agitated, that there are mysterious happenings, sudden piercing memories, hatreds, jealousies, agonies. They are all genuine. One believes in them. But these things take place behind an impenetrable curtain of words. The reader is shut off from them. He is excited, but he does not know why.[45] □

Although Swinnerton's praise is more qualified than Crickmay's, his final observations, while they might put off some readers, could also entice and challenge others to try and penetrate the curtain, to find reasons for one's excitement; and it would indeed be these tasks that many future critics would undertake.

Looking across the range of responses to *The Sound and the Fury* that have been sampled above, a number of important critical issues can be identified, some of which occur in more than one review. There is the issue of influence, or of what today might be called intertextuality – the relationships between *The Sound and the Fury* and other writers and texts. Seven reviewers compare Faulkner to Joyce – Scott (p. 15), Robbins (p. 18), Hansen (p. 21), Saxon (p. 21), Baker (pp. 23–24), Fitts (pp. 26, 27, 28) and Crickmay (p. 28) – and three compare him to Dostoevsky – Scott (p. 14), Saxon (p. 21) and Myers (p. 25). Other writers to whom Faulkner is compared are Blake (p. 14), Chaucer (pp. 19–20), Chekhov (p. 21), Proust (p. 21) and Thomas Wolfe (p. 26). There is the question of whether *The Sound and the Fury* is a tragedy, considered by Scott (p. 13), Robbins (p. 18), Davenport (p. 19), Smith (p. 20), Hansen (p. 21), Saxon (p. 21) and Fadiman (p. 22). There is the matter of Faulkner's use of a 'stream of consciousness' technique, discussed by Fadiman (p. 22) and Myers (p. 25), while Fitts (pp. 26, 27) and Crickmay (pp. 28–30) address the issue of Faulkner's obscurity or unintelligibility. The question of what might be called the 'Americanness' of Faulkner, of what makes him distinctively an American writer, is especially considered by Swinnerton (p. 30), while the relationship between Faulkner as an American writer,

Faulkner as a global or universal writer, and Faulkner as a provincial or regional writer, a writer of the American South, is alluded to by Saxon (p. 21) and explored more extensively by Smith (pp. 19–20). Fitts's analysis of a specific prose extract from *The Sound and the Fury* (pp. 27–28) is an important anticipation of the method of much future criticism of the novel, which will subject it to close reading and to detailed analysis, while the comments of Scott (pp. 16–20), Baker (p. 24) and Fadiman (pp. 22–23) on the novel's representation of African Americans and women, dubious though they may now seem, broached topics that would become of particular importance with the rise of feminism and of a powerful African American presence in American culture, literature and criticism.

When Faulkner's *As I Lay Dying* appeared in 1930, it provoked a similar range of reactions as *The Sound and the Fury*. The anonymous writer in the *New York Times Book Review* of 19 October 1930 found that the novel produced 'a commingled sense of respect for the author and an intense annoyance – emotional rather than intellectual – with him for spending his rich inventive faculty on such a witch's brew of a family'. This reviewer draws attention to a supposed disparity between the 'quality of Mr. Faulkner's own mind', which, 'even when it is latent, is of a high order', and the 'quality of the minds of the people he chooses to set before you, in fluid Joycean terms', which is 'on the contrary, of a very low sort'. In the reviewer's opinion, this disparity forces one to question the 'prevalent assumption that the artist may never be quarrel-[l]ed with for his selection of material'. It is Faulkner's 'selection of material' that compels the critic 'to put this book in a high place in an inferior category'. Faulkner has 'chosen subtle and extended means to develop the interrelated mental and emotional life of a family more amenable to the method Ring Lardner has used on his ball players'. Lardner was an American writer who had become famous for letters he had written under the pseudonym of 'Jack Keefe', supposedly a new-comer to a professional baseball team; the letters employed vernacular speech as their main mode of characterisation.

The writer in the *New York Times Book Review* charges Faulkner with a failure to individuate his characters and identifies the technique of the interior monologue as the main culprit: '[t]he chief trouble with the method of the interior monologue in dealing with these people is that it makes them . . . seem very much alike'. Moreover, the characters, 'are not always coherent' and it is almost impossible to predict how they would behave in situations other than those evoked in the novel, with the exception of Jewel and McGowan, who 'are put before us by more objective means than, say, Cash or Vardaman, or . . . Addie'. Faulkner finds himself, '[a]s he dips into the recesses of the consciousness of these various people', 'discovering more and more about less and less. He makes us yearn for a Dostoevsk[y] to rescue the stream of consciousness and to put it into literary channels whereby it can be handled by the human intellect'. While Faulkner 'is carrying on an experiment that has widened the boundaries of modern fiction' in seeking 'to get at the essence of his characters' thought', it is necessary that 'essences . . . be contained in outlines' or they become so dispersed that 'the pedestrian human mind' cannot follow them 'without going to pieces itself'.[46]

The review of 26 October 1930 in the 'Literature and Less' column of the New Orleans *Times-Picayune*, like the review in that column of *The Sound and the Fury* on 29 June 1930 (see pp. 23–25), is under the byline of John McClure but is attributed, this time by both Bassett and Inge, to Julia K. W[etherill] Baker.[47] Baker begins by asserting that most recent American writers of promise have 'shown an unfortunate tendency, after a splendid beginning, to go backwards or to stand still'. But Faulkner 'is a noteworthy exception' who 'has developed steadily and impressively, and has become in a very few years an important figure in contemporary fiction'. The outline of Faulkner's career that Baker then proceeds to offer is not, however, one of steady development, for she claims that the promise of *Soldier's Pay*, which showed both 'a remarkably keen and fine sense of tragedy' and 'a very intense zest for life', was not fulfilled by his next two novels, *Mosquitoes* and *Sartoris*. It was, however, 'amply fulfilled by *The Sound and the Fury*', which, as Baker points out, had been reviewed in the *Times-Picayune* some months before, and which, while 'too difficult in technique to become popular', was 'one of the finest pieces of tragic writing yet done in America', with 'minor faults' but 'major merit' because of its 'terrific intensity'.[48] Baker does not point out that she herself was (presumably) the author of the review of *The Sound and the Fury*, but she does summarise and reiterate key aspects of that review, and thus contributes further to enhancing the reputation of *The Sound and the Fury*. She then goes on to draw a series of interesting comparisons and contrasts between Faulkner's previous and his latest novel:

■ . . . *As I Lay Dying* . . . is a worthy companion piece to *The Sound and the Fury*. It lacks the intensity and the driving power that make the latter one of the most remarkable of American novels, but it has an integrity of conception and firmness of handling that make it a distinctive and noteworthy work. It fulfils the promise of *Soldier's Pay*. It represents, in construction and technique, an advance beyond *The Sound and the Fury*. Mr. Faulkner continues to develop towards simplicity and power. *The Sound and the Fury* dealt with the tragedy of the disintegration of an aristocratic family. *As I Lay Dying* deals with the tragedy of death among white trash ['white trash' is a derogatory term for the poverty-stricken white people of the southern United States]. The tragedy of character is deeper than the tragedy of death, for death is a commonplace, whether among white trash or cavaliers. It stands to reason that *The Sound and the Fury* with its strange reverberations of madness should be a more striking novel than *As I Lay Dying* in which the action is sordidly matter-of-fact.[49] □

Baker goes on to call *As I Lay Dying* a 'horrible' book that 'will scandalize the squeamish' but which is also 'admirable' and will 'delight those who respect life well interpreted in fine fiction without attempting to dictate what subjects an author shall choose'. The Bundrens are 'primitive souls' who 'are not sensitive enough to perceive the indecency, the enormity of their conduct', which 'is matter-of-fact to them'. Moreover, 'the fact of death' is 'offset throughout [the novel] by a fine zest for life which Mr. Faulkner shares with the primitive types he so successfully interprets'.

Baker observes that Faulkner's style in *As I Lay Dying*, except in the 'excellent' dialogue, 'is not strictly in dialect'. Rather, he 'repeatedly uses rhetorical devices of his own, and a vocabulary such as a Bundren never dreamed of, to render the thought in the mind', 'particularly when the thought is so vague that a Bundren would be inarticulate, merely sensible [aware] of his feelings'. These brief but perceptive remarks indicate a topic, also considered in Basil Davenport's review of *As I Lay Dying* (see pp. 36–37), that offers much scope for further critical analysis of Faulkner's style. Baker concludes by conceding that Faulkner 'has in a few instances exaggerated to attain the horror he desired', but she affirms that 'the story as a whole is convincing' and that *As I Lay Dying* 'is a distinguished novel' that, along with *The Sound and the Fury*, 'entitles William Faulkner to rank with any living writer of fiction in America', and above most of them: 'he far surpasses' '[a]ll but a scant half dozen',[50] including Dreiser, Anderson and Hemingway.

A much more reserved response came from Clifton P. Fadiman, who had earlier expressed his doubts about *The Sound and the Fury* and about Faulkner's general standing as a novelist (pp. 21–23). In *The Nation* of 5 November 1930, he remarks that *As I Lay Dying* 'has to an extent departed from the irritating obscurity which marked *The Sound and the Fury*' but that its technique is 'far more involved' than its 'material actually requires: impudent analysis might reduce this story to the dimensions of simple melodrama' – although, as Fadiman acknowledges, the same could be done with Shakespeare's *Hamlet* (about 1601). *As I Lay Dying* 'is a psychological jig-saw puzzle, the pieces of which are represented by the distorted mentalities of half a dozen characters'.[51] Fadiman's review also offers a general characterisation of Faulkner as a writer:

■ Mr. Faulkner has a set of romantic obsessions which he treats in a highly intellectual manner. He is fascinated by characters who border on idiocy; by brother-and-sister incest; by lurid religious mania; by physical and mental decay; by peasants with weird streaks of poetry; by bodily suffering; by the more horrifying aspects of sex. Though his approach is always objective, he specializes in emotional extremes – is a sort of prose Robinson Jeffers [an American poet who 'called for a poetry of "dangerous images"' and who has a 'preoccupation with the themes of lust, incest and the corrupt nature of man'[52]].[53] □

Fadiman does not raise the question of whether Faulkner's 'romantic obsessions' can be related to the cultural, social and economic context of the American South. His morbidity is 'interesting' but repetitive; '[m]entally disintegrated types (unless the disintegration is of a subtle and complicated character) are not a very rich mine for investigation'; his 'portrayal of defective mentalities' might seem 'very acute', but this was impossible to verify in view of the inaccessibility of '[t]he minds of idiots'. Fadiman judges that, '[d]espite the enthusiasm which has greeted Mr. Faulkner's work, it is difficult to believe him an important writer', and the only praise of the novelist that he offers is of a rather patronising kind: *As I Lay Dying* demonstrates that its author 'has a really interesting mind, apparently untouched by the major intellectual platitudes of our day'. Faulkner's 'cosmos is awry . . . but it is his own, self-created'; in contrast to 'our younger novelists' who mostly 'explain themselves too easily' and can be 'conveniently ticketed', Faulkner displays the rare quality of '[g]enuine idiosyncrasy' and 'cannot be so ticketed' – and 'that is one reason why he deserves attentive consideration'.[54]

In a concise but perceptive review in the *New Republic* of 19 November 1930, Kenneth White, like the anonymous writer in the *New York Times Book Review*, felt that Faulkner's subject matter was limited, but praised the way in which he heightened and articulated more fully the emotional states and experiences of his characters without falling into the obscurity into which his narrative technique might have led him:

■ Fiction dealing with Southern poor whites tends, whether it need to or not, to confine itself within a small circle of events beyond which few authors seem capable of carrying it. Mr. Faulkner has enlarged this circle but little and added practically not at all to the temper or range of activity peculiar, in literature at least, to these people, but he has increased the intensity and explicitness of their emotional states and experiences. Working within the frame of an extremely simplified external plot he has attempted to reconstruct the complete affective [emotional] and factual experience of a poor and ignorant family. The method used, telling the same events as seen through the minds of the different characters, offers many pitfalls of unintelligibility and obscurity of reference, which Mr. Faulkner has largely avoided. As the family's grim history unrolls in all its repellent details, one is forced to admire the ingenuity Mr. Faulkner displays in keeping his various strands tightly knit and in contriving the steadily increasing horror. The style, save for occasional passages of meaningless word juggling, is well adapted to the material; and the colloquial idiom these farmers speak is excellently handled. *As I Lay Dying* does not offer a pleasant or inspiring view of humanity, but it is an uncommonly forceful book.[55] □

Basil Davenport, who, as discussed earlier in this chapter (pp. 18–19) had reviewed *The Sound and the Fury* in the *Saturday Review of Literature* eleven months previously, reviewed *As I Lay Dying* in the same magazine on 22 November 1930. His review is worth printing in full in this Guide, both because its first and last paragraphs effectively comprise a discussion of both novels, making a range of effective points about each of them through comparisons and contrasts, and because of its specific comments upon *As I Lay Dying*, which lucidly explicate the relationship between the novel's technique and its subject matter:

■ Mr. Faulkner's new book is in essence much like his great achievement of last year, *The Sound and the Fury*, but it is far from being a mere repetition. Each deals with a family – in *The Sound and the Fury* of down-at-heel gentry, in *As I Lay Dying* of shiftless poor whites – which has sunk hopelessly into the mire, and must look forward only to poverty and sullenness for ever. In each there is a strain of insanity which actually brightens the black despair of the whole, like lightning at night. But in the story and presentation the two books are alike only in that each is boldly and brilliantly original.

In *As I Lay Dying* Addie Bundren dies; her coffin is made outside her window while she is dying; and then her husband and children put the body on a wagon and set out to take her to Jefferson, thirty miles away, where she was born. With the rare obstinacy of weak natures, her husband keeps on in spite of floods and accidents; one son breaks his leg; vultures follow overhead; but they reach Jefferson after nine days. The story is presented through the minds of the woman, her family, and neighbors, and people along the road; some of them appear many times, some but once; each reveals his mind for a few pages, and then gives place to another.

There is a disadvantage in this experimental method for a writer of Mr. Faulkner's remarkable imaginative power, which is that many of his characters would in fact be quite unable to find words for their deep and complex feelings; for Mr. Faulkner knows, as few poets do, that thoughts which lie too deep for tears are not the peculiar possession of those who can express them. In this difficulty, he cuts the knot; at times his people think in bad grammar and in dialect, as they would actually speak; at other times they think in sentences most skilfully constructed from a rich vocabulary to give as nearly as possible an impression of their incommunicable thoughts [Julia K. W[etherill] Baker's review of *As I Lay Dying* makes a similar point (pp. 33–34)]. The compromise cannot be called entirely successful, but the facing of the problem is another evidence of Mr. Faulkner's self-reliant experimentalism.

In all other respects, the method entirely justifies itself. As the characters speak, they disclose all the violent forces that have made their stagnant lives; the dying woman recalls the love-affair that led to the birth of one of the children; the daughter is continually gnawed with anxiety over her concealed pregnancy; the others show the secret antipathies and alliances that have been formed in the family. One boy [Darl] shows flashes of what may be genius, but by the end of the story he has gone mad.

Mr. Faulkner's power is especially in his presentation of mental abnormality. To his studies of it may be given the very high praise that they convince without demonstrating. That is, in the earlier classics of insanity, [Guy de] Maupassant's 'Le Horla' ['The Horla'] (1887) and Mrs. [Charlotte Perkins] Gilman's 'The Yellow Wallpaper' (1899), the disease may be seen developing step by step, one might almost say logically; they stop one's heart by the terrible necessity with which each stage follows upon the other. But Mr. Faulkner's equally breathtaking madmen are like Lear or Ophelia, in this respect at least, that one believes in them at once; they convince the feelings, which are harder to reach than the reason.

These qualities were present in *The Sound and the Fury*; the present book shows that Mr. Faulkner can repeat his success. This book differs from the other in being even more grim and unrelieved. There is the same extraordinary fertility of character, and even of a sardonic humor; but among all the characters there is none that stirs pity like Quentin, the young suicide, or commands admiration like the old negress [Dilsey] in the earlier book. Again, *The Sound and the Fury* was written upon two planes of time, connected in the timeless mind of the idiot son, showing at once the tragic crisis of twenty years ago and its effects today. Thus, although there is in *As I Lay Dying* the same contrast between the red coals of love and hate in the past and the gray cinders they have left behind, the contrast is less vivid; the total effect is in every way of a more monotonous bleakness. Some readers will prefer *The Sound of* [*sic*] *the Fury*, finding its effect heightened by the interludes in the past, and its brief passages of humor and tenderness; others will prefer the crushing, almost deadening effect of *As I Lay Dying*. But whichever one puts first, these two novels establish

Mr. Faulkner as one of the most original and powerful of our newer novelists.[56] □

Davenport's powerful and critically acute endorsement of *The Sound and the Fury* and *As I Lay Dying*, and his sense of their importance to Faulkner's overall standing set a precedent for much subsequent criticism. But his review omits one significant issue to be found both in immediate reactions to *The Sound and the Fury* and to *As I Lay Dying*, and in future Faulkner studies, in that it makes no mention of Faulkner as a novelist of the American South. It is under this category that John Donald Wade, in the *Virginia Quarterly Review*, places him when he considers *As I Lay Dying* along with six other novels by various writers, all but one of which, as Wade puts it, 'consciously occupy themselves with the South – with a section, that is, as the real protagonist overtopping all other characters whatever'.[57] The idea of 'a section' of the South – presumably a 'section' of Southern society – as the main protagonist in *As I Lay Dying* is an interesting one. With particular reference to Faulkner, Wade also raises the question of a 'perilously close kinship' between the 'superior "softness" of the Mississippians' and 'the most thorough-going aspects of degeneracy', and goes on to affirm that '[i]t is difficult indeed to find anywhere a more horrible pageant of degeneracy than Mr. Faulkner sets forth. His characters are all incompetents, morons, idiots, and he presents them with the relentless faithfulness of the great Russians who probe so carefully into all that normal people in America (perhaps ever so wickedly) have been so consistently bent to ignore'.[58] Nevertheless, Wade goes on, 'what Mr. Faulkner does, he does with great skill and great force, with Art, indeed, as great, likely, as anybody has achieved who has set out from a standard West-European background of respectability to identity himself with hopeless squalor and hopeless misery and hopeless impotence'.[59]

When *As I Lay Dying* was published in England in 1935, it received a patronising and dismissive review from Gerald Gould in the Sunday newspaper the *Observer* on 29 September. Gould suggests that Faulkner, if asked, would be unable 'to tell a straight tale and tell it straight' and that '[h]is importance is that he has created a school of worshippers' who react uncritically and enthusiastically to his work; he is a 'literary Pavlov' who has conditioned his admirers to respond in 'a purely reflex action', like dogs. *As I Lay Dying* is a novel from which it is difficult to extract a clear meaning or to determine the 'relations or reactions' of the characters, all of whom 'talk the same tough poor-white idiom when they remember (and the most execrable Bloomsbury when they forget)'. This is Gould's way of describing the novel's mixture of the kind of language its characters might actually use and the kind of language with which Faulkner endows them to express feelings that they could not, in actuality, put into words themselves – 'Bloomsbury' here is a way of indicating Faulkner's use of a 'poetic' stream-of-consciousness style that, in the English literary context of the 1930s, was associated primarily with Virginia Woolf, a member of the Bloomsbury Group. This mixture of different kinds of language was remarked on more favourably in the reviews of Julia K. W[etherill] Baker and Basil Davenport discussed earlier in this chapter (see pp. 34, 36–37); but Gould does not find the mixture justifiable, and it is the main object of his criticism of the novel. He acknowledges that Faulkner may well be 'a perfectly sincere artist', that one can dimly discern in *As I Lay Dying* 'the makings of something worth writing', and that 'underneath all the nonsense there is possibly a genuine gift'; otherwise 'one would not waste time in criticising Mr. Faulkner'. But Gould turns with relief to the 'perfect contrast' furnished by Robert Hichens's *Susie's Career*, the work of 'an artist' who '"knows his stuff"'.[60]

Edwin Muir's review in *The Listener* of 16 October 1935 was no less dismissive, though on different grounds. Muir, a poet, novelist, translator and critic who had undergone psychoanalysis and was interested in mythology, saw Faulkner as possessed by 'a very deep-seated obsession' with death. This obsession was not like that of the Jacobean writer of revenge tragedy, John Webster, or of the seventeenth-century Metaphysical poet John Donne, for whom death 'was inseparable from life'; Faulkner's obsession was with 'a sort of death absolute, or rather a sort of post-mortem life, that has no connection with human life at all'. Muir finds that 'the most interesting character' in *As I Lay Dying*, 'or at least the character in which [Faulkner] shows most interest, is the corpse, not in its former incarnation as a human being with feelings, affections and a soul, but simply in its dead, or rather gruesomely alive, state'. Muir does not consider the ways in which the novel reveals aspects of Addie Bundren's 'former incarnation as a human being' and does not mention the other characters in the novel at all, apart from quoting an extract that mentions Jewel. Muir attributes the complication of Faulkner's technique to 'something blind, something unaccounted for by his intellect, in his vision of the world, so that it can only take the form of a series of circular wanderings making towards a circumference which it can never reach'. He suggests this probably also accounts 'for the sulphurous and overcharged atmosphere' in Faulkner's novels, 'and the brilliance of the occasional flashes, for they always appear against this background of impenetrable darkness'. He then quotes from the scene of the fire (p. 205) to exemplify such a 'flash', and says that, while it is 'produced in the most wasteful and amateurish way possible, amid a terrific hubbub of adjectives and adverbs', Faulkner has demonstrated that he is 'a remarkable writer' in 'descriptions such as this of physical events'. Muir concludes, however, that '[l]ittle can be said for [*As I Lay Dying*] except for a few isolated accounts of violent action'.[61]

The hostility of Muir and Gould towards Faulkner was widely shared in the 1930s, in both the UK and the USA. Such hostility had started to develop early in the decade. In 1932, F.R. Leavis, the critic who was to have the greatest influence on literary criticism in England in the mid-twentieth-century, had written a review of *Light in August* that diagnosed what could be seen as more general Faulknerian faults and could certainly be applied to both *The Sound and the Fury* and *As I Lay Dying*:

■ [t]he technique that matters is the means of expressing a firmly realized purpose, growing out of a personal sensibility [whereas] Faulkner's 'technique' is an expression of – or disguise for – an uncertainty about what he is trying to do . . .. Faulkner is seldom for long sure of the point of view he is writing from, and will alter his focus and his notation casually, it would seem, and almost without knowing it . . .. This pervasive uncertainty of method goes down to a central and radical uncertainty [about his purpose].[62] □

In the same year that Leavis mounted this attack, Alan Reynolds Thompson, in an essay in *The Bookman* entitled 'The Cult of Cruelty', charged that Faulkner, along with Robinson Jeffers, had founded a new school of writing, a 'tendency which we may call the cult of cruelty'[63] (as shown earlier in this chapter (p.35), a comparison between Faulkner and Jeffers had been made in 1930 in Clifton P. Fadiman's review of *As I Lay Dying*). The 'cult of cruelty' was based on 'a pessimistic skepticism, to which morals and aspirations are merely customs and dreams, and the world is an inhuman mechanism'.[64] If Faulkner and Robinson Jeffers founded a new school of writing, Thompson's essay founded, or at least gave a name to, a whole school of anti-Faulknerians: the 'cult-of-cruelty' critics. For instance, Harry Hartwick, in his book *The Foreground of American Fiction* (1936) called his account of Faulkner 'The Cult of Cruelty' and claimed that *The Sound and the Fury* 'treats of a diseased, imbecilic group', while *As I Lay Dying* describes the 'macabre journey of a shiftless insane family, as they cart a putrefying corpse halfway across the state to bury it'.[65]

Other attacks on Faulkner, sometimes overlapping with those of the 'cult-of-cruelty' critics, came from humanist, left-wing and Marxist quarters. For example, in *The Nation* of 4 November 1931, Lionel Trilling – rather more to the left at this time than he would later become – judged that *Soldier's Pay* and *Sartoris* were damaged and diminished by an 'ideology' that entailed a 'sentimental nostalgia for past glory' and an evasion of the physical. Trilling did find that, in later books such as *The Sound and the Fury* and *As I Lay Dying*, Faulkner 'awoke from the aristocratic obliviousness to the physical which marred his two early books and . . . achieved both reality and generality of implication'; but even in these novels, which exemplify 'the best of Faulkner's work', 'other qualities of the ideology . . . still operate . . . to make [his work] essentially parochial'.[66] The humanist, left-wing, Marxist and 'cult-of-cruelty' criticisms of the 1930s were fused into a powerful indictment in Maxwell Geismar's account of Faulkner in his *Writers in Crisis*, which did not appear until 1942 but which drew together key elements of the anti-Faulkner criticism of the previous decade. Geismar charged Faulkner with 'a hatred of life so compelling . . . that there almost seems to be an inability in the writer to reach maturity itself' and accused him of using 'the Female and the Negro' as scapegoats. He traces what he calls 'a curious progression' in Faulkner's work from 'the troubled but tender and intensely human world of *The Sound and the Fury* . . . toward the perverse and the pathological', 'the denial of humanity' – and even *The Sound and the Fury* foreshadows that progression in some of its representations of women:

■ Faulkner . . . has focused his anger on the feminine portraits which mark his work as a whole. We recall . . . [t]he neurasthenic ['neurasthenic' means 'suffering from a feebleness of nerves causing fatigue, listlessness, etc.'; this is, of course, a questionable interpretation of Mrs Compson's condition] **Mrs. Compson of** *The Sound and the Fury*, **who is perhaps the most purely contemptible character in the novel** [compare this comment with Deborah Clarke's observations in chapter five of this Guide (pp.150–52)]. **And even Caddy herself, the object of such intense devotion, on the part of Benjy and Quentin, whose sexual weakness is nevertheless the direct cause of their destruction . . . And as Faulkner has been steadily concerned in the past with these female incubae** [evil spirits supposed to descend on sleeping persons; persons or things that oppress like nightmares], **so now** [with *Light in August*], **and drawn like these later women toward the black male, he will view the Negro with perhaps even greater bitterness . . . . . .**

What, then, is the meaning of these twin Furies of the Faulknerian deep southern Waste Land, this odd, and to Faulkner quite horrifying, conjunction of the female and the Negro? Of these symbols which he has taken to convey the entire complex of his southern revolt against modern society, and even maturity itself? . . . . . . What a strange inversion it is to take the Female and the Negro, who are if anything the tragic consequence, and to exhibit them, indeed to believe them as the evil cause![67] □

Geismar's attack posed challenging questions, which would later be taken up, in different idioms and with greater degrees of sophistication, in the 1980s and 1990s.

In the 1930s, Faulkner fared much better in France than in England or the USA. His French translator Maurice Coindreau, in an essay on

'France and the Contemporary American Novel', first published in the *Kansas City University Review* in 1937, observed that 'French criticism considers [Faulkner] today as one of the most interesting authors not only of American literature but of the literature of all countries'.[68] A translation of *As I Lay Dying* appeared, as *Tandis que j'agonise*, in 1933, and of *The Sound and the Fury*, as *Le bruit et le fureur*, in 1938 (with an introduction by Coindreau[69]). The latter novel attracted the attention of a young writer whose own first novel came out in the same year: Jean-Paul Sartre. Sartre had already written an essay on *Sartoris*:[70] June and July 1939 saw the publication in *La Nouvelle Revue Française* of his essay 'À propos de *Le Bruit et Le Fureur*: La temporalité chez Faulkner' – 'On *The Sound and the Fury*: Time in the Work of Faulkner'[71] – in which Sartre offered an evocative account of Faulkner's 'metaphysics of time'. The essay begins by considering the disruption of conventional chronology in the novel:

■ The first thing that strikes one in reading *The Sound and the Fury* is its technical oddity. Why has Faulkner broken up the time of his story and scrambled the pieces? Why is the first window that opens out on this fictional world the consciousness of an idiot? The reader is tempted to look for guidemarks and to re-establish the chronology for himself:

> Jason and Caroline Compson have had three sons and a daughter. The daughter, Caddy, has given herself to Dalton Ames and become pregnant by him. Forced to get hold of a husband quickly. . .

Here the reader stops, for he realizes he is telling another story. Faulkner did not first conceive this orderly plot so as to shuffle it afterwards like a pack of cards; he could not tell it in any other way. In the classical novel, action involves a central complication; for example, the murder of old Karamazov [in Dostoevsky's *The Brothers Karamazov* (1879–80)] or the meeting of Édouard and Bernard in [André Gide's] *The Coiners* (*Les Faux-Monnayeurs* (1926)). But we look in vain for such a complication in *The Sound and the Fury*. Is it the castration of Benjy or Caddy's wretched amorous adventure or Quentin's suicide or Jason's hatred of his niece? As soon as we begin to look at any episode, it opens up to reveal behind it other episodes, all the other episodes. Nothing happens; the story does not unfold; we discover it under each word, like an obscene and obstructing presence, more or less condensed, depending upon the particular case. It would be a mistake to regard these irregularities as gratuitous exercises in virtuosity. A fictional technique always relates back to the novelist's metaphysics. The critic's task is to define the latter before evaluating the former. Now, it is immediately obvious that Faulkner's metaphysics is a metaphysics of time.

Man's misfortune lies in his being time-bound: 'a man is the sum of his misfortunes. One day you'd think misfortune would get tired, but then time is your misfortune' (p.103). Such is the real subject of the book. And if the technique Faulkner has adopted seems at first a negation of temporality, the reason is that we confuse temporality with chronology. It was man who invented dates and clocks. '[C]onstant speculation regarding the position of mechanical hands on an arbitrary dial which is a symptom of mind-function. Excrement Father said like sweating' (p.75). In order to arrive at real time, we must abandon this invented measure which is not a measure of anything: 'time is dead as long as it is being clicked off by little wheels; only when the clock stops does time come to life' (p.85). Thus, Quentin's gesture of breaking his watch has a symbolic value; it gives access to a time without clocks. The time of Benjy, the idiot, who does not know how to tell time, is also clockless.

What is thereupon revealed to us is the present, and not the ideal limit whose place is neatly marked out between past and future. Faulkner's present is essentially catastrophic. It is the event which creeps up on us like a thief, huge, unthinkable – which creeps up on us and then disappears. Beyond this present time there is nothing, since the future does not exist. The present rises up from sources unknown to us and drives away another present; it is forever beginning anew. 'And . . . and . . . and then' [Sartre's ellipses]. Like [John] Dos Passos, but much more discreetly, Faulkner makes an accretion of his narrative. The actions themselves, even when seen by those who perform them, burst and scatter on entering the present:

> I went to the dresser and took up the watch, with the face still down. I tapped the crystal on the corner of the dresser and caught the fragments of glass in my hand and put them into the ashtray and twisted the hands off and put them in the tray. The watch ticked on. (p.80)

The other aspect of this present is what I shall call a sinking in [the French word translated by 'sinking in' here is '*l'enfoncement*' (Sartre's italics).[72] The translation in Hoffman and Vickery (1960) renders '*l'enfoncement*' as '*suspension*' (translator's italics).[73]]. I use this expression, for want of a better one, to indicate a kind of motionless movement of this formless monster. In Faulkner's work, there is never any progression, never anything which comes from the future. The present has not first been a future possibility, as when my friend, having been *he for whom*

I am waiting, finally appears. No, to be present means to appear without any reason and to sink in. This sinking in is not an abstract view. It is within things themselves that Faulkner perceives it and tries to make it felt.

> The train swung around the curve, the engine puffing with short, heavy blasts, and they passed smoothly from sight that way, with that quality of shabby and timeless patience, of static serenity . . . (p. 87)

And again,

> Beneath the sag of the buggy the hooves neatly rapid like the motions of a lady doing embroidery, *diminishing without progress* like a figure on a treadmill being drawn rapidly off-stage. (p. 124)

It seems as though Faulkner has laid hold of a frozen speed at the very heart of things; he is grazed by congealed spurts that wane and dwindle without moving.

This fleeting and unimaginable immobility can, however, be arrested and pondered. Quentin can say, 'I broke my watch', but when he says it, his gesture is *past*. The past is named and related; it can, to a certain extent, be fixed by concepts or recognized by the heart. We pointed out earlier, in connection with *Sartoris*, that Faulkner always showed events when they were already over.[74] In *The Sound and the Fury*, everything has already happened. It is this that enables us to understand that strange remark by one of the heroes [Quentin], *'Fui. Non sum'* (p. 173). ['Fui. Non sum' is Latin for 'I was. I am not'. Translated into French (as quoted in Sartre's essay) as 'Je ne suis pas, j'étais'[75] – 'I am not, I was'.] In this sense, too, Faulkner is able to make man a sum total without a future: '[t]he sum of his climactic experiences', '[t]he sum of his misfortunes', '[t]he sum of what have you'. At every moment, one draws a line, since the present is nothing but a chaotic din, a future that is past. Faulkner's vision of the world can be compared to that of a man sitting in an open car and looking backwards. At every moment, formless shadows, flickerings, faint tremblings and patches of light rise up on either side of him, and only afterwards, when he has a little perspective, do they become trees and men and cars.

The past takes on a sort of super-reality; its contours are hard and clear, unchangeable. The present, nameless and fleeting, is helpless before it. It is full of gaps, and, through these gaps, things of the past, fixed, motionless and silent as judges or glances, come to invade it. Faulkner's monologues remind one of aeroplane trips full of air-pockets. At each pocket, the hero's consciousness 'sinks back into the past' and rises only to sink back again. The present is not; it becomes. Everything *was*. In *Sartoris*, the past was called 'the stories' because it was a matter of family memories that had been constructed, because Faulkner had not yet found his technique.

In *The Sound and the Fury* he is more individual and more undecided. But it is so strong an obsession that he is sometimes apt to disguise the present, and the present moves along in the shadow, like an underground river, and reappears only when it itself is past. When Quentin insults Bla[n]d,[76] he is not even aware of doing so; he is reliving his dispute with Dalton Ames. And when Bla[n]d punches his nose [as Candace Waid suggests in chapter five of this Guide (p.169), at least one of Bland's blows lands on Quentin's eye rather than his nose; the French original has 'casse la figure'[77] which might be translated as 'smashes his face in';[78] the version in Hoffman and Vickery renders this (rather feebly) as 'hits him'[79]], this brawl is covered over and hidden by Quentin's past brawl with Ames. Later on, Shreve relates how Bla[n]d hit Quentin; he relates this scene because it has become a story, but while it was unfolding in the present, it was only a furtive movement, covered over by veils. Someone once told me about an old [school] monitor[80] who had grown senile. His memory had stopped like a broken watch; it had been arrested at his fortieth year. He was sixty, but didn't know it. His last memory was that of a schoolyard and his daily walk around it. Thus, he interpreted his present in terms of his past and walked about his table, convinced that he was watching students during recreation.

Faulkner's characters are like that, only worse, for their past, which is in order, does not assume chronological order. It is, in actual fact, a matter of emotional constellations. Around a few central themes (Caddy's pregnancy, Benjy's castration, Quentin's suicide) gravitate innumerable silent masses. Whence the absurdity of the chronology of 'the . . . assertive and contradictory assurance' (p.83) of the clock. The order of the past is the order of the heart. It would be wrong to think that when the present is past it becomes our closest memory. Its metamorphosis can cause it to sink to the bottom of our memory, just as it can leave it floating on the surface. Only its own density and the dramatic meaning of our life can determine at what level it will remain.[81] □

Sartre goes on to compare Faulkner with Proust, contending that both writers, despite their differences, have 'decapitated' time, 'deprived it of its future, that is, its dimension of deeds and freedom'.[82] Alluding to the famous comparison, in the above extract, of Faulkner's vision of the world to that of a man looking backwards from an open car, Sartre claims that 'Faulkner's heroes . . . never look ahead. They face backwards as the car carries them along'. Quentin, for example, does 'not for a second . . . envisage the possibility of *not* killing himself'. His impending suicide 'is not an *undertaking*, but a fatality'.[83] Sartre concludes, however, by rejecting what he sees as Faulkner's denial of the future: 'Faulkner uses his extraordinary art to describe our suffocation and a world dying of old age. I like his art, but I do not believe in his metaphysics. A closed future is still a future'.[84]

It took time for Sartre's essay to make an impact outside France. His own rise to fame did not occur until after the Second World War, and the essay was not translated into English until 1955. But its attempts to grasp the overall structure of Faulkner's world view, and its suggestive specific insights, have made it a classic point of reference, though it should not, of course, be accepted uncritically. John T. Matthews, for example, observes that 'Sartre concentrates almost exclusively on Quentin's section',[85] while Henry J. Underwood, Jr points out that all three of Sartre's quotations from Quentin's section 'are the words of Quentin's father Jason'[86] (or at least are attributed to Jason by Quentin); Sartre, Underwood contends, has wrongly assumed that Jason's philosophy is Faulkner's.

The year 1939, in which Sartre's essay was first published in France, also saw the first of a number of reappraisals of Faulkner in the USA that were to lay the ground for the growth of his critical fortunes after the Second World War. In the *Atlantic Monthly* for November 1939, Conrad Aiken, the poet, short-story writer and novelist, who had won the Pulitzer Prize for his *Selected Poems* ten years previously, published an essay called 'William Faulkner: The Novel as Form'. The word 'form' in Aiken's title signals his intention to try to move away from what he calls 'the usual concern' of 1930s discussions of Faulkner 'with the violence and dreadfulness of his themes'[87] – in other words, from 'cult-of-cruelty' criticism. Enlisting himself among 'the most passionate of Mr. Faulkner's admirers',[88] Aiken first remarks upon the difficulties, irritations and satisfactions of Faulkner's style, and proposes an analogy between the structure of his sentences and of his novels as wholes:

■ [His sentences] parallel in a curious and perhaps inevitable way, and not without aesthetic justification, the whole elaborate method of *deliberately withheld meaning*, of progressive and partial and delayed disclosure, which so often gives the characteristic shape to the novels themselves. It is a persistent offering of obstacles, a calculated system of screens and obtrusions, of confusions and ambiguous interpolations and delays, with one express purpose; and that purpose is simply to keep the form – and the idea – fluid and unfinished, still in motion, as it were, and unknown, until the dropping into place of the very last syllable.[89] □

Aiken goes on to compare Faulkner with a writer who might at first seem his antithesis in terms of themes:

■ Obviously, such a style, especially when allied with such a method, and such a *concern* for method, must make difficulties for the reader; and it must be admitted that Mr. Faulkner does little or nothing as a rule to make his highly complex 'situation' easily available or perceptible. The reader must simply make up his mind to go to work, and in a sense to cooperate; his reward being that there *is* a situation to be given shape, a meaning to be extracted, and that half the fun is precisely in watching the queer, difficult, and often so laborious, evolution of Mr. Faulkner's idea. And not so much idea, either, as form. For, like the great predecessor whom at least in this regard he so oddly resembles, Mr. Faulkner could say with Henry James that it is practically impossible to make any real distinction between theme and form. What immoderately delights him, alike in *Sanctuary, The Sound and the Fury, As I Lay Dying, Light in August, Pylon, Absalom, Absalom!* and now again in *The Wild Palms*, and what sets him above – shall we say it firmly – all his American contemporaries, is his continuous preoccupation with the novel *as form*, his passionate concern with it, and a degree of success with it which would clearly have commanded the interest and respect of Henry James himself.[90] □

As the above extracts show, Aiken develops a masterly general case for Faulkner. He shifts attention away from themes to style and structure, thus displacing the debate about the unpleasantness or oddity of Faulkner's subject matter; he concedes the difficulties that Faulkner's style and structure present, while arguing that these are not arbitrary and gratuitous but contribute to the overall artistic effect and meaning of his works. He presents a Faulkner who appeals to people who want both to read actively – 'to go to work' – and to gain pleasure from that active reading – 'half the fun is precisely in watching the queer, difficult and often so laborious evolution of Mr. Faulkner's idea'. The reader's work and pleasure lead to an appreciation of Faulkner's own 'immoderate delight' in form, his passionate concern with form and his considerable success in achieving form in his novels. It is this concern and success that elevates him towards the status of Henry James and which undoubtedly makes him pre-eminent among contemporary American writers. Aiken thus claims for Faulkner both national and – like Henry James – international status, and goes on to affirm that 'he is not in the least to be considered as a mere "Southern" writer: the "Southernness" of his scenes and characters is of little concern to him'.[91] Verisimilitude – 'the appearance of being true'[92] – is also of little concern to him: '[v]erisimilitude – or, at any rate, *degree* of verisimilitude – he will cheerfully abandon, where necessary, if the compensating advantages of plan or tone are a sufficient inducement'.[93]

Aiken identifies in Faulkner a 'tendency to what is almost a hypertrophy [an excessive enlargement] of form'[94] that gets out of hand when – as happens in *Light in August* – it is not sufficiently matched with characters and themes. But this does not occur in his best novels, among which *The Sound and the Fury* possibly ranks highest, with *As I Lay Dying* deserving a special mention:

■ In the best of the novels . . . – and it is difficult to choose between *The Sound and the Fury* and *The Wild Palms*, with *Absalom, Absalom!* a very close third, – this tendency to hypertrophy of form has been sufficiently curbed; and it is interesting, too, to notice that in all these three (and in that remarkable *tour de force, As I Lay Dying*, as well), while there is still a considerable reliance on time-shift, the effect of richness and complexity is chiefly obtained by a very skillful fugue-like alternation of viewpoint. [A fugue is a musical composition in which a short melodic theme (the 'subject') is introduced by one part and successively taken up by others and developed by interweaving the parts.] Fugue-like in *The Wild Palms* – and fugue-like especially, of course, in *As I Lay Dying*, where the shift is kaleidoscopically rapid, and where, despite an astonishing violence to plausibility (in the reflections, and *language* of reflection, of the characters) an effect of the utmost reality and immediateness is nevertheless produced.[95] □

If *As I Lay Dying* is like a fugue in structure, *The Sound and the Fury* is like a symphony:

■ *The Sound and the Fury* . . . with its massive four-part symphonic structure, is perhaps the most beautifully *wrought* of the whole series, and an indubitable masterpiece of what James loved to call the 'fictive art'. The joinery is flawless in its intricacy; it is a novelist's novel – a whole textbook on the craft of fiction in itself, comparable in its way to *What Maisie Knew* or *The Golden Bowl*.[96] □

Aiken's elevation of *The Sound and the Fury* as a novel of particular interest to those concerned with the craft of the novel, and his singling-out of *As I Lay Dying* as a *tour de force*, were important pointers for future criticism.

If Aiken opened up one new critical road with his focus on Faulkner's form, George Marion O'Donnell opened up another with his essay 'Faulkner's Mythology', which also appeared in 1939. Writing in the *Kenyon Review*, O'Donnell contended that Faulkner was 'really a traditional moralist, in the best sense' and that his work to date, including what was then his latest novel, *The Wild Palms*, was held together by '[o]ne principle' that gave his work 'unity' and, 'at times, the significance that belongs to great myth'. The unifying principle is 'the Southern social-economic-ethical tradition which Mr. Faulkner possesses naturally, as a part of his sensibility'. But, as 'a traditional man in a modern South', Faulkner 'could not fail to be aware' of the 'anti-traditional forces' at work '[a]ll around him'. Thus, O'Donnell argues, 'his novels are, primarily, a series of related myths (or aspects of a single myth) built around the conflict between traditionalism and the anti-traditional modern world in which it is immersed'.[97] O'Donnell then sketches out a further series of oppositions:

■ . . . In Mr. Faulkner's mythology there are two kinds of characters; they are Sartorises or Snopeses, whatever the family names may be. And in the spiritual geography of Mr. Faulkner's work there are two worlds: the Sartoris world and the Snopes world. In all of his successful books, he is exploring the two worlds in detail, dramatizing the inevitable conflict between them.

It is a universal conflict. The Sartorises act traditionally; that is to say, they act always with an ethically responsible will. They represent vital morality, humanism. Being anti-traditional, the Snopeses are immoral from the Sartoris point-of-view. But the Snopeses do not recognize this point-of-view; acting only for self-interest, they acknowledge no ethical duty. Really, then, they are a-moral; they represent naturalism or animalism. And the Sartoris-Snopes conflict is fundamentally a struggle between humanism and naturalism.

As a universal conflict, it is important only philosophically. But it is important artistically, in this instance, because Mr. Faulkner has dramatized it convincingly in the terms of particular history and of actual life in his own part of the South – in the terms of his own tradition.[98] □

O'Donnell applies the Snopes/Sartoris distinction to *The Sound and the Fury*:

■ In *The Sound and the Fury*, Quentin Compson represents all that is left of the Sartoris tradition. The rest of his family have either succumbed entirely to the Snopes world, like Jason Compson, or else have drugs to isolate them from it – Mr. Compson his fragments of philosophy, Uncle Maury his liquor, Mrs. Compson her religion and invalidism, Benjy his idiocy. But Quentin's very body is 'an empty hall echoing with sonorous defeated names'.[99] [O'Donnell's essay refers the reader at this point to a footnote in which he explains that 'the quotations are from *Absalom, Absalom!*, the other novel in which Quentin appears; but they are necessary for an understanding of his function in *The Sound and the Fury*'.[100]] His world is peopled with 'baffled, outraged ghosts'; and although Quentin himself is 'still too young to deserve yet to be a ghost',[101] he is one of them. However, it is evident that Quentin's traditionalism is far gone in the direction of formalization, with its concomitant lack of vitality; he is psychologically akin to Bayard Sartoris [in *Sartoris*] and to Narcissa Benbow [in *Sanctuary* and *The Wild Palms*]. When he discovers that his sister Candace has been giving herself to the town boys of Jefferson, Mississippi, and is pregnant, he attempts to change her situation by telling [or imagining that he is telling] their father that he has committed incest with her. It is a key incident. Quentin is attempting to transform Candace's yielding to the a-morality of the Snopes world into a sin, within the Sartoris morality; but the means he employs are more nearly pseudo-traditional and romantic than traditional; and he fails.

Quentin tells his father: 'it was to isolate her out of the loud world so that it would have to flee us of necessity' (p.176). Precisely. The loud world is the Snopes world, with which the Compson house has become thoroughly infected and to which it is subject. Quentin is really *striving toward the condition of tragedy* for his family; he is trying to transform meaningless degeneracy into significant doom. But because his moral code is no longer vital, he fails and ends in a kind of escapism, breaking his watch to put himself beyond time, finally killing himself to escape consciousness. Only he is aware of the real meaning of his struggle, which sets up the dramatic tension in *The Sound and the Fury*.

In a way, Quentin's struggle is Mr. Faulkner's own struggle as an artist . . . [102] □

O'Donnell also discusses *As I Lay Dying*, which he, like Conrad Aiken, sees as slightly different from Faulkner's other novels, but which he attempts to assimilate to the overall mythological framework he has outlined:

■ *As I Lay Dying* stands a little apart from the rest of Mr. Faulkner's novels, but it is based upon the philosophical essence of his Sartoris-Snopes theme – the struggle between humanism and naturalism. The naif hill folk who appear in the book are poor and ungraceful, certainly; they are of low mentality; sexually, they are almost animalistic. But when Anse Bundren promises his dying wife that he will bury her in Jefferson, he sets up for himself an ethical duty which he recognizes as such – though not in these terms. It is the fulfillment of this obligation, in spite of constant temptation to abandon it, and in spite of multiplied difficulties put in his way by nature itself, that makes up the action of the novel.

Fundamentally, *As I Lay Dying* is a legend; and the procession of ragged, depraved hillmen, carrying Addie Bundren's body through

water and through fire to the cemetery in Jefferson, while people flee
from the smell and buzzards circle overhead – this progress is not
unlike that of the medieval soul towards redemption. The allegories of
Alanus de Insulis [(1128–1203), also known as Alan of Lille, a French
religious writer, author of *Anticlaudianus*, a long allegorical poem about
'the creation of the soul by God out of nothing'[103]] and the visions of
Sister Hildegard of Bingen [(1098–1179), Abbess of Rupertsberg,
whose *Scivias*, dictated between 1141 and 1151, described twenty-six
visions, 'with denunciations of the world and enigmatic prophecies of
disaster'[104]] would yield a good many parallels. On a less esoteric
plane, however, the legend is more instructive for us. Because they are
simpler in mind and live more remotely from the Snopes world than
the younger Sartorises and Compsons, the Bundrens are able to carry a
genuine act of traditional morality through to its end. They are
infected with a-morality; but it is the a-morality of physical nature, not
the artificial, self-interested a-morality of the Snopeses. More heroism
is possible among them than among the inhabitants of Jefferson.[105] □

In the brief compass of their essays, O'Donnell and Aiken sowed the
seeds of two possible overall approaches to Faulkner's work, one mythological, the other structural; and their comments on specific novels, as
the examples above show, also provided fertile suggestions for future
development. But Faulkner's critical standing remained uncertain: it was
not until 1946 that the event that, as Lawrence H. Schwarz says, 'many
literary historians and critics see as the turning point in Faulkner's literary reputation'[106] occurred – a more decisive turning point than that of
1939 exemplified by the essays of Aiken and O'Donnell. This event was
the publication of Malcolm Cowley's *The Portable Faulkner*.

Cowley had already published three essays on Faulkner by the time
the *Portable* appeared, in the *New York Times Book Review* in October 1944,
the *Saturday Review* in April 1945, and the *Sewanee Review* in July 1945.[107]
Parts of these essays were incorporated into his influential introduction
to the *Portable*. In that introduction, Cowley claims that 'Faulkner
performed a labor of imagination that has not been equaled in our time,
and a double labor: first, to invent a Mississippi county that was like a
mythical kingdom, but was complete and living in all its details; second,
to make his story of Yoknapatawpha County stand as a parable or legend
of all the Deep South'.[108] But Cowley also stresses the lack of recognition
that Faulkner has suffered: '[h]is early novels, when not condemned,
were overpraised for the wrong reasons; his later and in many ways better novels have been ridiculed or simply neglected; and in 1945 all his
seventeen books were effectively out of print, with some of them unob-
tainable in the secondhand bookshops'.[109] Moreover, '[e]ven his warm
admirers, of whom there are many – no author has a higher standing

among his fellow novelists – have shown a rather vague idea of what he is trying to do; and Faulkner himself has never explained'.[110]

Cowley emphasises that '[a]ll [the] books in the Yoknapatawpha cycle are part of the same living pattern', and that '[i]t is this pattern . . . that is Faulkner's real achievement'.[111] It is a pattern that, although 'presented in terms of a single [mythical] Mississippi county', 'can be extended to the Deep South as a whole'.[112] In novel after novel, he has elaborated a 'whole fictional framework' that has made his work 'a myth or legend of the South'.[113] Although Cowley's introduction does not specifically apply this myth to *The Sound and the Fury* and *As I Lay Dying*, it is worth reprinting his summary of the myth here as it provides one influential and useful overall context for a study of the two novels that are the subject of this Guide:

■ The Deep South was ruled by planters some of whom were aristocrats like the Sartoris clan, while others were new men like Colonel Sutpen. Both types were determined to establish a lasting social order on the land they had seized from the Indians (that is, to leave sons behind them). They had the virtue of living single-mindedly by a fixed code; but there was also an inherent guilt in their 'design', their way of life; it was slavery that put a curse on the land and brought about the Civil War . . .

After the War was lost, partly as a result of the Southerners' mad heroism . . . the planters tried to restore their 'design' by other methods. But they no longer had the strength to achieve more than a partial success, even after they had freed their land from the carpet-baggers who followed the Northern armies. ['Carpet-bagger' is 'the name given to the northern political adventurers who sought a career in the Southern states after the [Civil War] ended (1865)'. Their only 'property qualification' was their 'carpet bag' of personal belongings, and they were regarded by the southerners as parasites and exploiters.[114]] As time passed, moreover, the men of the old order found that they had Southern enemies too; they had to fight against a new exploiting class descended from the landless whites of slavery days. In this struggle between the clan of Sartoris and the unscrupulous tribe of Snopes, the Sartorises were defeated in advance by a traditional code that kept them from using the weapons of the enemy. As a price of victory, however, the Snopeses had to serve the mechanized civilization of the North, which was morally impotent in itself, but which, with the aid of its Southern retainers, ended by corrupting the Southern nation.

Faulkner's novels of contemporary Southern life – especially those written before 1945 – continue the legend into a period that he regards as one of moral confusion and social decay. He is continually seeking in them for violent images to convey his sense of outrage . . .

In his novels dealing with the present – I am speaking of those written before 1945 – Faulkner makes it clear that the descendants of the old ruling caste have the wish but not the courage or the strength to prevent this new disaster . . . [115] □

Cowley opened up the possibility of seeing Faulkner's work as a whole and of interpreting individual novels in terms of that whole.

While Cowley offers no extended discussion of *The Sound and the Fury* in his introduction, he does use it as one example to justify his claim that 'almost all [Faulkner's] novels have some obvious weakness in structure'.[116] Cowley says: 'In *The Sound and the Fury*, which is superb as a whole, we can't be sure that the four sections of the novel are presented in the most effective order; at any rate, we can't fully understand the first section until we have read the three that follow'.[117] This charge against *The Sound and the Fury* will be taken up and answered by Lawrence E. Bowling in his significant 1948 essay, 'Faulkner: Technique of *The Sound and the Fury*' (see pp. 56–57). Cowley's work on *The Portable Faulkner* also had one important consequence for the study of *The Sound and the Fury* in relation to Faulkner's other work, as he explains:

■ In the present volume I wanted to use part of *The Sound and the Fury*, the novel that deals with the fall of the Compson family. I thought that the last part of the book would be most effective as a separate episode, but still it depended too much on what had gone before. Faulkner offered to write a very brief introduction that would explain the relations of the characters. What he finally sent me is the much longer passage printed at the end of the volume: a genealogy of the Compsons from their first arrival in America. Whereas the novel is confined (except for memories) to a period of eighteen years ending on Easter Sunday, 1928, the genealogy goes back to the battle of Culloden in 1745, and forward to the year 1943, when Jason, last of the Compson males, has sold the family mansion, and Sister Caddy has last been heard of as the mistress of a German general. The novel that Faulkner wrote about the Compsons had long ago been given what seemed its final shape, but the pattern or body of legend behind the novel – and behind his other books – was still developing.[118] □

Clearly the Compson Appendix was a major coup for Cowley, a 'paratextual'[119] addition that came long after the original text of *The Sound and the Fury* but which, endowed as it was with authorial authority, could not but affect interpretation of that novel and of Faulkner's other fiction.[120]

The Portable Faulkner did not at once produce a Faulkner revival. Only 20,000 copies were sold between 1946 and the announcement in November 1950 of Faulkner's Nobel Prize for Literature. Although a

Modern Library edition combining *The Sound and the Fury* and *As I Lay Dying* came out in 1946, no more novels appeared until *Intruder in the Dust* (1948). But Cowley's introduction and selection of material, and the Compson Appendix provided by Faulkner himself, made the *Portable* a key point of reference in contemporary discussion of Faulkner. Cowley's work on Faulkner found an admirer in the poet, novelist and critic Robert Penn Warren, whose authority as a writer was growing: his novel *All the King's Men* (1946) would win the Pulitzer Prize in 1947 and he would become known in the 1950s as one of the founding fathers of the New Criticism. In the same year as the appearance of *All the King's Men* and of *The Portable Faulkner*, Warren published a two-part essay on Faulkner in the *New Republic* that would further advance Faulkner's critical reputation.[121]

Warren's first sentence identifies Faulkner as America's pre-eminent living writer: '[a]t the age of fifty-three, William Faulkner has written nineteen books which for range of effect, philosophical weight, originality of style, variety of characterization, humor, and tragic intensity are without equal in our time and country'. As if to disarm potential critics, Warren then immediately concedes that Faulkner has 'grave defects' – '[s]ometimes the tragic intensity becomes mere sensationalism, the technical virtuosity mere complication, the philosophical weight mere confusion of mind' – and that he is 'a very uneven writer'. But this unevenness 'is, in a way, an index to his vitality, his willingness to take risks, to try for new effects, to make new explorations of material and method'. It is also, 'sometimes at least, an index to a very important fact about Faulkner's work', which is that he 'writes of two Souths: he reports one South and he creates another. On one hand he is a perfectly straight realistic writer, and on the other he is a symbolist'.[122] It is in this perspective that Warren explores Faulkner's work as a whole and comments on specific novels. Here are his remarks on *The Sound and the Fury*:

■ . . . the whining Mrs. Compson, the mother in *The Sound and the Fury* . . . with her self-pity and insistence on her 'tradition' surrenders all the decency which the tradition would have prescribed, the honor and the courage. Or the exponents of the tradition may lose all contact with reality and escape into a dream world of alcohol or rhetoric or madness or sexual dissipation. Or they fall in love with defeat and death, like Quentin Compson, who commits suicide at Harvard. Or they lose nerve and become cowardly drifters. Or, worst of all, they try to come to terms with reality by adopting Snopesism, like the last Jason of *The Sound and the Fury*, whose portrait is one of the most terrifying in all literature – the paranoidal self-deceiver, who plays the cotton market and when he loses, screams about those 'kikes'[123] in New York who rob him, who himself robs the daughter of his sister

Caddy over the years and in the end makes her into the desperate and doomed creature she becomes, who under the guise of responsibility for his family – the ailing mother, the idiot brother, the wild niece – tortures them all with an unflagging sadistic pleasure.[124] □

In taking up what he himself defines as 'the question of class and race',[125] Warren claims that '[t]he actual role of the Negro in Faulkner's fiction is consistently one of pathos or heroism' and cites as his first example of this 'Dilsey [in *The Sound and the Fury*], under whose name in the Compson genealogy Faulkner writes, "They endured"'.[126] Warren discusses *As I Lay Dying* in relation to class, at one point drawing a contrast with some of the protagonists of *The Sound and the Fury*:

■ There is a current misconception . . . that Faulkner's Snopesism is a piece of snobbery. It is true that the Snopeses are poor whites, descendants of bushwhackers (those who had no side in the Civil War but tried to make a good thing out of it), but any careful reader should realize that a Snopes is not to be equated with a poor white. For instance, the book most fully about the poor white, *As I Lay Dying*, is charged with sympathy and poetry . . . . . .

The whole of *As I Lay Dying* is based on the heroic effort of the Bundren family to fulfil the promise to the dead mother to take her body to Jefferson; and the fact that Anse Bundren, after the effort is completed, immediately gets him a new wife, 'the duck-shaped woman' (p. 247), does not negate the heroism of the effort or the poetry in which it is clothed . . . the Bundrens come off a little better than the latter-day Compsons, the whining, selfdeluding mother, the promiscuous Caddy, the ineffectual Quentin, and the rest, including the vile Jason. The Bundrens at least are capable of the heroic effort. What the conclusion indicates is that even such a fellow as Anse Bundren, in the grip of an idea, in terms of promise or code, can rise above his ordinary level; Anse falls back at the end, but only after the prop of obligation has been removed.[127] □

In the conclusion of his essay, Warren speaks of Faulkner's hatred of 'modernism', in Faulkner's special sense, in which 'modernism' is, as Warren puts it, 'the enemy of the human', comprising 'abstraction', 'mechanism', 'irresponsible power' and 'the cipher on the ledger or the curve on a graph'. But Faulkner does not, for Warren, merely 'come to a dead end, setting up traditional virtues against the blank present'.[128] While he offers no easy solutions, he does give a sense of the future, as the last sentence of Warren's essay puts it: '[a]nd *The Sound and the Fury*, which is Faulkner's *Waste Land*, ends with Easter and the promise of resurrection'.[129] By comparing *The Sound and the Fury* with T. S. Eliot's *The*

Waste Land, which in the postwar era was to come to be regarded, along with *Ulysses*, as the pre-eminent modernist text, Warren turns Faulkner, the supposed hater of modernism in the sense of 'modernity', into a high-ranking exemplar of modernism in the sense in which the term was to be increasingly used in postwar literary criticism: as a mode that combined a certain measure of technical innovation with a world view in which a traditional past was set against a decayed present that still held a faint hope of transcendence.

While Warren included his remarks on *The Sound and the Fury* and *As I Lay Dying* within a more general appraisal of Faulkner, Laurence E. Bowling, in an essay in the *Kenyon Review* in 1948, focused on *The Sound and the Fury* as 'an appropriate test case' for an evaluation of Faulkner's technique. Bowling contends that all Faulkner's critics, whatever their other differences, agree on one point – 'that [Faulkner's] narrative technique is extremely intricate and perplexing'. But they then 'divide into two groups: those who feel that this complexity is justified and those who hold that it is an unnecessary obstacle'.[130] Taking up Bowling's own metaphor of the 'test case', it can be said that Bowling in his essay acts as defence attorney and seeks to justify the ways of Faulkner to those critics who feel that his involved technique is unnecessary. In the extract from Bowling's essay that follows, he argues that Benjy's section has to come first because of the way in which it foreshadows later sections; he first takes issue with Malcolm Cowley's contention, quoted above (see p. 53) that 'we can't be sure that the four sections of the novel are presented in the most effective order':[131]

■ What disturbs Mr. Cowley is not the violation of surface chronology but the fact that 'we can't fully understand and perhaps can't even read the first section until we have read the other three'.[132] By 'most effective order' he seems to mean the order in which a section would be most easily understood and most effective individually. One may very well agree with Mr. Cowley that some other order of arrangement might have made Benjy's section more comprehensible on the first reading; however, the shifting of this section would merely mean that some other section would then come into first position, and the same trouble would start all over again, for each of the four sections is interdependent upon the other three. This is true even of the fourth and simplest section – as Cowley discovered when he considered printing this unit in *The Portable Faulkner*. 'I thought that the last part of the book would be most effective as a separate episode, but still it depended too much on what had gone before'.[133]

Let us consider some of the ways in which the present position of Benjy's section does contribute to the desired effect of the novel as a whole. If the childhood experiences are to be included at all, it does seem definitely preferable that they be presented early, before the reader advances too far into the problems of adult life dealt with in the following three sections. But Benjy's section is far more than a mere background summary of ordinary childhood experiences. From one point of view, it is the whole novel in miniature. It presents all the main characters in situations which foreshadow the main action. This is particularly true of the recalled water-splashing episode which took place when Caddy was seven, Quentin nine, Jason about five, and Benjy about three. These children and a little colored boy, Versh, are playing in the branch [of the river] one evening. Caddy gets her dress wet and, in order to avoid punishment, pulls off the dress to let it dry. Quentin is perturbed because she gets her dress wet and also because she pulls it off before Versh and the other children. He slaps her and she falls down in the water, getting her bodice and drawers wet. He then feels partly responsible for Caddy's guilt and says that they will both get whipped. She says it was all his fault. However he and she and Versh agree not to tell; but Jason decides to tell if Caddy and Quentin do not give him a bribe. When the children go to bed, Dilsey the Negro cook discovers the stain on Caddy's buttocks, but she is unable to remove the spot.

The parallels between this and the main plot are obvious. When Caddy becomes a young woman, she soils her honor with a serious stain which will not come off; Quentin assumes responsibility for her shame and finally commits suicide in an attempt to expiate her sin; Jason, true to form, makes the most of Caddy's shame by blackmailing her for all he can get. In the childhood experience, Jason walks with his hands in his pockets (as if 'holding his money'(p. 34)) and once falls down because he does not have his arms free to balance himself (p. 21); in the main action later, his 'holding his money' (by keeping it at home in a box instead of banking it) results in his being robbed by his niece. Since this childhood experience is obviously intended to for[e]shadow the adult action, it can accomplish this purpose only if it comes before the other three sections.

The Sound and the Fury is a novel about disorder, disintegration, and the absence of perspective. As an introduction to this theme, what could be more appropriate than the flat, perspectiveless language of Benjy's section? The novel is essentially about the internal chaos of the characters – their intellectual, moral, and spiritual confusion. It is therefore appropriate that the first section be presented from the point of view of an idiot who symbolizes this general disorder and exemplifies the simplest variation of it – intellectual confusion; Benjy is incapable of intellectual discrimination, constantly mistaking the past for the present.[134] □

If Cowley and Warren had offered important general appraisals of Faulkner's fiction, Bowling demonstrated how a close focus on one novel – *The Sound and the Fury* – could reward the critic by revealing a fascinating complexity. It would be a combination of these two approaches – general appraisal and the close analysis of specific works – that was to prove central to the significant books about Faulkner that would be produced in the 1950s and 1960s by Irving Howe, Olga Vickery, Cleanth Brooks and Michael Millgate. The next chapter considers the accounts of *The Sound and the Fury* and *As I Lay Dying* that these critics offer. But in the late 1940s, there were no books devoted to Faulkner. Many of his commentators in the Thirties and Forties sound, on the surface, like Quentin or Jason, fastidiously shrinking from the flesh into archaic abstraction, or slickly shirking emotion through a sharp, streetwise patter. These dignified or demotic tones, however, do not quite conceal a silence, punctuated by howls and bellows, that finds its closest counterpart in Benjy: the silence of a prisoner of inarticulacy, overwhelmed by memory and desire, lost for words, trying to say. The words in which critics might speak of Faulkner adequately and at length had not yet been found. But the pressure to find those words would redouble as the 1950s began: the new decade would thrust Faulkner into the spotlight of world fame.

CHAPTER TWO

Taming the Furies: Faulkner Criticism in the 1950s and 1960s

ON SATURDAY 10 December 1950, William Faulkner made his Nobel Prize speech in Stockholm. It was barely audible at the time,[1] but the response to the printed version soon made it clear that the master of rhetoric had found the right words, not only for the occasion, but also for the historical moment. Faulkner began by saying that he felt that the Prize had not been made to him as a man, but to his work – 'a life's work in the agony and sweat of the human spirit, not for glory and least of all for profit, but to create out of the materials of the human spirit something which did not exist before'. He then turned his attention to 'the young men and women already dedicated to the same anguish and travail', the struggling writers, one of whom would 'some day stand here where I am standing', to receive the Nobel Prize. But there was a contemporary 'tragedy' that threatened to cripple the creativity of these young writers – 'a general and universal physical fear' that had driven out 'problems of the spirit' and left only the question: 'When will I be blown up?'. Faulkner was alluding, of course, to the fear of nuclear war. That fear, Faulkner charged, had resulted in a form of amnesia: 'the young man or woman writing today has forgotten the problems of the human heart in conflict with itself which alone can make good writing because only that is worth writing about, worth the agony and the sweat'. Young writers must relearn those problems and teach themselves 'that the basest of all things is to be afraid';[2] there should be no room 'for anything but the old verities and truths of the heart, the old universal truths lacking which any story is ephemeral and doomed – love and honor and pity and pride and compassion and sacrifice'. Faulkner went on to affirm his belief that man would not only 'endure' but 'prevail'[3] and that it was the writer's duty to help him do this.

In his Nobel speech, Faulkner cast himself as the spokesman of mankind, and implicitly outlined the terms in which his work would be interpreted over the next two decades. But at first the spotlight of fame that had fallen on him left most critics skulking in the shadows. As the previous chapter of this Guide demonstrated, Faulkner had been the object of considerable critical hostility in the USA and the UK in the 1930s and 1940s; and those who did express admiration for his work tended to do so defensively, conceding much to his opponents, as Robert Penn Warren did in the opening paragraph of his 1946 essay (see p. 54), or acting like a lawyer arguing a case for an awkward client, as Lawrence Edward Bowling did in his analysis of *The Sound and the Fury* (see p. 56). But the Nobel Prize seemed to confirm that Faulkner was perceived, in the world at large if not in the USA, as a great American writer; it helped to strengthen a desire to honour the prophet in his own country, to produce a body of critical commentary commensurate with Faulkner's high international reputation. Moreover, the difficulty of Faulkner's work, which had posed such an obstacle to his widespread critical acceptance in the 1930s and 1940s, proved an asset as the prime site of literary criticism shifted in the 1950s from the little magazine to the academy. The development of New Criticism as the dominant critical method in the universities encouraged close attention to the complexities of language and structure in literary texts and Faulkner's texts – especially, perhaps, *The Sound and the Fury* – required and rewarded such attention. A further affinity between Faulkner and New Criticism was due to the fact that the most prominent New Critics in the USA – Robert Penn Warren, Cleanth Brooks, John Crowe Ransom, Allen Tate – were all from the US South, and remained concerned, as they had been since the 1920s, to contest the image of the South as merely racist and reactionary. Faulkner could be deployed to improve the image of the South by demonstrating that a great modern writer of international stature could emerge from this supposedly backward region. In the wider cultural politics of the Cold War, Faulkner's distance from the political commitments of the 1930s, or from any obvious political commitment, was a further factor in his favour: he could be represented as a writer who transcended partisan positions in his concern for 'the old universal truths', 'love and honor and pity and pride and compassion and sacrifice'.

Among the books on Faulkner that began to appear in the early 1950s, the most important was Irving Howe's *William Faulkner: A Critical Study*, which first appeared in 1952, and, in revised editions, in 1962 and 1975. Howe can be classified as one of the 'New York intellectuals', the 'critics and writers drawn to [the journal] *Partisan Review* in the late 1930s (after its clear break with the Communist Party) and throughout the 1940s'.[4] Like other intellectuals of this ilk – most notably Lionel Trilling – Howe would move into academic life in the postwar era. In his study, Howe, as Cowley had done before him, stresses how Faulkner has created an imaginary world, and how this world is 'the setting for a

complex moral chronicle in which a popular myth and an almost leg-
endary past yield something quite rare in American literature: a deep
sense of the burdens and grandeur of history'.[5] Howe goes on to explore
Faulkner's background, the 'Southern Tradition', 'Faulkner and the
Negroes' and 'The Moral Vision'. The second part of his study focuses on
specific novels. He cites Faulkner's own reply to a group of Mississippi
students who asked which novels he thought his best – '"*As I Lay Dying*
was easier and more interesting. *The Sound and the Fury* still continues to
move me"':[6] Faulkner's judgement, Howe affirms, 'is correct: these are
his best novels, *The Sound and the Fury* is his masterpiece'.[7] Like Lawrence
Edward Bowling, Howe then goes on to discuss the positioning of
Benjy's narrative as the first section of the novel, asking why the novel
starts in this way, a problem that is, Howe says, 'of far more than "technical" interest'[8] – perhaps a veiled reference to Bowling, the title of
whose essay had announced a focus on technique (pp. 56–57). Like
Bowling, however, Howe justifies the priority of the Benjy section partly
by the way in which it foreshadows what comes later in the novel:

■ Since the collapse of the Compson family is to be shown as a completed history, Faulkner can forgo the orderly accumulation of
suspense that might be had from a conventional narrative. Beginning
near the end of his story, he must employ as his first perceiving mind
a Compson who has managed to survive until Easter 1928. Mrs.
Compson is too silly and Jason too warped to preserve, let alone present, the family history. Quentin is dead, Caddy gone, and Dilsey
must be saved for her role as chorus of lament. Only Benjy remains –
and this, far from being accidental, is a symbolic token of the book.

Of all the Compsons, Benjy alone is able to retain the past; he
alone has not suffered it in conscious experience. Being an idiot he is
exempt from the main course of action and untainted by self-interest.
Because he cannot color or shape his memories, his mind serves the
novel as an entirely faithful glass [mirror]. Unable to order events in
sequence, he must grope for fragments, stumbling over stray chips
from the quarry of the past. All these effects of perspective Faulkner
might have gained from a narrator of superior intelligence who would
look upon the Compsons from a distance – all but the poignant immediacy that only Benjy can provide. In *Absalom, Absalom!* the Sutpen
history ricochets off the consciousness of Quentin Compson; in *The
Sound and the Fury* the Compson history is already 'in' Benjy's mind.
Where Quentin, as introductory or perceiving mind, makes for distance and historical summation, Benjy creates disordered closeness
and, perhaps, identification.

But can one identify with an idiot? If Benjy's memories were tightly
locked in the shell of his mind, if their quality were determined by his

idiocy, it would clearly be impossible. Benjy does not act or talk or reflect; his only function is to lead directly and without comment into the past. He brings no sharply formulated point of view to his memories, in the sense that Quentin and Jason will; his remembering does not organize or condition that which he remembers. To 'identify' with Benjy is, therefore, to abandon him as a person and yield oneself to the Compson experience. Yet this abandonment becomes a way of learning to appreciate his role and value. We gain our experience of the Compsons mainly from the materials coursing through his mind, and it is these materials alone that enable us to see that behind his fixed rituals there are genuine meanings, half-forgotten tokens of the past which survive for him as realities of the present. Whenever Benjy has to change the motions of his routine – going around the town square toward the left rather than the right, for example – he is stricken with agony, and he registers it in the only way he can, by bellowing. The pattern of order to which he is so attached may signify nothing in itself, nor need the pain consequent on its disruption signify anything – unless there are those present who understand and can remember what Benjy clings to. Without knowing observers, Benjy is simply the past forsaken. None of the Compsons has remained to care and only Jason so much as remembers; soon it is we, the alien readers, who together with Dilsey must take the burden on ourselves. Only then can we understand Benjy.

Lacking any sense of time, Benjy feels the reality of 1902 or 1912 as closely as that of 1928, the death of grandmother as sharply as Luster's "'projecking'" (p. 53) with his graveyard. Only through a mind such as his could the past be raised to a plane of equality with the present and the two dissolved in a stream of chaotic impression. Were either Quentin or Jason to open the novel, an apparent order would be imposed on the past, but an order reflecting their private interests. An external observer, used somewhat like Captain Marlow in [Joseph] Conrad's novels, might provide breadth and balance of judgment, but with some loss in immediacy.[9] Such an observer might report the Compson history but could not present it; his very role as commentator would change the shape of the book. But Benjy, precisely because he lacks formed personality and has no need for detachment, can reveal the Compsons in both intimacy and distance, completeness and chaos.

The Benjy section forces the reader to participate in the novel, to become, as it were, a surreptitious narrator; otherwise he cannot read it at all. Given the material of the past, or at least a shrewdly formed simulation of its chaos, he is then required to do the work which in an ordinary novel is done by the writer or narrator. This method exacts from him the reader an increment [increase] of attention, prodding him to compose in his mind a conventional narrative which accompanies, registers, but finally submits to the narrative of the book. The bewilderment, produced by Benjy's flow of memory, sharpens one's responses, teaches one to look for clues, parallels and anticipations.

Though the last section contains a few incidents not anticipated in the earlier ones, these are merely bitter footnotes to a text of disaster; almost everything else is foreshadowed by Benjy. *The Sound and the Fury* does not launch an action through a smooth passage of time; it reconstructs a history through a suspension – or several suspensions – of time. In the water-splashing incident to which Benjy so persistently returns, the behavior of the Compson children is an innocent anticipation of their destinies; each shows himself as he will later become. The Benjy section thus forms not merely one part or one movement among four, but the hard nucleus of the novel. Later sections will add to the pathos of Quentin's reflections and the treachery of Jason's conduct, but merely as variations or extensions of what has already been present from the beginning.

Of greater specific weight than the others, the Benjy section is ultimately clearer in its perceptions and more delicate in sensibility; from it there begins an emotional decline which graphs the novel's meaning. Benjy is the past recaptured; Quentin, imprisoned in his own consciousness, cannot hold the past with the purity Benjy can; Jason violently breaks from the past; and the concluding section completes the book's movement from a claustrophic [*sic* – presumably 'claustrophobic'] private world to a sterile public world, from the subjective heart of Compson life to a cold record of its death. Each of the first two sections is primarily a retrospect, yet both manage to carry the story forward to clarity and resolution. When he wishes to create an atmosphere of closeness and involvement Faulkner depends on stream-of-consciousness; but toward the end, except when describing the Negro revival meeting, he writes in a style of clipped notation, a style – later to be harshened in *Sanctuary* – signifying distance and revulsion. Coming, as it must, at the beginning of the book and shortly before the visible collapse of the Compsons, the Benjy section is a last reminder of what their world once was.[10] □

Howe then praises the 'classical . . . rigor, impersonality, and austerity' of the Benjy section,[11] and homes in on its stylistic spareness and structural juxtapositions:

The impression Faulkner seeks to establish, at least the first one, is that Benjy's memories are formless; yet only through precise form can this impression take root and thrive in the reader's mind. Satisfying the needs of both character and author, a simulation of disorder comes to convey an order of significance.

Toward this end Faulkner drafts all his ingenuity, and refrains, moreover, from the rhetorical bombardments that mar a number of his other books. Self-effacing and rigidly disciplined, he directs his language to the uses of his subject, and the result is that his writing is more delicate and controlled than anywhere else in his work. He stakes everything on elemental presentation. He avoids complex sentence structures explicitly involving logic, sequence, and qualification. In place of an elaborate syntax, there is a march of short declarative sentences and balanced compounds following the journey of Benjy's senses. Monotony is the obvious risk of this grammatical stripping, but it is escaped in several ways: frequent time shifts in Benjy's memories, a richness of concrete pictorial imagery, and an abundance of sharply inflected voices. The internal regularity of individual sentences is thus played off against the subtle pacing and tonal variety of the sequence as a whole – the sentences invoking Benjy and the sequence that which exists beyond Benjy. Though the rhythm and shape of the sentences vary but little, there is a wide range of speed. Beginning with relatively large units, Benjy's memories break into increasingly small fragments until, at the climax,[12] brief sentences of recalled incident whirl feverishly about one another, mixing events from 1898, 1910, and 1928. And then the agitated spinning of Benjy's mind comes to an abrupt stop, resting in memories of childhood.

No elaborate symbols or metaphors, no hyperbole [exaggeration] or euphuism [artificial or affected style of writing]; the few symbols are worked with niggardly concentration, and, thereby, with all the greater effectiveness. Pared and precise, eluding abstraction and reverie, the writing absorbs its color from the life it appropriates, the pictures of behavior and accents of speech. It favors concreteness and spareness, particularly nouns naming common objects, and adjectives specifying blunt sensations.

Through such nouns and adjectives Faulkner manages his transitions in time. Places, names, smells, feelings – these are the chance stimuli that switch Benjy from one track of memory to another. As they impress themselves on him, jolting his mind backward or forward in time, they seem mere accidental distractions, and it is important for the credibility of the section that they continue to seem so; but they are also carefully spaced and arranged so as to intensify Faulkner's meanings by effects of association, incongruity and, above all, juxtaposition.

Juxtaposition is here both method and advantage. Through it we gain sudden insights and shocks which, in small symbolic presentiments or recapitulations, crystallize the meanings of the sequence – insights of the kind a man may have when he looks back upon a life's work and knows, indisputably, that it is waste, or shocks of the kind a man may feel when he looks upon his child and considers the blows to which it is certain to be exposed. By making the past seem simultaneous with the present, Faulkner gains remarkable moments of pathos, moments sounding the irrevocable sadness that comes from a recognition of decline and failure. And remarkable, one must add, for the ways small incidents and contrasts, little more than the slurred minutiae of life, suggest the largest issues in human conduct.

In a fragment that may roughly date 1902, Mrs. Compson chides Caddy for proposing to take the seven-year-old Benjy into the winter cold without overshoes: '"Do you want to make him sick, with the house full of company"'. Formal sentiment followed by actual motive, the sentence reveals Mrs. Compson to her marrow. As if aware that she may have betrayed herself, she then takes the idiot boy's face into her hands and calls him '"[m]y poor baby"' (p.6). A page beyond, in a scene set eleven years later, the neurasthenic Mrs. Compson is still calling Benjy '"the baby"' (p.7). But when this '"baby"' starts moaning during a trip to the family graveyard, she is helpless and it is Dilsey who knows how to placate him: '"Give him a flower to hold"' (p.8).

At the climax of the Benjy section, fragments from 1900 and 1928 alternate. The strands from 1900 show Caddy feeding her little idiot brother with kindness and care, those from 1928 show Caddy's daughter, Quentin, asking at a family meal: '"Has he got to keep that old dirty slipper on the table . . . Why don't you feed him in the kitchen. It's like eating with a pig"' (p.68).

A few pages earlier there occurs a similar contrast between Caddy and her daughter. In 1909 Caddy and a boy are making love on a swing in the Compson backyard. Discovering them, Benjy 'cried and pulled Caddy's dress'. Caddy tries to break away from her lover and when he remarks that Benjy '"can't talk,"' she replies in agitation, '"He can see."' (p.45) Running into the house and holding each other in the dark, Caddy and Benjy weep together. '"I won't any more, ever,"' the girl whispers. A few lines below, in a fragment from 1928, the girl, Quentin, is sitting on the same swing with a circus man. Scolding Luster for letting Benjy follow her, she cries out, '"You old crazy loon . . . I'm going to tell Dilsey about the way you let him follow everywhere I go. I'm going to make her whip you good"' (p.46).

Shortly after Caddy's wedding Benjy stands at the gate of the Compson house, crying loudly. His Negro keeper explains, 'Ain't nothing going to quiet him . . . He think if he down to the gate, Miss Caddy come back'. To which Mrs. Compson, with her usual sensitiveness, replies, 'Nonsense' (p.49). On the following page, in a passage set two or three years later, Jason and Mrs. Compson are discussing how Benjy managed to get out of the yard and 'attack' some little girls coming home from school. 'How did he get out, Father said. Did you leave the gate unlatched when you came in, Jason' (p.50).

In each of these juxtapositions, the whole Compson story is enacted: in Mrs. Compson's whining over her '"baby"' (pp. 6, 7), in the treatment of Benjy by his sister and niece, in the varying significance the gate has for Benjy. Such contrasts reveal the family's history in all its vulnerability, and the result is not an account but a picture of experience, a series of stripped exposures. When Benjy's mind comes to rest, the final effect of these juxtapositions is overwhelming. To specify that effect accurately requires a somewhat startling comparison. In Jane Austen's *Persuasion* (1818) the writing forms a highly polished and frequently trivial surface of small talk, and only toward the end does one fully realize that beneath this surface has occurred a romance of exquisite refinement. In the Benjy sequence, the writing forms a surface that is rough, broken, and forbidding, and only toward the end does one fully realize that beneath it Faulkner has retrieved a social history of exquisite pathos. At opposite poles of technique, the two pieces have in common an essential trait of art: they reveal more than they say.[13] □

Howe's combination of a detailed analysis with a comparison to Jane Austen helps to enhance Faulkner's status, suggesting that he is a highly conscious and accomplished artist. He goes on to discuss Quentin's section in some detail, though he thinks it less successful than the Benjy sequence, which, 'by picturing a disintegration specific to one family yet common to our age, gains its strength from a largeness of reference. The Quentin section abruptly reduces the scope of the novel to a problem that is "special" in a clinical sense and not necessarily an equivalent or derivative of the Compson history'.[14] Nonetheless, Howe concludes his chapter by ranking *The Sound and the Fury* among those 'American novels of the [twentieth] century which may be called great, which bear serious comparison with the achievements of twentieth-century European literature'. Echoing those early reviews that defined the novel as a 'tragedy' (pp. 13, 18, 19, 20, 21), Howe finds that it is 'one of the three or four American works of prose fiction written since the turn of the century in which the impact of tragedy is felt and sustained'. Furthermore, despite his criticisms of some aspects of the Quentin section, Howe finds *The Sound and the Fury* 'the one novel in which his vision and technique are almost in complete harmony, and the vision itself whole and major'. Its vision, as Howe defines it, is of a particular kind, one perhaps particularly appropriate to a postwar world torn by conflicts and threatened with nuclear war: '[w]hether taken as a study of the potential for human self-destruction, or as a rendering of the social disorder particular to our time, the novel projects a radical image of man against the wall'.[15]

Turning to *As I Lay Dying*, Howe homes in on what he sees as 'the crux of the novel':

■ That *As I Lay Dying* is something more than a record of peregrine [outlandish] disaster we soon discover. As it circles over a journey in space, the novel also plunges into the secret life of the journeyers. Each of them conducts the action a little way while reciting the burden of his mind; the novel resembles a cantata in which a theme is developed and varied through a succession of voices [a cantata is a musical term for 'a choral work, [a] kind of short oratorio [semi-dramatic musical composition], or lyric drama set to music but not intended for acting']. In *As I Lay Dying* the theme is death, death as it shapes life. The outer action, never to be neglected and always fearsomely and absurdly spectacular, is a journey in a wagon; the inner action is the attempt of the Bundrens to define themselves as members of a family at the moment the family is perishing.

Neither fire nor flood is the crux of the novel, nor any physical action at all; it is Addie Bundren's soliloquy, her thoughts as she lay dying (pp. 157–65). This soliloquy is one of Faulkner's most brilliant rhetorical set-pieces, placed about two-thirds of the way through the novel and establishing an intense moment of stillness which overpowers, so to speak, the noise of the Bundren journey. Until that moment in the book, Faulkner lightly traces the tangled relationships among the Bundrens – the father, the daughter, Dewey Dell, the sons, Cash, Darl, Jewel[,] and . . . Vardaman. It seems at first that Darl, the most introspective of the sons, is the cause and catalyst of family tensions. He guesses Dewey Dell's pregnancy and silently taunts her with his knowledge; he hovers over Jewel with eager attentiveness and broods upon the rivalry between them. But Addie's soliloquy makes clear that the conflicts among the children are rooted in the lives of their parents, in the failure of a marriage. It is Addie who dominates the book, thrusting her sons against each other as if they were warring elements of her own character. From her soliloquy until the end of the novel, the action is a physical resolution of the Bundrens' inner troubles, a resolution which must be achieved if the body is to be buried in some sort of peace.

Dying, Addie remembers her youth. Always she had searched for a relation with people by which to impress her will; at no point did her energy find full release. The search for meaning was for her a search for impact, a fierce desire that not all her desires be dissipated in words. Hard, single-minded, intolerant, Addie is one of these Faulknerian characters concerning whom one finds little to admire except their utter insistence upon taking and struggling with life until the end. As a schoolteacher she 'would look forward to the times when they faulted, so I could whip them. When the switch fell I could feel it upon my flesh; when it welted and ridged it was my blood that ran, and I would think with each blow of the switch: Now you are aware of me! Now I am something in your secret and selfish life' (p. 157). But when she married Anse she learned that, for all her fierce willfulness, she would never penetrate to his secret and selfish life . . . . . .

Softened and dulled, Addie's emotional yearnings reappear among her children, as indeed they suffuse the entire novel. Though it contains a group of figures who in all the obvious ways are among the least conscious in Faulkner's work, the book is, nonetheless, devoted – almost as if it were a Jamesian novel – to the effort of several characters to achieve a break-through in consciousness. They brush against each other for friction and light; the very irritation one produces in another forces all of them to some glimmer of awareness; and the climax of the mother's death, herding them into a brief closeness, serves to intensify this discovery through pain. Not the least of Faulkner's achievements is that he locates the striving for a fine consciousness in a family like the Bundrens, realizes the incongruity of this, and then transforms the incongruity into the very terms of his triumph.

Addie's sons, in their struggle toward self-definition, discover that to answer the question, *Who am I?*, they must first consider, *What was my mother and how did she shape me?* The rivalry between Darl and Jewel, which recurs throughout the book like an underground tremor, is a rivalry in sonship, and it is Darl's sense of being unwanted which drives him to his obsessive questionings and finally his collapse. As the children try, each in his fumbling or inarticulate way, to learn the meaning of living as son or brother, Addie's authority persists and grows; indeed, her power is never greater than during the moment after her death, when the Bundrens realize how thoroughly the dead live on, tyrants from the past. In their search for selfhood the Bundrens demonstrate their mother's conviction that language is vanity while action is the test of life: 'I would think how words go straight up in a thin line, quick and harmless, and how terribly doing goes along the earth, clinging to it' (p. 162). The sentence prefigures the Bundren history and announces the theme of the book – though not the entire theme. For at the end Cash is able to reach toward that harmonious relation between word and action which none of the Bundrens, not even Addie, sees enough to desire.

Tyrannical in its edict of love and rejection, the will of the mother triumphs through the fate of her children. Cash, the accepted son, endures a preposterous excess of pain largely because of his own inattention and the stupidity of the others. He thereby learns the meaning of kinship, his brothers impinging on him through the torment they cause him; and at the end he takes his place as the mature witness of the wreckage of the family. Jewel, by breaking from his violent obsession, fulfills his mother's prophecy: '"He is my cross and he will be my salvation. He will save me from the water and from the fire"' (p. 156). Literally, that is what Jewel does, and when he parts from his horse in order to speed Addie's burial he achieves a direct expression of filial love. Dewey Dell, munching her banana, continues to move in an orbit of egoism; Vardaman remains pathetic and troubled; and Anse gets himself another wife, 'duck-shaped' and with 'hard-looking pop eyes' (p. 247).

Darl is the family sacrifice. An unwanted son, he seeks continually to find a place in the family. The pressures of his secret knowledge, the pain of observing the journey, the realization that he can never act upon what he knows – these drive Darl close to madness. Now he dares taunt Jewel: '"whose son are you? . . . . . . Your mother was a horse, but who was your father, Jewel?"' (p. 198). From the sobriety of Cash, Darl moves to the derangement of Vardaman . . . . . .

Betrayed by Dewey Dell and assaulted by Jewel, Darl is taken away to the asylum. Only Cash understands him; only Cash and Vardaman pity him. Speaking of himself in the third person, a sign of extreme self-estrangement, Darl says:

> Darl is our brother, our brother Darl. Our brother Darl in a cage in Jackson where, his grimed hands lying light in the quiet interstices, looking out he foams.
>
> 'Yes yes yes yes yes yes yes yes.' (p. 242)

To the end it is a search for kinship that obsesses Darl, and his cryptic row of affirmatives may signify a last, pathetic effort to proclaim his brotherhood.[16] □

If, for Howe, *As I Lay Dying* is not as great a work as *The Sound and the Fury*, it is nonetheless a remarkable achievement, of a distinctive kind:

■ Because he writes of the Bundrens with a comely and tactful gravity, a deep underlying respect, Faulkner is able to blend extreme and incongruous effects – the sublime and the trivial, anguish and absurdity, a wretched journey through the sun and a pathetic journey toward kinship. An American epic, *As I Lay Dying* is human tragedy and country farce. The marvel is, that to be one it had to be the other.[17] □

A second important critic of Faulkner to emerge in the 1950s was Olga W. Vickery. An essay on *As I Lay Dying* had appeared in the journal *Perspective* in Autumn 1950, and another on *The Sound and the Fury* in *PMLA* in December 1954. Both these essays were gathered into her study *The Novels of William Faulkner: A Critical Interpretation*, which first appeared in 1959 and then, in a revised edition, in 1964. By Vickery's own account, the essay on *The Sound and the Fury* was shortened for the book and the essay on *As I Lay Dying* 'much altered'.[18] In her discussion of *The Sound and the Fury*, as it appears in her 1964 study, Vickery, like Howe, aims to justify the structure of the narrative and the ordering of its four sections and she does so in a lucid and illuminating way, relating it to the theme and patterns of the novel:

■ The structure of the novel is clearly reflected in the organization of the events of the evening on which Damuddy dies. These events reveal the typical gestures and reactions of the four children to each other and to the mysterious advent of death. They chart the range and kind of each of their responses to a new experience. In this way the evening partakes of the dual nature of the novel: primarily it is an objective, dramatic scene revealing the relations and tensions which exist among the children, but at the same time it is a study in perspective. Between the fact of Damuddy's death and the reader stands not only the primitive mind of the narrator, Benjy, but the diverse attitudes of the other children and the deliberate uncommunicativeness of the adults.

Within the novel as a whole it is Caddy's surrender to Dalton Ames which serves both as the source of dramatic tension and as the focal point for the various perspectives. This is evident in the fact that the sequence of events is not caused by her act – which could be responded to in very different ways – but by the significance which each of her brothers actually attributes to it. As a result, the four sections appear quite unrelated even though they repeat certain incidents and are concerned with the same problem, namely Caddy and her loss of virginity. Although there is a progressive revelation or rather clarification of the plot, each of the sections is itself static. The consciousness of each character becomes the actual agent illuminating and being illuminated by the central situation. Everything is immobilized in this pattern; there is no development of either character or plot in the traditional manner. This impression is reinforced not only by the shortness of time directly involved in each section but by the absence of any shifts in style of the kind that, for example, accompany the growing maturity of Cash Bundren in *As I Lay Dying*.

By fixing the structure while leaving the central situation ambiguous, Faulkner forces the reader to reconstruct the story and to apprehend its significance for himself. Consequently, the reader recovers the story at the same time as he grasps the relation of Benjy, Quentin, and Jason to it. This, in turn, is dependent on his comprehension of the relation between the present and the past events with which each of the first three sections deals. As he proceeds from one section to the next, there is a gradual clarification of events, a rounding out of the fragments of scenes and conversations which Benjy reports. Thus, with respect to the plot the four sections are inextricably connected, but with respect to the central situation they are quite distinct and self-sufficient. As related to the central focus, each of the first three sections presents a version of the same facts which is at once the truth and a complete distortion of the truth. It would appear, then, that the theme of *The Sound and the Fury*, as revealed by the structure, is the relation between the act and man's apprehension of the act, between the event and the interpretation. The relation is by no means a rigid or inelastic thing but is a matter of shifting perspective, for, in a sense, each man creates his own truth. This does not mean that truth does not exist or that it is fragmentary or that it is unknowable; it only insists that truth is a matter of the heart's response as well as the mind's logic.

In keeping with this theme each of the first three sections presents a well demarcated and quite isolated world built around one of these splinters of truth. The fact that Benjy is dumb is symbolic of the closed nature of these worlds; communication is impossible when Caddy who is central to all three means something different to each. For Benjy she is the smell of trees; for Quentin, honor; and for Jason, money or at least the means of obtaining it. Yet these intense private dramas are taking place in a public world primarily concerned with observable behavior. Accordingly, in the fourth section we are shown what an interested but unimplicated observer would see of the Compsons. For the first time we realize that Benjy has blue eyes, that Mrs. Compson habitually wears black dressing gowns, and that Jason looks somewhat like a caricature of a bartender. Moreover, since we are prevented from sharing in the consciousness and memories of the characters, Caddy is no longer an immediate center. Nevertheless, through the conflict between Jason and Miss Quentin the final repercussions of her affair penetrate into the life of Jefferson and even Mottson. And out of the Compson house, itself a symbol of isolation, one person, Dilsey, emerges to grasp the truth which must be felt as well as stated.

Out of the relation that Benjy, Quentin, and Jason bear to Caddy yet another pattern emerges: a gradual progression from the completely closed and private world of the first section to the completely public world of the fourth. The latter, in a sense, both reverses and repeats the former: in the one Benjy is restricted by his retarded mind to immediate facts and sensations, in the other the reader is similarly limited. But Benjy's subjectivity has been replaced presumably by the reader's objectivity. Quentin's section is very close to Benjy's, for although he performs the gestures expected of him by other people, his world is essentially as isolated and irrational as his brother's.

Jason, on the other hand, moves nearer to the public world of the fourth section insofar as he is able to act effectively, if unethically, in a social situation.

Moreover, each of these shifts from the private to the public world is accompanied by a corresponding shift in the form of apprehension. With Benjy we are restricted entirely to sensation which cannot be communicated; quite appropriately therefore Benjy is unable to speak. The closed world which he builds for himself out of various sensations becomes at once the least and the most distorted account of experience. He merely presents snatches of dialogue, bits of scenes exactly as they took place. Such reproduction is not necessarily synonymous with the truth. Benjy, however, makes it his truth and his ethics, for it is in terms of sensation that he imposes a very definite order on his experience. Despite the apparent chaos of fragments, Benjy himself lives in a world which is inflexible and rigid. The extent of its inflexibility is indicated by his bellows of protest whether over a wrong turn taken by Luster, Caddy's use of perfume, or her sexual promiscuity.

Quentin's world is almost as isolated and inflexible as Benjy's, but its order is based on abstractions rather than sensations. While Benjy can comprehend only the physical aspects of his experience, Quentin sees the physical only as a manifestation of ideas. Thus, his section is filled with echoes, both literary and Biblical, phrases, names quoted out of context but falling neatly into the pattern of his thought. These echoes assume the quality of a ritual by which he attempts to conjure experience into conformity with his wishes. When Caddy's behavior disarranges his world, his protest partakes of Benjy's outrage and agony. He stands despairing before the abyss which has suddenly separated experience and his conception of what experience ought to be, and when all his efforts to coerce experience with a word, 'incest', fail, he chooses death which alone can terminate his unwilling involvement in circumstance.

The third section shows a greater degree of clarity though not of objectivity. The reason for this is that Jason operates in terms of a logic which forms the basis of social communication. We may not approve the direction in which his logic takes him, but that his actions are the results of clear, orderly thinking in terms of cause and effect cannot be disputed. The steps in his reasoning follow one another naturally: since it was because of Caddy that he was deprived not only of his inheritance but of his promised job, his recompense must come from Caddy; and since Miss Quentin was the actual cause of Herbert's displeasure, it is through her that he simultaneously gains his wealth and his revenge. It is part of the general satiric intent of this section that Jason's obvious distortion of Caddy should be associated with logic and reason, for it throws a new perspective not only on the actions of the Compsons but on Jason, the representative of the 'rational' man.

The objective nature of the fourth section precludes the use of any single level of apprehension, and accordingly it provokes the most complex response. Dilsey, almost as inarticulate as Benjy, becomes through her actions alone the embodiment of the truth of the heart which is synonymous with morality. The acceptance of whatever time brings, the absence of questioning and petty protests, enables her to create order out of circumstance rather than in defiance of it, and in so doing she gains both dignity and significance for her life. In a sense, Dilsey represents a final perspective directed toward the past and the Compsons, but it is also the reader's perspective for which Dilsey merely provides the vantage point. This fact suggests another reason for the objective narration in this section: to use Dilsey as a point of view character would be to destroy her efficacy as the ethical norm, for that would give us but one more splinter of the truth confined and conditioned by the mind which grasped it.[19] ☐

Like her analysis of *The Sound and the Fury*, Vickery's account of *As I Lay Dying* focuses on the structure of the novel and the relationship of its structure to its theme. Her interpretation is, once again, clear and insightful; and it is especially notable for its discussion of 'the language of the unconscious' in *As I Lay Dying* and for its dissent from the view that the Bundrens' journey to Jefferson is a positive one, an affirmation of humanity or morality:

■ *As I Lay Dying* possesses basically the same structure as *The Sound and the Fury* but in a more complex form. Instead of four main sections, three of which are dominated by the consciousness of a single character, there are some fifty short sections apportioned among fifteen characters. Each of these brief chapters describes some part either of the funeral preparations or of the procession itself, even as it explores and defines the mind of the observer from whose point of view the action is described. Accordingly, the clear sweep of the narrative is paralleled by a developing psychological drama of whose tensions and compulsions the characters themselves are only half-aware. The need to co-operate during the journey merely disguises the essential isolation of each of the Bundrens and postpones the inevitable conflict between them. For the Bundrens, no less than the Compsons, are living in a private world whose nature is gauged in relation to Addie and to the actual events of the journey to Jefferson. The larger frame of reference, provided in *The Sound and the Fury* by the impersonal, third person narration of the fourth section, is here conveyed dramatically through eight different characters who comment on some aspect of the funeral in which they themselves are not immediately involved. Their diverse reactions to and judgments of the Bundrens chart the range of social responses, passing from friendliness to indifference to outraged indignation.

As in *The Sound and the Fury*, each private world manifests a fixed and distinctive way of reacting to and ordering experience. Words, action, and contemplation constitute the possible modes of response, while sensation, reason, and intuition form the levels of consciousness. All of these combine to establish a total relationship between the individual and his experience; for certain of the characters in *As I Lay Dying*, however, this relationship is fragmented and distorted. Anse, for example, is always the bystander, contemplating events and reducing the richness of experience to a few threadbare clichés. In contrast, Darl, the most complex of the characters, owes his complexity and his madness to the fact that he encompasses all possible modes of response and awareness without being able to effect their integration. It is Cash, the oldest brother, who ultimately achieves maturity and understanding by integrating these modes into one distinctively human response which fuses words and action, reason and intuition. In short, the Bundren family provides a locus for the exploration of the human psyche in all its complexity without in the least impairing the immediate reality of character and action.

The different levels of consciousness are rendered by Faulkner through variations in style ranging from the dialect of actual speech to the intricate imagery and poetic rhythms of the unconscious. When the characters are engaged in conversation or concerned with concrete objects, the vocabulary used is limited and repetitious and the style is realistic and colloquial. These same qualities, though to a lesser extent, characterize the expression of conscious thought, for whatever a person is aware of, he articulates in his habitual way, which in a number of instances involves a groping for words. There is, however, some loss of immediacy and vividness since on this level language strives to achieve the impersonal order and clarity of reason rather than the concreteness of sensation. With the unconscious or intuitive, the personal element is at once restored and transcended. Making its appeal to emotion and imagination, the language of the unconscious relies heavily on symbols with their power to evoke rather than to define reality. Thus, Faulkner is able to indicate the particular combination of sensation, reason, and intuition possessed by each of his characters, as well as their range of awareness through a subtle manipulation of language and style.

Quite naturally, the three modes of response to experience – words, action, and contemplation – are implemented not by the style but by the series of events with which the characters are confronted.

Each of the Bundrens is concerned with Addie's death and with her funeral, events which are by no means identical. As Doctor Peabody suggests, the former is a personal and private matter: 'I can remember how when I was young I believed death to be a phenomenon of the body; now I know it to be merely a function of the mind – and that of the minds of the ones who suffer the bereavement' (p. 38). Thus, it is Addie not as a mother, corpse, or promise but as an element in the blood of her children who dominates and shapes their complex psychological reactions. Their motivation lies within her life, for she is the source of the tension and latent violence which each of them feels within himself and expresses in his contacts with the rest of the family. Obsessed by their own relationships to Addie, they can resolve that tension only when they have come to terms with her as a person and with what she signifies in their own consciousness.

In contrast to her death, her funeral is a public affair, participated in and, indeed, supervised by the neighbors as well as the family. On this level she is simply the corpse which must be disposed of in accordance with a long established ritual of interment. While the neighbors prepare themselves to comfort the bereaved, the Bundrens are expected to assume the traditional role of mourners, a role which carries with it unspoken rules of propriety and decorum. Only Anse, for whom Addie never existed as an individual, finds such a role congenial. His face tragic and composed, he easily makes the proper responses to condolences and recites his litany of grief, though somewhat marred by his irrepressible egotism. There is even a sense in which Anse thoroughly enjoys the situation since as chief mourner he is, for once in his life, a person of importance. It is not, however, that simple for Addie's sons, who find that the conventions of mourning and burial can neither channel nor contain their grief. Thus, Cora Tull, the self-appointed champion and arbiter of propriety, finds that each of them fails, at some point, to behave in a fitting manner.

Because the agonizing journey to Jefferson does fulfill the promise to Addie, because it does reunite her in death with her family, some critics have seen in it an inspiring gesture of humanity or a heroic act of traditional morality. In reality, however, the journey from beginning to end is a travesty of the ritual of interment. Any ritual, as Addie herself suggests, can become a travesty, even though it has been ordained and sanctioned in its fixed order from the beginning of time. Since there is no virtue attached simply to the meticulous repetition of its words and gestures, it is the individual who must give meaning and life to ritual by recognizing its symbolic function. But the spirit which should give meaning to Addie's funeral is either absent, as in Anse and Dewey Dell, or in conflict with it, as in Cash and Darl. As this becomes clear, the series of catastrophes that befall the Bundrens becomes a source of macabre humor, for it is only when the ritual is disengaged from its symbolic function that the comic aspect becomes apparent.[20] □

Vickery's readings of *The Sound and the Fury* and *As I Lay Dying*, and of Faulkner's work as a whole, helped to advance Faulkner criticism into a new stage, where his stature could be, to some extent, taken for granted, and critics could focus on the task of providing their own interpretations and dissenting from those of others – as Vickery does, in the above extract, when she takes issue with those who would interpret the journey to Jefferson in an affirmative light. Like other critics, Vickery seeks to insert her readings of specific novels into a larger overall pattern; this sense of Faulkner's work as comprising a totality, a whole 'world', is magisterially developed in Cleanth Brooks's *William Faulkner: The Yoknapatawpha Country*, first published in 1963. By 1963, of course, Faulkner was dead; on 6 July 1962, the day after going into hospital with acute back pain, he had died suddenly of a heart attack; he was 64. His death meant that he did not have to find a response to the cultural and political ferment of the USA in the later 1960s; had he lived into that period, his public stances on race, already the source of much controversy in the 1950s, might well have come under far stronger attack.[21] In critical terms, of course, Faulkner's demise cleared the way for his canonisation; and there was no better man to perform the task than Cleanth Brooks, a Southerner, and a New Critic of immense authority.

Brooks announces that his study 'attempts to deal with William Faulkner's characteristic world, the world of Yoknapatawpha Country', and then at once acknowledges the difficulty of this task: '[h]ow does one go about describing a world?' Brooks thinks that there is no inevitable way or one best way and says that 'the disposition of the chapters of this book represents no more than a possible – and I hope useful – way to explore Faulkner's world'.[22] He thus opens for his readers the exciting prospect of following his trail but also, at times, looking for alternative paths.

Rather than taking the novels in chronological order, Brooks, after three introductory chapters, focuses on what he sees as a 'mature work', *Light in August*, that contains 'many of the characteristic topics and themes of [Faulkner's] fiction'. He then explores the conflict and contrast between 'the old order and the new', and the 'theme of honor', in *The Unvanquished*, *Sartoris* and *Sanctuary*, and goes on to examine how that 'theme of honor . . . is transposed into the world of the poor white in . . . *As I Lay Dying*':[23]

■ The code of honor receives heavy stress in [*As I Lay Dying*]. The need of the male to prove himself . . . comes to a high focus in this story of the Bundren family. It is not enough simply to bury the mother reverently and with some show of decent grief; the promise she has exacted must be honored to the letter: come fire or flood, hell or highwater, her body must be taken to the spot which she has designated as her final resting place, and no circumstance, not even the most frustrating, is allowed to cancel the obligation. By any rational test, the undertaking is quixotic, but in carrying it out, two of the children, Cash and Jewel, exhibit true heroism – Cash in his suffering, Jewel in his brave actions. Both brothers go far beyond the claims of rationality and common sense. Their brother Darl, of course, does not. His role is that of the critic of the action, who does not believe in honor and has the supreme lucidity of the mad.

The general importance of honor in the novel deserves stress, especially since many readers associate a concern for honor only with Faulkner's aristocrats and are not sufficiently aware of the sensitivity on that score exhibited by Faulkner's poor whites. An episode late in the book will illustrate, and the comic overtones need not obscure the seriousness of the issues here for the Bundrens. The wagon with its stinking burden is just approaching Jefferson. A passer-by, shocked by the odor, exclaims: '"Great God . . . what they got in that wagon?"'. Jewel whirls toward him with the cry: '"Son of a bitches"' (p.215). It is a term which cannot be ignored, and for a moment it looks as if Jewel and the stranger will fight: Jewel swings at him and the stranger promptly draws a knife. It is interesting to see what happens. Darl apologizes for Jewel by explaining that he is ill and not himself. When this excuse does not suffice, he adds: '"[Jewel] thought you said something to him"' (p.216). This explanation opens a way for mutual accommodation, but in what follows the touchiness of the code of honor is nicely illustrated.

Darl promises that Jewel will take back the offending words but insists that the retraction must not be made under duress, for when the stranger demands that Jewel take back the words, Darl says: '"Put up your knife, and he will"'. The stranger does so, and now Darl conjures Jewel to tell him '"you didn't mean anything"'. '"I thought he said something," Jewel says. "Just because he's –"' But Darl hushes him and says: '"Tell him you didn't mean it"'. And Jewel at last makes the necessary concession by saying that he didn't mean it. The angered man then remarks: '"He better not . . . Calling me a –"'. But the Bundrens must not seem to concede too much and it is now Darl who quickly asks: '"Do you think he's afraid to call you that?"' Whereupon there is a slight retreat on the other side as the stranger cautiously replies: '"I never said that"'. Jewel follows up the advantage with: '"Don't think it, neither"'. But Darl, now that honor has been saved, orders Jewel to '"[s]hut up"' (p.217) and urges his father to drive on. The code involved is quite as elaborate as that humorously described in the fifth act of Shakespeare's *As You Like It* (first performed about

1599). It has its own degrees corresponding to such niceties as Touchstone's 'Reproof Valiant' and his 'Countercheck Quarrelsome' (Act 5, Scene 4, lines 91–92).[24]

The episode is significant in another way. Though we are by this time in the novel perfectly aware of the hostility that exists between Jewel and Darl, and though in another hour or so Jewel will be leaping upon Darl to turn him over to the officers, at this moment Darl is quite as much involved as any other member of the family in preserving the family honor and seeing to it that no stranger takes liberties with it. Even Darl, who does not believe in the quixotic journey and who sees the absurdity of any literal fulfillment of the promise made to his mother – even Darl responds automatically to a defense of the family honor.[25] □

In his discussion of *The Sound and the Fury*, Brooks again takes up, among other things, the question of the 'theme of honor', this time as it relates to the Compson family:

■ Quentin [Compson] was apparently very close to his father and the influence of his father on him was obviously very powerful. The whole of the Quentin section is saturated with what 'Father said' and with references to comparisons that Father used and observations about life that Father made. Though his father seems to have counseled acquiescence in the meaninglessness of existence, it is plain that it was from him that Quentin derived his high notion of the claims of honor. Quentin has not the slightest doubt as to what he ought to do: he ought to drive Caddy's seducer out of town, and if the seducer refuses to go, he ought to shoot him. But Quentin is not up to the heroic role. He tries, but he cannot even hurt Ames, much less kill him. Caddy sees Quentin as simply meddling in her affairs, the quixotic little brother who is to be pitied but not feared or respected . . . . . .

Quentin is emotionally committed to the code of honor, but for him the code has lost its connection with reality: it is abstract, rigidified, even 'literary'. Quentin's suicide results from the fact that he can neither repudiate nor fulfill the claims of the code. The idiot Benjy, of course, has no code at all. His is an inarticulate love, a love that is as direct and wordless as an odor ('Caddy smelled like trees' (pp. 4, 7, 17, 40, 41, 42, 46, 70)). Nevertheless, Benjy's love is recognizably human in that it asks something of the loved one. Benjy can sense Caddy's betrayal of honor: he screams in horror when he smells the perfume that she has worn for her lover, and is not appeased until she has washed it off.

The third brother, Jason, has repudiated the code of honor. He has adopted for himself a purely practical formula for conduct. Money is what counts. He wants none of Quentin's nonsense nor of the other kinds of nonsense in which people believe – or in which they pretend to believe. But though Jason's ostensible code is purely practical, reducing every action to its cash value, his conduct has in fact its nonpractical aspect. For Jason harbors a great deal of nonpractical and irrational bitterness, even sadism. When, in order to see the disappointment upon Luster's face, Jason deliberately drops the passes to the minstrel show into the fire, he is satisfying his perverted emotion even though he pretends to be merely throwing away what cannot be sold. His stealing systematically the money that Caddy is sending for the benefit of her daughter answers to his mercantilism, but Jason is not content to steal Quentin's allowance. He also wants the enjoyment of teasing and hurting the girl.[26] □

The relationship of the three Compson brothers to the 'code of honor' might seem to be one of the aspects of *The Sound and the Fury* that makes it a novel about the decline of the old US South. Brooks, however, is sceptical of such an interpretation, and he contests it in two ways. First, he suggests that the Compsons are not so much representative of the Old South but more of a special case:

■ The basic cause of the breakup of the Compson family – let the more general cultural causes be what they may – is the cold and self-centered mother who is sensitive about the social status of her own family, the Bascombs, who feels the birth of an idiot son as a kind of personal affront, who spoils and corrupts her favorite son, and who withholds any real love and affection from her other children and her husband. Caroline Compson is not so much an actively wicked and evil person as a cold weight of negativity which paralyzes the normal family relationships.[27] □

Brooks's second way of challenging the view that the fall of the Compson family is representative of the fall of the South is the polar opposite of his first way: he proposes that the fall of the Compson family is not a special case, but a universal one. He then complicates matters further, however, by suggesting that it is not altogether universal, since it is a fall that is made worse because it takes place in a society that still clings to 'old-fashioned ideals', Brooks then proceeds to suggest that it can be related specifically to the 'contemporary American scene':

■ The downfall of the house of Compson is the kind of degeneration which can occur, and has occurred, anywhere at any time . . . The real significance of the Southern setting in *The Sound and the Fury* resides, as so often elsewhere in Faulkner, in the fact that the breakdown of a family can be exhibited more poignantly and significantly in a society which is old-fashioned and in which the family is still at the center. The dissolution of the family as an institution has probably gone further in the suburban areas of California and Connecticut than it has in the small towns of Mississippi. For that very reason, what happens to the Compsons might make less noise and cause less comment, and even bring less pain to the individuals concerned, if the Compsons lived in a more progressive and liberal environment. Because the Compsons have been committed to old-fashioned ideals – close family loyalty, home care for defective children, and the virginity of unmarried daughters – the breakup of the family registers with greater impact.

The decay of the Compsons can be viewed, however, not merely with reference to the Southern past but to the contemporary American scene. It is tempting to read it as a parable of the disintegration of modern man. Individuals no longer sustained by familial and cultural unity are alienated and lost in private worlds. One thinks here not merely of Caddy, homeless, the sexual adventuress adrift in the world, or of Quentin, out of touch with reality and moving inevitably to his death, but also and even primarily of Jason, for whom the breakup of the family means an active rejection of claims and responsibilities and, with it, a sense of liberation. Jason resolves to be himself and to be self-sufficient. He says: 'Besides, like I say I guess I don't need any man's help to get along I can stand on my own feet like I always have' (p. 206). Jason prides himself in managing matters by himself and – since this is the other side of the same coin – refuses to heed the claims of anyone but himself . . . Jason is done with religion in every way, including its etymological sense as a 'binding back'. Jason is bound back to nothing. He repudiates any traditional tie. He means to be on his own and he rejects every community.[28] □

Brooks skilfully turns back any suggestion that the fall of the Compson family is an indictment of the South by arguing that it is an indictment of a more general disintegrative trend in modern American society – and it could be said, although Brooks does not say it, that this trend was strengthened by the victory of the North over the South in the American Civil War. But the effectiveness of Brooks's polemical strategy here should not conceal the more general uncertainty he evinces as to the social referent of *The Sound and the Fury*, the way in which he takes up, successively, a range of positions that are not easily compatible: that the Compsons are a special case; that their decline could happen anywhere at any time; that it is particularly painful in a traditional environment; and that it could be a parable of the contemporary American society and of the disintegration of modern man (Brooks very quickly assumes that the state

of contemporary American society and the state of modern man are synonymous). Brooks's uncertainty is perhaps indicative of a more general
but fruitful critical difficulty in determining how far *The Sound and the
Fury* is specific or general, particular or universal, in its import.

Brooks follows up his suggestion that the novel is representative of
the disintegration of modern man with a discussion of Dilsey – a discussion that, in the USA of the early 1960s in which issues of race,
particularly in respect of African Americans, were increasingly prominent, demanded a good deal of critical, and political, tact.

■ The one member of the Compson household who represents a unifying and sustaining force is the Negro servant Dilsey. She tries to take
care of Benjy and to give the girl Quentin the mothering she needs. In
contrast to Mrs. Compson's vanity and whining self-pity, Dilsey
exhibits charity and rugged good sense. She is warned by her
daughter Frony that taking Benjy to church with her will provoke
comments from the neighbours. '"Folks talkin,"' Frony says; to which
Dilsey answers: '"Whut folks? . . . . . . And I know whut kind of folks
. . . Trash white folks. Dat's who it is. Thinks he ain't good enough fer
white church, but nigger church ain't good enough fer him"'. Frony
remarks that folks talk just the same, but Dilsey has her answer: '"Den
you send um to me . . . Tell um de good Lawd don't keer whether he
smart er not. Don't nobody but white trash keer dat"' (p.290). All of
which amounts to sound manners and to sound theology as well.

Faulkner does not present Dilsey as a black fairy-godmother or as
a kind of middle-aged Pollyanna full of the spirit of cheerful optimism.
[*Pollyanna* (1913) was a novel by the American writer Eleanor H[odg-
man] Porter, the child heroine of which plays her favourite 'Glad Game'
of always looking on the bright side in her many difficulties. As *The
Reader's Encyclopedia* (1977) points out, the 'word Pollyanna has become
a synonym for the fatuous, irrepressible optimist who always makes the
best of things for him[her]self and other people'.[29]] Even his physical
description of her looks in another direction. We are told that she had
once been a big woman, but now the unpadded skin is loosely draped
upon the 'indomitable skeleton' which is left 'rising like a ruin or a
landmark above the somnolent and impervious guts, and above that
the collapsed face that gave the impression of the bones themselves
being outside the flesh, lifted into the driving day with an expression
at once fatalistic and of a child's astonished disappointment'
(pp.265–66). What the expression means is best interpreted by what
she says and does in the novel, but the description clearly points to
something other than mindless cheeriness. Dilsey's essential hopeful-
ness has not been obliterated; she is not an embittered woman, but her
optimism has been chastened by hurt and disappointment.

Faulkner does not make the mistake of accounting for Dilsey's virtues through some mystique of race in which good primitive black folk stand over against corrupt wicked white folk. Dilsey herself has no such notions. When her [grand]son Luster remarks of the Compson household: '"Dese is funny folks. Glad I ain't none of em,"' she says: '"Lemme tell you somethin, nigger boy, you got jes es much Compson devilment in you es any of em"' (p.276). She believes in something like original sin: men are not 'naturally' good but require discipline and grace.

Dilsey, then, is no noble savage and no *schöne Seele* [German for 'beautiful soul']. Her view of the world and mankind is thoroughly Christian, simple and limited as her theological expression of her faith would have to be. On the other hand, Dilsey is no plaster saint. She is not easy on her own children [and grandchildren]. ('"Don't stand dar in de rain, fool,"' she tells Luster (p.269).) [Brooks does not make it clear here that Luster is Dilsey's grandchild, the son of her daughter Frony and an unknown man.[30]] She does not always offer the soft answer that turneth away wrath. She rebukes Mrs. Compson with '"I don't see how you expect anybody to sleep, wid you standing in de hall, holl'in at folks fum de crack of dawn,"' (p.270) and she refuses Mrs. Compson's hypocritical offer to fix breakfast, saying: '"En who gwine eat yo messin? . . . Tell me dat"' (p.271). Dilsey's goodness is no mere goodness by, and of, nature, if one means by this a goodness that justifies a faith in man as man. Dilsey does not believe in man; she believes in God.

Dilsey's poverty and her status as a member of a deprived race do not, then, assure her nobility, but they may have had something to do with her remaining close to a concrete world of values so that she is less perverted by abstraction and more honest than are most white people in recognizing what is essential and basic. In general, Faulkner's Negro characters show less false pride, less false idealism, and more seasoned discipline in human relationships. Dilsey's race has also had something to do with keeping her close to a world still informed by religion. These matters are important: just how important they are is revealed by the emphasis Faulkner gives to the Easter service that Dilsey attends.

The Compson family – whatever may be true of the white community at large in the Jefferson of 1910 – has lost its religion. Quentin's sad reveries are filled with references to Jesus and Saint Francis, but it is plain that he has retreated into some kind of Stoicism, a version which is reflected in his father's advice to him: '"we must just stay awake and see evil done for a little while"'. Quentin's reply is that '"it doesnt have to be even that long for a man of courage"' (p.175), and the act of courage in the Roman style takes Quentin into the river. Mrs. Compson, when she finds that the girl Quentin has eloped, asks Dilsey to bring her the Bible, but obviously Mrs. Compson knows nothing about either sin or redemption. Her deepest concern is with gentility and social position. And Jason, as we have seen, worships only the almighty dollar.[31] □

Brooks has a characteristic New Critical nostalgia for a unified traditional society and for Christianity. At the same time, he shares the New Critical dislike of definite commitments in literature, and he is careful to say, as his chapter on *The Sound and the Fury* draws to a close, that 'Faulkner makes no claim for Dilsey's version of Christianity one way or the other. His presentation of it is moving and credible, but moving and credible as an aspect of Dilsey's own mental and emotional life'.[32] Christianity, Brooks observes, does not help those who will not let it help them, for example Mrs. Compson and Jason.

As the above extracts from Brooks's study show, his approach to Faulkner is mainly in terms of characters and themes, and questions of technique are secondary to that. To some extent, the same is true of Michael Millgate's study, *The Achievement of William Faulkner* (1966), though Millgate is also interested in Faulkner's own statements about his work, and in how Faulkner revised his work. He looks at earlier drafts of Faulkner's novels where available. For example, he comments on Faulkner's extensive additions and amendments to the Quentin section of *The Sound and the Fury*, and especially on the introduction, in revision, of references to Quentin's father. This leads him into his discussion of characters and themes in the novel. He suggests, interestingly, that Quentin, in all his acts, is concerned for the act's 'significance as a gesture rather than for its practical efficacy' (that is, whether the act produces the desired effect); he considers Quentin's obsession with time; and he addresses the issue of the success of the characterisation of Caddy and of her exclusion from the privileges of interior monologue:

■ Throughout the [Quentin] section, as revised in the carbon type-script and the published book, Quentin's mind runs on his father almost as much as it does on Caddy. Quentin is, of course, very much like his father in many ways, and in his obsession with family tradition and honour it is understandable that he should refer to his father, the head of the family, as a transmitter of that tradition and as a source of authority and advice. The irony of this situation, however, and a major cause of Quentin's tragedy, is that just as his mother has failed him as a source of love so his father fails him utterly in all his roles of progenitor [ancestor], confessor and counsellor. He has become, indeed, Quentin's principal enemy, his cold and even cynical logic persistently undermining the very basis of all those idealistic concepts to which Quentin so passionately holds. Throughout the section there is a battle in progress between Quentin's romantic idealism and Mr. Compson's somewhat cynical realism, a battle which is not finally resolved in *The Sound and the Fury* and which is resumed on an even larger scale in *Absalom, Absalom!*. Indeed, if we are to understand that the discussion between Quentin and his father at the end of the section is purely a figment of Quentin's imagination and never actually took place, then it has to be said that in *The Sound and the Fury* the battle is never properly joined – as, according to Mr. Compson himself, no battle ever is – and that it is, rather, a series of skirmishes in which Quentin suffers a progressive erosion of his position and a steady depletion of his reserves. Father and son are, in any case, too much alike in their fondness for words, for abstractions, and in choosing to evade life – the one in drink, the other in suicide – rather than actively confront it.

Whenever Quentin acts, his concern is for the act's significance as a gesture rather than for its practical efficacy. He seeks pertinaciously [stubbornly] for occasions to fight in defence of his sister's honour, knowing in advance that he will be beaten and concerned in retrospect only that he has performed the act in its ritualistic and symbolistic aspects. It is the fight with Gerald Bland which reveals most clearly the degree to which Quentin's obsessions have divorced him from actuality, since throughout the struggle it is the remembered fight with Dalton Ames which remains for Quentin the superior reality. Throughout a whole day of quite extraordinary incident – with two fights, an arrest, a court hearing, much movement and many encounters – Quentin's mind remains preoccupied with the past. It is almost as though Faulkner were playing on the idea that a drowning man sees his whole life pass before him, and we come to realize that this last day of Quentin's is a kind of suspended moment before death.

Quentin's own obsession with time derives primarily from his recognition of it as the dimension in which change occurs and in which Caddy's actions have efficacy and significance. His search is for a means of arresting time at a moment of achieved perfection, a moment when he and Caddy could be eternally together in the simplicity of their childhood relationship; his idea of announcing that he and Caddy had committed incest was, paradoxically, a scheme for regaining lost innocence:

> it was to isolate her out of the loud world so that it would have to flee us of necessity and then the sound of it would be as though it had never been . . . if i could tell you we did it would have been so and then the others wouldnt be so and then the world would roar away (p. 176)

The similarity between this conception and the image of motion in stasis which haunted Faulkner throughout his life, especially as embodied in Keats's 'Ode to a Grecian Urn' (1820), suggests – as do the echoes of Joyce – that Quentin is in some measure a version of the artist, or at least the aesthete, as hero. But Quentin's conception is artificial, rigid, life-denying: as Mr. Compson observes, '[p]urity is a negative state and therefore contrary to nature. It's nature is hurting you not Caddy . . . ' (p. 115). The inadequacy of Quentin's position is exposed in terms of Caddy and her vitality and humanity. In the Benjy section we recognize Caddy as the principal sustainer of such family unity as survives: we glimpse her as the liveliest spirit among the children and their natural leader, as the protector and comforter of Benjy, and even as the pacifier of her mother, and it is highly significant for us as well as for Benjy that she is persistently associated with such elemental things as the fire, the pasture, the smell of trees, and sleep. Her sexual freedom appears as the expression of a natural rebellion against the repressive, contradictory, and essentially self-centred demands made upon her by the different members of her family; it certainly seems spontaneous and affirmative by the side of Quentin's fastidious or even impotent avoidance of sexual experience – we note, for example, his revulsion at his childish experiments with Natalie and the fact that he is known at Harvard for his indifference to women – or Jason's rigid compartmentalization of his sexual life and strict subordination of it to his financial interests.

Caddy finds an outlet from family repression in sexual activity, but she is also both a principle and a symbol of social disruption. Her assertion of individuality is much less positive and urgent than that of such a character as Ursula Brangwen in D.H. Lawrence's *The Rainbow* (1915); even so, she is brought, like Ursula, to break with traditional patterns and, in so doing, to demonstrate just how moribund those patterns have become, how irrelevant both to modern conditions and to the needs of the human psyche. It is possible to feel, however, that although Caddy is the core of the book she is not herself a wholly successful creation. Faulkner often spoke of Caddy, outside the novel, with an intensely passionate devotion: 'To me she was the beautiful one,' he said at the University of Virginia, 'she was my heart's darling. That's what I wrote the book about and I used the tools which seemed to me the proper tools to try to tell, try to draw the picture of Caddy'.[33] The original image of the little girl with the muddy drawers grew into the rich and complex conception of Caddy, beautiful and tragic both as child and woman, but although this conception is already present in the first section of the novel it is evoked, necessarily, in somewhat fragmentary fashion, as we glimpse Caddy in various family situations, as we sense how much she means to Benjy, as we come to associate her, through Benjy, with images of brightness, comfort and loss. In the second section Caddy is more clearly visible, and there are passages of remembered dialogue as revealing of Caddy's character as of Quentin's, but the world of Quentin's section is so unstable, so hallucinatory, that the figure of Caddy, like so much else, is enveloped in uncertainty. In Jason's section Caddy's agony is most movingly evoked, but only briefly so, while in the final section of the book she is no more than a memory.

It was an essential element in Faulkner's overall conception of the novel that Caddy never be seen directly but only through the eyes of her three brothers, each with his own self-centred demands to make upon her, each with his own limitations and obsessions. Asked at Virginia why he did not give a section to Caddy herself, Faulkner replied that it seemed more 'passionate' to do it through her brothers,[34] and one is reminded of his remarks at Nagano about the beauty of description by understatement and indirection: 'Remember, all Tolstoy said about Anna Karenina was that she was beautiful and could see in the dark like a cat. That's all he ever said to describe her. And every man has a different idea of what's beautiful. And it's best to take the gesture, the shadow of the branch, and let the mind create the tree'.[35] It certainly seems likely that to have made Caddy a 'voice' in the novel would have diminished her importance as a central, focal figure. As the book stands, however, Caddy emerges incompletely from the first two sections, and in the last two attention shifts progressively from her to her daughter, Quentin. The different limitations in the viewpoints of Benjy, Quentin and Jason make unavoidable the shadowiness, the imprecision, of Caddy's presentation: because the mind of each is so closed upon its own obsessions it is scarcely true to speak of their interior monologues as throwing light upon Caddy from a variety of angles; it is rather as though a series of photographs in differing focus were superimposed one upon the other, blurring all clarity of outline or detail. The novel revolves upon Caddy, but Caddy herself escapes satisfactory definition, and her daughter's tragedy, simply because it is more directly presented, is in some ways more moving.[36] □

The issue of the representation of Caddy – or of the failure to represent her – is one that will be taken up by later critics, especially, of course, from feminist perspectives.

When Millgate moves on to discuss *As I Lay Dying*, he refers to a number of attempts 'to establish specific relationships' between this novel and *The Sound and the Fury*,[37] singling out especially Carvel Collins's essay 'The Pairing of *The Sound and the Fury* and *As I Lay Dying*' (1957).[38] Millgate himself draws a number of fruitful comparisons and contrasts in the following extract:

■ *The Sound and the Fury* and *As I Lay Dying* . . . do invite comparison as products of the same immensely creative period in Faulkner's career, as two of his most ambitious stylistic experiments, and as his only substantial adventures in 'stream of consciousness' techniques. It is arguable, too, that *As I Lay Dying* follows up *The Sound and the Fury* in its treatment of a tightly-knit family situation revolving upon a single female figure. Here the central figure is Addie, the mother, instead of Caddy, the sister, and Faulkner seems to have attempted to avoid repeating whatever inadequacies there may have been in his presentation of Caddy, at least to the extent of giving Addie one of the fifty-nine sections of interior monologue into which the novel is divided. *As I Lay Dying* might also be said to mark a development from *The Sound and the Fury* in that Faulkner is now at pains to establish the setting and social context of the novel from the beginning . . . . . . [The] drama of Darl's personal breakdown recalls that of Quentin Compson in *The Sound and the Fury*, and Darl's vision, his perception of the world and of himself, undoubtedly has something in common with Quentin's state of mind on the day of his suicide . . . . . . [There are] also . . . certain thematic similarities between the two books. The idea of 'twilight', for example . . . is . . . important [in *The Sound and the Fury* and] in *As I Lay Dying*: [an extract from Millgate's earlier discussion of 'twilight' in *The Sound and the Fury* is inserted here to reinforce his comparison]. In Quentin's section, in particular, [in *The Sound and the Fury*] twilight, as a condition of light and a moment in time, takes on very considerable importance[39] . . . The phrase [in Quentin's monologue] about 'all stable things' becoming 'shadowy paradoxical' (p. 169) aptly defines the hallucinatory world of the Quentin section, but it is also relevant to the treatment of 'fact', of 'truth', throughout the novel. Like *Absalom, Absalom!*, *The Sound and the Fury* is in part concerned with the elusiveness, the multivalence, of truth, or at least with man's persistent and perhaps necessary tendency to make of truth a personal thing: each man, apprehending some fragment of the truth, seizes upon that fragment as though it were the whole truth and elaborates it into a total vision of the world, rigidly exclusive and hence utterly fallacious.[40] [The text now returns to Millgate's discussion of *As I Lay Dying*.] Addie Bundren [in *As I Lay Dying*] is herself at the twilight point, the poised moment, between life and death; it is at the hour of twilight that she dies; and throughout the early part of the book the dying of the day and of the daylight is persistently linked with the moment of her death, somewhat in the manner of Shakespeare's sonnet 73 [lines 5–8 of this sonnet run: 'In me thou seest the twilight of such day/As after sunset fadeth in the west,/Which by and by black night doth take away/Death's second self, that seals up all in rest'.[41]].

More important, however, is the extent to which the whole

journey to Jefferson with Addie's body becomes for Darl, and for the reader, an outrageous 'denial of the significance [it] should have affirmed' [from Quentin's monologue in *The Sound and the Fury*, p. 169]. We are challenged throughout the book, as throughout *The Sound and the Fury*, to confront and, so far as possible, to bridge the gulf that divides our personal systems of value from those adhered to by the characters; we are equally challenged to perceive and resolve the contradictions that necessarily follow from the use of multiple points of view. A major source of ironic, and often comic, effects in *As I Lay Dying* is the frequency with which characters are completely mistaken in their judgments of each other, and of themselves. We quickly realize, for example, that Cora Tull is utterly wrong about the kind and quality of the relationships within the Bundren family, while her own obsession with the cakes she has made prepares the way for the throw-away humour of Addie's brief but shattering reference to 'Cora, who could never even cook' (p. 162). Of a similar order is the recurrent association of Jewel with images of rigidity – the description of him in Darl's opening section (p. 1) . . . is reinforced by many subsequent allusions to his wooden face and eyes, his wooden back, and so on – in direct contrast to the inward passion and fury of his nature.

In *As I Lay Dying*, then, as in *The Sound and the Fury*, we are confronted with the problems of the elusiveness of truth, the subjectivity of what individuals call fact, and there is a sense in which these two novels together with the later *Absalom, Absalom!* can be regarded as a trilogy on this theme. In *Absalom, Absalom!*, as in the two earlier novels, the narrative is assembled from fragments; the central situation is progressively illuminated by the light thrown upon it from a number of different viewpoints, none of them possessing final authority. *As I Lay Dying* represents a development from *The Sound and the Fury* in that the authorial voice is entirely dispensed with, but *Absalom, Absalom!* goes a step further than *As I Lay Dying* in that we ultimately remain in doubt as to what has 'really' happened, something which is not seriously at issue in *As I Lay Dying*. Here the concern with the many faces of truth merges with, and is eventually superseded by, the examination of the many meanings of experience – specifically, of the widely divergent purposes which the various members of the Bundren family hope to achieve in the course of their joint expedition to Jefferson. Regarded in this light, the multiplicity of viewpoints, which is much more marked than in *The Sound and the Fury* or *Absalom, Absalom!* and which may give an initial appearance of fragmentation, begins to appear rather as a means both of dramatizing diversity and of focusing it upon a single course of action. A further focusing effect is achieved by the way in which the relationships within the Bundren family radiate about Addie, the mother, as both their physical and their symbolic core. Addie's powerful personality and the principle of family unity which she embodies have long held the family together and continue so to hold it at least until her body has been buried, and it is entirely natural that she should not only occupy the foreground of the novel throughout but become, in effect, the battlefield on which her husband and her children – especially Jewel and Darl – fight out their personal rivalries and antagonisms. What finally gives the technique its unifying force is the way in which the successive segments not only advance the action, the progress towards Jefferson, but continually cast light inwards upon the central situation, deepening our understanding of the characters and intensifying our awareness of their often violent interrelationships.

It has sometimes been suggested that the sheer profusion of points of view in *As I Lay Dying* is self-defeating, and there is perhaps a sense in which the *tour de force* draws attention to itself by its very brilliance [a *tour de force* is 'a feat of strength or skill'; in one of the drafts for his Introduction to the proposed but unpublished 1933 Modern Library edition of *The Sound and the Fury*, Faulkner himself said: '[w]hen I began *As I Lay Dying* . . . I set out deliberately to write a tour-de-force. Before I ever set down the first word I said, I am going to write a book by which, at a pinch, I can stand or fall if I never touch ink again'.[42]]. But Faulkner succeeds marvellously in catching the tone of voice of such characters as Anse – it is the skills evident in the Jason section of *The Sound and the Fury* which are being exploited here – and the use of a wide range of viewpoints gives moral as well as narrative perspective, offers scope for rich ironic effects, and broadens the sense of social reality. A clear distinction must be made, however, between viewpoints, such as those of Darl, Cash, and other members of the Bundren family, which display a developing internal drama, a progression from one segment to the next, and those, such as MacGowan's and Samson's, which are single expressions of an outside view. The technique of the novel represents, of course, *a tour de force* of conception as well as of execution, and in his determination to avoid any authorial intrusion Faulkner perhaps allowed a certain dilution of the tensions arising from the internal psychological dramas of his major characters. The centripetal [moving or tending to move towards a centre] effect of the technique might have proved still more powerfully cohesive if the segmentation had been less radical, if the points of view had been fewer, if they had been identified from the start, and if each one had recurred more frequently. On the other hand, the book as it stands offers a vivid evocation of the widening circle of impact of the Bundrens' adventure, an effect which harmonizes with the circular and radiating techniques of the book as a whole and with its recurring images of the circle, from the circling buzzards to the wheels of the wagon itself.[43] □

The important work of Howe, Vickery, Brooks and Millgate ensured that by the end of the 1960s Faulkner was firmly established as a major author whose work had demonstrated its capacity to generate substantial critical commentary and debate. The comparative neglect of the 1930s and 1940s had been amply compensated for and the accolade of the Nobel Prize had been endorsed and amplified by an ever-expanding body of critical acclaim. The battle for Faulkner's standing seemed to have been won; but there was now the question of where Faulkner criticism might go in the future. The social, cultural and political developments in the 1960s, especially the intensification of the African American struggle, and the emergence, at the end of the decade, of a new and vigorous feminism, implicitly posed challenges to what had now become established Faulkner criticism; but it would take time for these challenges to be articulated in ways that would have a significant influence on such criticism: they would be felt most strongly in the 1980s and 1990s. In a sense, as the Sixties ended, the disturbances provoked by Faulkner's texts, the furies they had originally unleashed, seemed to have been tamed; but, as the next chapter will show, critical soundings in the 1970s would start to arouse them once again.

CHAPTER THREE

Sounding the Depths: *The Sound and the Fury* and *As I Lay Dying* in the 1970s

IN 1972, Faulkner's leading French critic, André Bleikasten, surveyed the current state of Faulkner criticism and scholarship, and diagnosed what he called 'a certain dispersion'. Despite the growth of such criticism and scholarship, he believed that no general assessment of Faulkner had emerged that could rank with those of Olga W. Vickery, Cleanth Brooks and Michael Millgate, extracts from which were provided in the previous chapter of this Guide. '[T]hose looking for sound scholarship and fresh critical insights', Bleikasten opined, 'are now more likely to find them in journals than elsewhere', but 'essays, provocative as they may be, are necessarily limited in their scope' since they could not 'investigate their subject in breadth as well as depth'. Bleikasten suggested, however, that 'this fragmentary approach and the concomitant failure to produce new general studies of enduring interest' was probably 'a necessary phase in Faulkner criticism' and that the 'time has not yet come for a systematic and thorough reevaluation of the whole of Faulkner's fiction'.[1] But in the meantime, another important critical task could be performed: 'to return to his novels and give each of them the close and sustained attention it deserves'. This was a task Bleikasten himself discharged, producing two book-length studies, originally written in French as part of his doctoral thesis[2] but translated into English, of Faulkner novels: *Faulkner's 'As I Lay Dying'* in 1972 (the comments above are from his preface to this volume) and *The Most Splendid Failure: Faulkner's 'The Sound and the Fury'* in 1976. Taken together, Bleikasten's books provide some of the most penetrating criticism of these two novels to appear in English in the 1970s.

Bleikasten's account of *As I Lay Dying* looks, in turn, at the genesis and sources of the novel, at its language and style, at its technique, at its characters, at its setting, at its themes, and at its critical reception. The extracts that follow are from the chapter on the novel's technique and consider its structures and its handling of points of view. In the first extract, Bleikasten suggests an intriguing distinction between the direction of the narrative – which has the forward movement of a journey – and the order of the novel, which is, he suggests, of a circular kind:

■ . . . at the center of *As I Lay Dying*, of its structure and of its themes, lies the figure, at once present and absent, of Addie Bundren, the 'I' of the book's title. If the *narrative* apparently follows the linear progression appropriate to a journey, the *novel* is ordered according to a circular scheme focused on this figure. This scheme in some ways brings to mind the one Henry James has diagrammed in his Preface to *The Awkward Age* (1899)

> I drew on a sheet of paper . . . the neat figure of a circle consisting of a number of small rounds disposed at equal distance about a central object. The central object was my situation, my subject in itself, to which the thing would owe its title, and the small rounds represented so many distinct lamps, as I liked to call them, the function of each of which would be to light with all due intensity one of its aspects.[3]

The central object here is Addie's corpse both as a material thing, as the constant mainspring of and object at stake in the physical action, and in its symbolic function, as a reminder of the event which has just upset the existence of the Bundrens, as a visible sign of the great void left by Addie's death, which each member of the family after his fashion tries to fill. As for the circle, it is made up of all those still alive who gather around the body, suddenly brought face to face with the enigma of death. Each consciousness caught in the novel's sweep is one of those little lamps of which James speaks; each one, in its flickering light, illuminating one particular aspect of the central figure and situation. But instead of lamps one might also suggest a comparison with reflecting mirrors: most of the sections, in addition to throwing an oblique and intermittent light on Addie's personality, testify to the persistent effects of her dark radiance. It is precisely in terms of reciprocal illumination that one could define the relationship between Addie's single monologue and the rest of the novel. Were it not for this monologue, the book would lack focus, and much of its meaning would be lost on the reader, since the family drama can be understood only by reference to the personal tragedy suggested by the dead woman's confession. But conversely Addie's monologue needs the echoing space of the whole work for its significance to be fully grasped.

A double movement is thus set up. On the one hand, within the circle there is a simultaneous centrifugal [moving or tending to move from a centre] and centripetal [moving or tending to move towards a centre] movement, a nonstop to-ing and fro-ing between circle and center; on the other hand, there is a circular movement governing the whole novel and making it turn around its fixed axis. Similar dynamics can be observed in Faulkner's earlier novels . . . *The Sound and the Fury* revolved around the absent-present figure of Caddy Compson, the 'lost girl'. *As I Lay Dying* turns likewise around Addie and her death, and the rapid shift of viewpoint, with its recurrences and reverberations, introduces this gyration [circling or spiralling] into the very structure of the novel.

That this circular pattern possesses thematic significance hardly needs to be stressed. In this connection it is interesting to note that the circle also appears in the imagery of the novel. The whole story of the journey is punctuated by the repeated evocation of the circles traced in the sky by the buzzards which follow the funeral cortège, and the circling vultures ceaselessly intersecting the straight line of the Bundrens' progression could almost be seen as an emblem [*Translator's Note*: 'Emblem' only partially translates [Bleikasten's original term] 'mise en abyme', retaining its primitive heraldic sense but losing the connotations it has in modern French criticism. André Gide, the first to apply the phrase to literature, used it in this way to define the device of internal reflection in a play or a novel. See his *Journal: 1899–1939* (Paris: Gallimard, Bibliothèque de la Pléiade, 1948), p.41[4]] of the book's structure. In addition, it is significant that Darl associates his dead mother with a wheel: 'the red road lies like a spoke of which Addie Bundren is the rim' (p.96). In her soliloquy Addie herself refers to the circle of her solitude; by Cash's birth, she remarks, her 'aloneness had been violated and then made whole again by the violation: time, Anse, love, what you will, outside the circle' (p.160). The metaphor of the circle would apply almost equally well to most of the other Bundrens: each time one of them voices his thoughts and feelings, he becomes for a while, to borrow another of James's phrases, 'the central intelligence'[5] of the novel, and each time his inner speech is enclosed by the circle of his private desires and secret obsessions – a circle of self-absorption and solitude he is either unwilling or unable to break. If the pattern of *As I Lay Dying* suggests first of all a moving circle whose center is Addie, it could also be described as a series of waves and eddies: it is as if a handful of pebbles were thrown into still water, rippling its surface, making concentric circles which overlap and interact in unexpected ways as they expand.

Both narrative and novel, then, have their own structure. In spatial terms the difference is that between a straight line and a circle. Yet this opposition is obviously too crudely stated not to require qualification.

In fact narrative structure and fictional structure do not exist independent of each other: the latter contains the former, the novel envelops the narrative and ends by changing its course. Although linear in its basic development, the story seems nonetheless to describe a double loop. The first of these loops is Addie's journey, a return journey which takes the dead woman back to the place of her birth. The second comes full circle at the very end of the novel, when Anse introduces his new wife to his children: "'Meet Mrs. Bundren'" (p. 248). Present at the beginning, Mrs. Bundren had gradually moved further away until she finally disappeared in Jefferson cemetery. Here she is back again. Certainly she is not the same at all. But by replacing Addie, who is dead and buried and has now left her family for good, the new Mrs. Bundren comes along to occupy a place left vacant. From life to death, from death to life, the cycle is closed (and at the same time open to the possibility of other returns and reversals), and the ending sends us back to the beginning. But not quite: the closing situation reproduces the opening one, but in another, lower key. The substitution is like a usurpation; the pop-eyed, duck-shaped new Mrs. Bundren is only Addie's grotesque understudy. And the whole journey suggests a process of degradation, best symbolized by the increasingly repulsive smell of the rotting corpse. Cash's gangrenous broken leg gets worse and worse in its cement cast; Dewey Dell, frustrated in her efforts to get an abortion and seduced by a drugstore clerk, will bear her bastard child; Jewel, badly burned by the fire, loses his treasured horse. The tensions within the family reach their climax in Dewey Dell's and Jewel's murderous assault on Darl. Darl himself goes mad and is finally disowned – the replacement of the mother thus coinciding with the repudiation of one of her sons. Ironically, Anse is the only one to gain something by the adventure.

Perhaps it is the figure of the spiral which best indicates the repetition-with-a-difference. *As I Lay Dying* carries us along in a helical movement or, more exactly, down in a spinning dive. The end of the narrative draws near its starting point and at that very moment veers away. Everything starts again and nothing is the same. The end of the novel is a false restoration (just as Anse's new teeth are false), a ludicrous dénouement echoing with Darl's mad laughter: ambiguity is given a final twist and irony is raised to its highest pitch.[6] □

In the next extract, Bleikasten examines the use of interior monologue in *As I Lay Dying*, suggesting that it serves the purposes both of psychological representation and of narrative advancement:

■ Earlier, in *The Sound and the Fury*, Faulkner had resorted to a fragmented point of view. In *As I Lay Dying* this fragmentation is taken a stage further: instead of four sections, there are fifty-nine. They are of varying importance, but never very long [the inconsistent use of numerals or words for numbers in what follows is from Bleikasten's original text] (the average is 2 to 4 pages, the maximum 7, the shortest a mere 5 words), and are shared among fifteen different narrators. The distribution is as follows: Darl 19, Vardaman 10, Vernon Tull 6, Cash 5, Dewey Dell 4, Cora Tull 3, Anse 3, Peabody 2, Addie 1, Jewel 1, Whitfield 1, Samson 1, Armstid 1, Moseley 1, MacGowan 1. Seven of the narrators belong to the Bundren family (actor-narrators); the eight others are outsiders, either episodic participants in the action or mere witnesses (spectator-narrators). Yet if the two categories of narrators are numerically almost equal, the share of sections given to the Bundrens (43) is far in excess of that of the outsiders (16). It is noteworthy, too, that Darl, with nineteen sections, takes on single-handed one-third of the narrative and thus occupies a highly privileged position as narrator.

One of the effects of this multiple point of view upon the reader is that he is prevented from identifying himself with any one narrator. The shifts are too frequent to permit his settling to a single point of view. *The Sound and the Fury* plunged us into the stream of consciousness of Benjy, Quentin, and Jason in turn, and the immersions lasted long enough for the reader to adopt (and forget) the point of view of the narrator. In *As I Lay Dying* these immersions are too short; the stream does not carry one with it. The broken construction of the novel keeps the reader at a distance and puts him in the position of a spectator rather than of a participant, thus preventing the emotional involvement generally associated with the interior monologue. Faulkner was nonetheless at pains to retain some unity of vision by making Darl his principal narrator and setting him – rather like Quentin Compson in *Absalom, Absalom!* – at the point of junction between narrative and novel. Although he is only given a third of the narration, his detachment and insight, his gifts of observation and expression, and his faculty of second sight single him out quite naturally for the function of 'central intelligence'.[7] Like the dramatized narrators in Conrad and James, Darl is the one who sees and knows the most, and it is through him that we are most completely, if not most reliably, informed, not only of the external development of the action but also of the secret links which bind the Bundrens together and of the hidden motivations which guide their behavior.

At the same time Darl's monologues tell us about Darl himself, about his reveries and obsessions and about his vain quest for identity. A two-way mirror, each section reflects external events as well as their impact upon a consciousness; each section strives to link up with the object of the narration – the story of which it is presumed to be a fragment – and tends at the same time to flow back to its source, to be reabsorbed into the narrator's voice. What counts here at least as much as what is said is the word itself, the use made of it by each person and the sort of relay race in which it is passed from one to the other. The use of interior monologue – a point of view which at any given moment betrays itself as such – has the effect of splitting the novel between the impersonality of *history* and the subjectivity of *discourse*.[8] There is a twofold subjectivity, both of a linguistic order (indicated by the constant recourse to the personal pronoun 'I' and the predominance of the present tense) and of a psychological order, since in its essence the *interior* monologue, as it has been understood since Joyce, claims paradoxically to be an immediate transcription of prelogical or even preverbal mental processes.

In *As I Lay Dying*, however, the form taken by the interior monologue seldom fully corresponds to such a definition. If Faulkner uses the monologue as an instrument of psychological revelation, he also gives it a narrative function. In most of the sections one finds therefore differently weighted combinations of narrative and discursive elements. Among the narrative elements are accounts of current and past actions and reported conversations; among the discursive elements are descriptions, reflections, and comments made by the narrators, and everything pertaining to interior discourse as such (reveries, recollections, fantasies). There is, of course, no clear dividing line between these two areas. In the Darl sections especially only a closely detailed textual analysis would allow one to discriminate between narrative and nonnarrative components ([compare] sect[ions] 3, 10, 12, 34, 46, 57). In other sections, however, they are not so inextricably interwoven, and according to the dominant category one might make a distinction between the monologues whose function is essentially narrative and those which are primarily psychological in character and interest.

The first are used either to relate a scene as it happens or to link different moments of the action and unite them in a coherent perspective. Darl is the character most often responsible for direct, moment-to-moment reporting and for giving us a sense of participation in the action as it develops. Among the Bundrens, Darl and, to a lesser extent, Cash, who takes over towards the end of the novel, are alone in assuming in any real sense the function of narrators. Beside them, marginal to the action, are all the characters who form the chorus: Vernon and Cora Tull, Samson, Armstid, Peabody, Moseley, and MacGowan. They are there not so much to give us objective views as to provide a broader perspective, a wider frame of reference. The sections allotted to them are much more like dramatic soliloquies than interior monologues; they are in fact more often than not retrospective accounts in the first person. Meant for the ear rather than the eye, they sound like oral accounts, freely improvised, with the colloquial tone, the repetitiveness, and the fumbling prolixity of unpremeditated talk. Furthermore, . . . they are 'spoken' in a vernacular idiom whose lexical and syntactic resources are exploited by the author with brilliant ingenuity. One therefore constantly feels the presence of the narrator's voice. And not only does each narrator's speech connote his social and geographical background but, far from being neutral, each witness reacts to the Bundrens' adventures according to his own temperament (perplexity tempered with neighborly kindness in the case of the farmers, a mixture of compassion and indignation in Doctor Peabody, self-righteous reproof in Cora Tull and Rachel Samson, outraged respectability in Moseley, cynical amusement in MacGowan), comments on them, and explains them according to his own lights (which are not always the right ones, as is amply shown by Cora's misrepresentations in section 6). As a group all these characters represent the rural community they belong to; they are its spokesmen, harboring its virtues and prejudices; they embody respectability confronted with scandal, collective wisdom challenged by the Bundrens' folly. Through their mingled voices the anonymous voice of the community is heard with its rules and values – an indispensable reference which, as always with Faulkner, emphasizes the opposition between social and individual, public and private.

Passing from the monologues of these outsiders to those of the Bundrens, one finds a change of scale, a sharper focus, and more frequent close-ups. Simplifying, one might say that a view from within replaces one from without. The heroes of the novel are no longer seen from a distance; their story is no longer related by third parties. They themselves come and say what happens to them. But can they? In point of fact, most of the Bundrens are too directly involved in the journey, too busy acting, too much absorbed by their thoughts and emotions to be in a position to give an ordered account of what they are living through. Therefore there is a great deal more subjectivity in the sections attributed to them. The interest shifts from narration to narrator and from narrator to character, discourse takes precedence over narrative, and insofar as the latter persists, the way in which events impinge on the consciousness asserts itself to the detriment of their objective reality. One may also note that the differentiation of points of view is effected here both more distinctly and more subtly: each viewpoint is determined conjointly by the character's supposed degree of consciousness, by his psychological makeup, and by the mood of the moment.

Of these points of view, Darl's is by far the most flexible and complex. Darl, as we have seen, is the principal narrator, but his monologues are far from being a mere record of events. Nothing is less objective than his narrative. Its transparency is almost constantly blurred by the welter of descriptive touches, epithets, comparisons, and metaphors; images, thoughts, and memories well up at every turn of the narration, sometimes bursting out with short-lived brilliance, sometimes lingering for meditation and reverie. Darl's mind is so supple and fluid that it slips effortlessly from one thing to another and changes place and time in a trice. Consider, for example, section 3 (pp. 7–10): the very short opening paragraph is both descriptive (of Tull and Anse sitting on the back porch) and narrative (with Darl dipping his gourd into the water bucket to drink): a conversation is started by Anse's question to Darl ('"Where's Jewel?"', but the answer is delayed for a page by the past suddenly breaking in on the present ('When I was a boy . . . ' (p. 7). Darl, drinking, reflects on the taste of water and remembers scenes from his childhood. The return to the present is marked by a close-up on 'Pa's feet', the narrative is resumed ('I fling the dipper dregs . . . ') and the question about Jewel is finally answered ('"Down to the barn," I say. "Harnessing the team"' (p. 8)), Darl's answer inducing the superb description of Jewel and his horse on which the section ends. Darl's mind is seen working in four registers – perception, reflection, memory, and second sight – and passing from one to another with no other logic than the unpredictable one of mental association. Not all his monologues, to be sure, contain so many breaks and bifurcations [divisions into two branches]. Yet all he says and describes bears the hallmark of an intensely personal vision. Almost every time Darl starts speaking, reality is transmuted: space begins to waver, the scenery takes on a disturbing life of its own, and everything stands out against an indistinct and shifting background with the strange clear-cut quality and fierce colors of a bad dream.

Hyperconscious and hypersensitive, Darl is almost always perfectly at ease with language. There is even in him a kind of intoxication with words. The same is not true of the younger Bundrens, Jewel, Dewey Dell, and, particularly, Vardaman. In them, the interior monologue sinks to a darker zone of greater confusion. It seeks to reflect the gropings of a nascent language, to capture the scarcely perceptible whispers and whimpers of a bemused consciousness which has difficulty in collecting itself around the kernel of a stable self. Neither Jewel nor Dewey Dell nor Vardaman is master of his words and all three have only a very dim and deformed awareness of the events with which they are confronted. If Darl's point of view has the broadest scope, theirs is certainly the most restricted. Jewel is all turbulence and action; only once does he break his silence, and his brief monologue peppered with invective and breathless with rage reveals nothing but his hatred of the others and his jealous love of Addie. As for Dewey Dell, everything for her centers on the obsession with her body, her pregnancy and intended abortion. In her monologues, and notably in sections 14 and 30, there is neither articulate thought nor definable feeling but a profusion of organic and tactile sensations . . . or else elemental images . . . It is through these sensations and images that the reader gradually discovers Dewey Dell's anxieties, anxieties which she is unable to translate into words.

This incapacity to extricate oneself from the chaos of lived experience is found again in young Vardaman. Not that his monologues are always pure confusion. He sometimes recounts what he is doing very clearly: 'Then I begin to run. I run toward the back and come to the edge of the porch and stop. Then I begin to cry' (p. 48). Snatches of narrative like this have the 'flat' and objective quality which is characteristic of the idiot Benjy's monologue in *The Sound and the Fury*: a series of gestures suggested by simple words and sentences, all based on the same paratactic pattern, and adding together without ever adding up ['paratactic' is the adjective from the grammatical term 'parataxis', which means the placing of clauses etc. one after another, without words, to indicate coordination or subordination]. But this appearance of objectivity is warped repeatedly by the strange equation Vardaman makes between his dead mother and a fish. His is the fluid prelogical world of a child in which all metamorphoses are possible. And like Dewey Dell's desire for an abortion, this *idée fixe* [fixed idea, obsession] in Vardaman's mind linking mother and fish returns again and again as a leitmotif in his monologues, his whole perception of reality revolving around this metaphor.

Thus section 35 (pp. 138–39), where Vardaman gives his own version of the river scene, is certainly a fragment of the narrative, but disrupted by the violent emotion which overcomes the child when he sees the coffin swallowed up by the water. Until the relationship between outside reality (coffin, water) and private fantasy (mother, fish) has been recognized by the reader, the monologue hardly makes sense. For it is the panic caused by the perception of this analogy which erupts into the narrative and causes it to disintegrate. Corresponding to the utter confusion in Vardaman's mind here is a breakdown of language of which the most obvious signs are irregularities in spelling ('darl' for 'Darl' (p. 138)), the absence of punctuation (except in the last five lines), and the dislocation of syntax. A riot of words dash and crash into each other, disappear and reappear; sentences are started and lost, repeated and mixed up, unable to find their rightful place or order. Reference to reality is certainly still present; in the midst of this whirling confusion we still perceive the echo of words spoken, the reflection of things seen, but so jumbled and scattered that their sequential logic escapes us altogether. The narrative value of such a section is almost nil; the discourse itself is reduced to frenzied verbal gesticulation, to stammering punctuated by shouts ('hollering' (pp. 138, 139)). Nothing is left but the dizzy anguish of a consciousness caught up in the event.

Each point of view, then, achieves its unity through its underlying linguistic and psychological configuration; each narrator may be identified by his voice (or by what linguists would call his idiolect [language as used by an individual person]). True, another voice sometimes interrupts that of the character. Thus in one of the Vardaman sections there is the lavish description of a horse (p. 51). Clearly this piece of rhetoric bears no relation to the inchoate language of a child; the voice speaking here is none other than the author's. Faulkner, contrary to what one might have expected, does not restrict himself to colloquial realism. It is not unusual for his characters to start thinking and speaking beyond their means, to express themselves in a style incompatible with their level of consciousness as well as with their social status. Is the novelist to be censured for these fits of ventriloquy? Do they not threaten to destroy the coherence of the different points of view? In fact, the author's voice *augments* those of the narrators more than it obliterates them. No doubt Darl's speculations on being and nothingness far exceed the capacity for abstraction and reasoning of an uneducated young Mississippi farmer, but they convey eloquently the character's secret obsessions, bringing into the light of language all the unspoken obscurity seething within his tortured mind.

It is true that by probing the innermost thoughts in this way, there is a risk of reviving the absolute viewpoint of the traditional novel, but the author's self-effacement in *As I Lay Dying* is in any case only a clever pretense. Giving up, apparently, the privilege of the novelist-God, Faulkner most often hides behind his characters, and pretends to listen to them and let them tell the tale in his stead. Yet how could anyone without uncommon powers of divination transport himself into the minds of fifteen different narrators? Is the extreme multiplicity of points of view not, in the end, omniscience in disguise?[9] The technique used in *As I Lay Dying* conceals the novelist so that he can operate more freely in the wings. It is by no means a guarantee of realism; it is simply a creative method suited to the writer's purpose. Far from encroaching upon the novelist's prerogatives, it makes him all-powerful by making him invisible.[10] □

The Most Splendid Failure, the book with which Bleikasten followed up his study of *As I Lay Dying*, takes its title from Faulkner's response to a question about which work he considered his best: he replied that *The Sound and the Fury* 'made the most splendid failure'.[11] As a Frenchman, Bleikasten was aware, more fully than many North American or English critics in the 1970s, of the development of structuralism, of the 'French

Freud' of Jacques Lacan, and of the French *nouvelle critique* (new criticism) represented by Roland Barthes; and he acknowledged, in the Preface to his study, 'a general debt to the *nouvelle critique* and to what has come to be known as structuralism'. But he felt free to adopt an eclectic critical approach, since '[t]o accommodate the teeming complexities of Faulkner's work, no approach can be inclusive enough'.[12] His interpretation of *The Sound and the Fury* remains valuable not only for its specific insights but also for the way in which it offers an informed but accessible appropriation of a range of critical perspectives from the more traditional to the most up-to-date. In its disciplined eclecticism, it anticipates some of the best criticism of the 1990s.

In *The Most Splendid Failure*, Bleikasten offers an account of Faulkner's development up to the writing of *The Sound and the Fury*, discussions of Caddy, Benjy, Quentin and Jason, and explorations of the themes of time, reality and redemption. The extract below is from his account of Caddy, whom he sees as a kind of Eurydice, the wife of the poet Orpheus in classical myth, the lost object of desire whom her husband tried to bring back from the underworld. Bleikasten points out that the novels written in the late 1920s, especially *The Sound and the Fury* and *As I Lay Dying*, 'are novels *about* lack and loss, in which desire is always intimately bound up with death', and suggests that 'they have sprung *out of* a deep sense of lack and loss', that they are 'texts spun around a primal gap'.[13] He then links this 'primal gap' with Caddy:

■ In *The Sound and the Fury* this gap is reduplicated and represented in the pathetic and intriguing figure of Caddy Compson, the lost sister . . . . . . Caddy is just a name, or the deceptive echo of a name. On the day when the novel begins – April 7, 1928 – the person to whom it refers has been missing from the Compson family for many years. Benjy's moaning points at once to an absence, an absence which the perception of anything however remotely related to his lost sister instantly quickens and thickens in his vacant mind. To Benjy, Caddy is the nearest of absences. His memory has no memories. He cannot remember; he cannot forget. For him it is as though Caddy had only departed a few seconds ago: her trace is forever fresh, and the merest sensation – something seen, heard, smelled – recalls her presence with agonizing immediacy. In surprisingly similar ways, Caddy also haunts her brother Quentin, holding him in her spell, leaving him no rest and no escape except in death. And even to Jason, for all his declared indifference and contempt, she will be a festering wound.

Yet at the same time – precisely because she is nothing but a haunting memory – Caddy remains to the end a being out of reach, an elusive figure not unlike Proust's 'creatures of flight'. She is the presence of what is not there, the imperious call of absence, and it is from her tantalizing remoteness that she holds her uncanny power over those she has left.

All the scenes out of the past which come to beset memory both bring her closer and remove her further away. Of Caddy nothing remains but a series of snapshots, vivid and unreal, in which her fleeting image is forever fixed:

> *Only she was running already when I heard it. In the mirror she was running before I knew what it was. That quick, her train caught up over her arm she ran out of the mirror like a cloud, her veil swirling in long glints her heels brittle and fast clutching her dress onto her shoulder with the other hand, running out of the mirror* (p. 79)

Barely glimpsed, Caddy the (no longer 'unravish'd') bride at once vanishes, and all that a glance could grasp was a silent rush reflected in a mirror. What lingers in the memory is at best the reflection of a reflection.

Or consider this other obsessive image of the lost sister, likewise linked to an event that Quentin cannot forget, the loss of her virginity: Caddy no longer caught running away, but immobilized in the silent suddenness of her appearance: '[*o*]*ne minute she was standing in the door*' (p. 78).[14] Whether Caddy's silhouette is fleetingly reflected in a mirror or emerges unexpectedly in the doorway, there is each time the same disturbing oscillation between absence and presence, the same paradoxical sense of receding proximity or close remoteness.

It is noteworthy too that Caddy is associated time and again with the immaterial and the impalpable: reflections (pp. 62, 75, 79, 148), shadows (pp. 79, 156), moonlight, a cloud (p. 79), a breath (p. 148), '*a long veil like shining wind*' (p. 37; see also pp. 38, 81). Caddy's evanescence in space constantly parallels her inaccessibility in time. Not that she is ever etherealized into a conventionally 'poetic' creature. But insofar as she must remain the ambiguous and evasive object of desire and memory, she can be approached and apprehended only in oblique ways. Caddy cannot be described; she can only be *circumscribed*, conjured up through the suggestive powers of metaphor and metonymy. A realistic rendering of the character is out of the question. Only the ruses and indirections of poetic discourse can do justice to the burning absence which Caddy 'embodies' in the novel.

To the very extent that Caddy is literally nowhere, she is metaphorically everywhere. Her presence/absence becomes diffused all over the world, pointing, like so many feminine figures of Faulkner's earlier and later work, to an elemental complicity between Woman and the immemorial Earth. Her swiftness and lightness relate her to the wind; her vital warmth to 'the bright, smooth shapes' (pp. 55, 62) of fire;[15] her muddy drawers and treelike odor (pp. 4, 7, 17, 40, 41, 42, 46, 70) to the fecundity and foulness of the land.[16] Yet above all Caddy is the most enticing and most pathetic of Faulkner's nymphs. In the entire novel there is scarcely a scene in which Caddy does not appear in close conjunction with *water*. It is in the branch near the Compson house that she wets her dress and drawers on the day of Damuddy's death (pp. 15–18); it is in the same branch that Quentin and Caddy wash off the stinking mud of the pig trough after the Natalie incident (p. 137);[17] and it is there again that Quentin finds his sister, sitting in the water, one summer evening, after the family has discovered her affair with Dalton Ames (p. 148). Lastly, in the third section, Jason remembers her standing over her father's grave in a drenching rain (pp. 201–02). Throughout the novel, water is Caddy's element, and like Caddy herself, it is drawn into an extremely ambiguous symbolic pattern. In the branch scenes it is primarily the lustral [of, or used in, ceremonial purification] water of purification rituals, and it would be easy to supply further illustrations of its cleansing function: Caddy, at fourteen, washing off the perfume to quiet Benjy (p. 40); Caddy, washing her mouth after kissing Charlie in the swing (p. 46); and, finally, Benjy pulling at his sister's dress, dragging her into the bathroom after the loss of her virginity (p. 67). After these ritual ablutions, Caddy 'smell[s] like trees' again, except in the last scene where Benjy keeps on crying even after Caddy has bathed herself.

Water, however, is not only a symbol of purity. If it possesses a restorative power, at least in the eyes of the novel's characters, and if Faulkner at times suggests its function in Christian baptism (it rains on the night Benjy's name is changed), there are also many significant intimations of its erotic quality. Bathing, in particular, as evoked in the novel, seems to prompt a kind of soft, sensuous, almost sensual intimacy between water and flesh, and to prurient [given to or arousing from indulgence of lewd ideas] eyes the spectacle of this tender complicity may become both a scandal and a temptation. In the insidious caress of water, in the way it reveals the body in its embrace, there is something all but immodest which, even in the early childhood scene at the branch, disturbs and alarms young Quentin. For him, who then begins to act as guardian of Caddy's 'honor', the sight of his sister and of the drenched dress clinging to her body is no longer an innocent spectacle. And when he slaps her for having undressed, he introduces by this very gesture the first suspicion of evil into a hitherto intact childhood world.

In Quentin's reminiscences and reveries, flesh and sex are repeatedly linked to suggestions of dampness and fluidity, and as the hour of his death draws nearer, it almost seems as if the waters were slowly rising, submerging his mind and memory, bringing him ever closer to the instant of his drowning. Thus, in the long breathless memory sequence in which he relives his poignant encounter with Caddy at the branch and his subsequent meeting with Dalton Ames near the bridge (pp. 148–62), water saturates the whole atmosphere with a silent drizzle. Quentin inhales the smell of the rain, breathes in the scent of honeysuckle wafted on the humid warmth of twilight. And out of all this mugginess emerges the body of his nymph-sister – water made flesh:

> . . . I ran down the hill in that vacuum of crickets like a breath travel-ling across a mirror she was lying in the water her head on the sand spit the water flowing about her hips there was a little more light in the water her skirt half saturated flopped along her flanks to the water's motion in heavy ripples going nowhere renewed themselves of their own movement I stood on the bank I could smell the honeysuckle on the water gap the air seemed to drizzle with honeysuckle and with the rasping of crickets a substance you could feel on the flesh (p. 148)

As in Faulkner's early sketch 'Nympholepsy', woman's body – 'her hips', 'her flanks' – is associated with running water, and as Quentin watches his sister lying there, he cannot help thinking back to the day long past when as a little girl she had soiled her dress and drawers: 'do you remember the day damuddy died when you sat down in the water in your drawers' (p. 150). Quentin himself is aware of the sym-bolic relationship between the two scenes; in retrospect the childhood episode acquires a premonitory meaning, Caddy's muddy drawers becoming a symbol of her physical and moral defilement, of what Quentin considers to be an indelible stain on her honor: her fall from sexual innocence. This irremediable loss is the focal point of Quentin's obsession, an obsession eagerly feeding on every sense impression: the sight of flowing water, the smell of rain and honeysuckle, the chirp of crickets, shadows, warmth, moisture, everything melts into 'a substance you could feel on the flesh'. It is clear that Quentin's obses-sion, as it is described here, is by no means the abstract, disembodied mania for which it has been all too often mistaken by critics. Experienced at first in the sultry profusion of immediate sensations, the traumatic shock is relived by Quentin's memory with hallucina-tory vividness and intensity.

There is no Proustian reunion, though, for Faulkner's hero. Caddy risen out of the past through the sortileges [spells] of memory is not Caddy recaptured. Memory serves only to exacerbate a sense of irrevoc-able loss. The past is recollected in fever and pain, never in tranquillity, and the camera obscura of memory turns out to be a torture chamber [a camera obscura is a darkened box with an aperture for projecting an image of a distant object on to a screen within the box]. It is never a shelter; happy memories have no place in it. As far back as it can reach, Quentin's memory encounters a Caddy *already* all but lost: as if she had resented her brother's jealous vigilance from the outset and were impatient to flee from the prison of innocence in which he would forever keep her, she is always seen rebelling against his demands, always on the point of running away. In this respect, the scene of the muddy drawers – one of the earliest among the childhood incidents recalled in his monologue – is equally prophetic: it marks the beginning of the ineluctable movement which is to separate him from his sister. From this childhood scene to Caddy's wedding, nearly all the fragments of the past which erupt into Quentin's mind are related to Caddy's gradual 'betrayal', and each of his painful memories reenacts one moment in the process of her desertion.

Presence in absence, nearness in distance, nothing perhaps better sums up the paradox of Quentin's haunted memory than *odor*. A subtle emanation from things and beings, odor, as Jean-Paul Sartre writes, is 'a disembodied body, vaporized, remaining entire in itself, yet turned into volatile essence'.[18] Like memory, it is a diffuse presence, a felt absence, a tantalizing intimation of being. Like symbols, it acts by indirection, through allusion and suggestion: to the extent that it always has the power to evoke something other than itself, to point an absence, one might consider it a 'natural' metaphor. Small wonder, then, that the fragrance of *honeysuckle* is the most pregnant and most poignant symbol in the Quentin section.

Quentin associates Caddy with the odor of honeysuckle, just as Benjy associated her with the smell of trees. But whereas in the first section 'she smelled like trees' functions as an index to Caddy's sexual innocence and vanishes as soon as the latter is compromised (see, for example, the perfume incident (pp. 44–46)), the meaning of honeysuckle in Quentin's monologue changes as Caddy changes, and its scent is irremediably corrupted when it comes to reek in Quentin's nostrils as the smell of her sex and sin. It is noteworthy that the term 'honeysuckle', which occurs approximately thirty times in section 2, is nowhere as frequent as in the scene immediately following Quentin's discovery of his sister's loss of virginity (pp. 148–62): the scent of honeysuckle then becomes the pivot in a shifting complex of sense impressions. After blending into the uncertain grayness of twilight (pp. 168–69), it combines with the humidity of the atmosphere (p. 152), 'coming up in damp waves' or drizzling like the rain (p. 153). Through the cross-play of synaesthesia ['a blending or confusion of different kinds of sense-impression, in which one type of sensation is referred to in terms more appropriate to another' – for example, when colours are called 'loud' or 'warm', or sounds 'smooth'[19]], honeysuckle is made to encompass and condense the entire field of sensory experience: something at once smelled, seen, and felt, it suffuses the whole scene. Yet, while metamorphosing and expanding across space, the smell also seems to flow back to Caddy as to its source, and Quentin refers to it as though it were a carnal secretion on the surface of her skin, a substance exuded from her flesh: *'the smell of honeysuckle upon her face and throat'* (p. 146); 'it was on her face and throat like paint' (p. 150). Quentin thus comes to resent the cloying odor as a disturbing indiscretion, an almost obscene exuding of the innermost secrets of the flesh. Associated with Caddy's lovemaking in the swing by the cedars and eventually equated with Caddy herself, it symbolizes in his mind 'the bittersweet mystery of sisterly sex'[20] as well as the unbearable scandal of its violation. It quickens his obsession, becomes the very emblem of his anguish and torment: 'after the honeysuckle got all mixed up in it the whole thing came to symbolize night and unrest' (p. 168). In his confrontation with Caddy about Dalton Ames, his sister reminds him that he once liked the smell (p. 152); now he hates it, cursing *'that damn honeysuckle'* (p. 147; see also pp. 152, 153). So hateful has it become to him that it even oppresses him physically, making him gasp for breath: 'I had to pant to get any air at all out of that thick grey honeysuckle' (p. 150). The sweet 'honey' of sisterhood, which Quentin so avidly 'suckled' in his childish greed, has thickened into a suffocating substance, and now has the bitter taste of loss.

Trees, water, twilight, honeysuckle – all the nature imagery related to Caddy, so far from calling attention to itself as symbolic, seems to grow out of the soil of subjective experience while being at the same time inextricably bound up with the sensible world. It never hardens into the fixed patterns of allegory; its mobile and manifold symbolism originates in the dynamic exchanges between a self and its concrete environment. If some of these images run through several sections, they can never be separated from the singular voice in whose discourse they occur: they reflect the changing moods or the stubborn obsessions of a particular consciousness; they belong to the shifting landscapes of an individual mind.

Yet the central ambiguity to which all these images ultimately refer is that of Caddy herself. Caddy, as we have already seen, is first and foremost an image; she exists only in the minds and memories of her brothers. We can find out what she represents for Benjy, Quentin, and Jason; we never discover what she actually is. Hence her many and contradictory faces: she is in turn sister and mother, virgin and whore, angel and demon; she at once embodies fecundity and foulness, the nostalgia for innocence and the call to corruption, the promise of life and the vertigo of death. She is in fact what woman has always been in man's imagination: the figure par excellence of the Other, a blank screen onto which he projects both his desires and his fears, his love and his hate. And insofar as this Other is a myth and a mirage, a mere fantasy of the Self, it is bound to be a perpetual deceit and an endless source of disappointment. Caddy, to borrow a phrase from Paul Claudel, is 'the promise that cannot be kept, and her grace consists in nothing else'.[21]

Even so, she is more than the sum of these fantasy images. Faulkner's triumph in creating Caddy is that her elusive figure eventually transcends the abstract categories and rigid patterns in which her brothers attempt to imprison her, just as she escapes any facile sentimentalizing or demonizing on the author's part. Not that the reader is enabled to infer a 'true' picture of Caddy from the information he is given in the novel. There is little doubt, of course, that she possesses the vitality, the courage, the capacity for love and compassion which her self-centered brothers and parents so sadly lack.[22] It is quite obvious, too, that she is both the tragic victim of her family and the unwitting agent of its doom. But to focus exclusively on Caddy's assumed psychology or to dwell at length on her moral significance is to miss the point. Caddy was elusive to her creator; so she is to her brothers in the novel, and so she must remain to the reader. She cannot be assessed according to the same criteria as the other characters. However complex her characterization (and it is indeed more complex than has been generally acknowledged), Caddy belongs in the last resort to another space, to what might be called the novel's utopia. 'The true life is absent,'[23] Rimbaud wrote. In *The Sound and the Fury* Caddy is a pathetic emblem of that desired other life, while her fate poignantly confirms its impossibility in a world of alienation and disease.

Henry James thought that 'a story-teller who aims at anything more than a fleeting success has no right to tell an ugly story unless he knows its beautiful counterpart'.[24] The story of the Compsons is indeed 'an ugly story'; Caddy, the daughter and sister of the imagination, the figure projected by 'the heart's desire', is 'its beautiful counterpart'. Let us remember, however, that from the very beginning she was conceived of as 'a beautiful *and* tragic little girl'. Caddy is a dream of beauty wasted and destroyed. Her presence/absence at the center and periphery of the novel signals the unfulfillment of the writer's desire as well as the inescapable incompletion of his work. Caddy's beauty is the beauty of failure.[25] □

Although Bleikasten's account of Caddy is perceptive and wide-ranging, and although he is familiar with much of the latest French critical and cultural theory of the period, he does not raise the possibility of applying feminist perspectives to his analysis of Caddy. Nonetheless, his exploration of her significance does offer scope for the application of such perspectives, and later chapters of this Guide will see feminist critics at work on Faulkner.

If Bleikasten sees Caddy as Eurydice, John T. Irwin sees Quentin as Narcissus, the youth who fell in love with his own reflection in a fountain and drowned trying to reach it – and whose name Sigmund Freud borrowed for his concept of 'narcissism', an eroticised fixation on oneself. As John E. Bassett observes, Irwin's *Doubling and Incest/Repetition and Revenge* (1975) quickly 'established itself as one of the major points of reference for serious criticism'.[26] Lucid, trenchant and evocative, drawing on psychoanalysis in an illuminating way, Irwin's study focuses on *The Sound and the Fury* and *Absalom, Absalom!*. Irwin claims that 'the deepest level' of meaning in the latter novel 'is to be found in the symbolic identification of incest and miscegenation' – sexual relations between siblings are equated with sexual relations between those of different races: this relates, of course, to Quentin, who is an embodiment, both in *Absalom, Absalom!* and in *The Sound and the Fury*, of the 'archetype of the brother who must kill to protect or avenge the honor of his sister'.[27] This is Irwin's analysis of Quentin:

■ Like Narcissus, Quentin drowns himself, and the internal narrative of his last day, clearly the narrative of someone who has gone insane, is dominated by Quentin's obsessive attempts to escape from his shadow, to 'trick his shadow', as he says. When Quentin leaves his dormitory on the morning of his death, the pursuit begins:

> The shadow hadn't quite cleared the stoop. I stopped inside the door, watching the shadow move. It moved almost perceptibly, creeping back inside the door, driving the shadow back into the door (p. 79) . . . . . . The shadow on the stoop was gone. I stepped into sunlight, finding my shadow again. I walked down the steps just ahead of it. (p. 80)

Later, standing by the river, he looks down:

> The shadow of the bridge, the tiers of railing, my shadow leaning flat upon the water, so easily had I tricked it that would not quit me. At least fifty feet it was, and if I only had something to blot it into the water, holding it until it was drowned, the shadow of the package like two shoes wrapped up lying on the water. Niggers say a drowned man's shadow was watching for him in the water all the time. (p. 88)

Like Narcissus staring at his image in the pool, Quentin stares at his shadow in the river and, significantly, makes a reference to Negroes in relation to that shadow. I say 'significantly' because at crucial points during Quentin's last day this connection between the shadow and the Negro recurs, most notably on the tram ride down to the river when Quentin sits next to a black man:

> I used to think that a Southerner had to be always conscious of niggers. I thought that Northerners would expect him to. When I first came East I kept thinking You've got to remember to think of them as coloured people not niggers, and if it hadn't happened that I wasn't thrown with many of them, I'd have wasted a lot of time and trouble before I learned that the best way to take all people, black or white, is to take them for what they think they are, then leave them alone. That was when I realized that a nigger is not a person so much as a form of behaviour; a sort of obverse reflection of the white people he lives among. (p. 84)

. . . since Quentin's own shadow has Negro resonances in his mind, it is not surprising that on the day of his suicide Quentin, who is being pursued by his shadow, is told by one of the three boys that he meets walking in the country that he (Quentin) talks like a colored man, nor is it surprising that another of the boys immediately asks the first one if he isn't afraid Quentin will hit him (p. 119).

If Quentin's determination to drown his shadow represents the substitutive punishment, upon his own person, of the brother seducer (the dark self, the ego shadowed by the unconscious) by the brother avenger (the bright self, the ego controlled by the superego), then it is only appropriate that the events from Quentin's past that obsessively recur during the internal narrative leading up to his drowning are events that emphasize Quentin's failure as both brother avenger and brother seducer in relation to his sister Candace – failures which his drowning of himself is meant to redeem. On the one hand, Quentin is haunted by his inability to kill Candace's lover Dalton Ames and by his further inability to prevent Candace from marrying Herbert Head, whom he knows to be a cheat. But on the other hand, he is equally tormented by his own failure to commit incest with his sister. In this connection it is significant that one of the obsessive motifs in the narrative of Quentin's last day is the continual juxtaposition of Quentin's own virginity to his sister's loss of virginity . . .

In Quentin's world young men lose their virginity as soon as possible, but their sisters keep their virginity until they are married. The reversal of this situation in the case of Quentin and Candace makes Quentin feel that his sister has assumed the masculine role and that he has assumed the feminine role. Quentin's obsessive concern with

Candace's loss of virginity is a displaced concern with his own inability to lose his virginity, for . . . Quentin's virginity is psychological impotence. Approaching manhood, Quentin finds himself unable to assume the role of a man. Consider his failure as the avenging brother when he encounters Dalton Ames on the bridge – Ames whom Quentin has earlier associated with the figure of the shadow (pp. 153, 154). He tells Ames to leave town by sundown or he will kill him. Ames replies by drawing a pistol and demonstrating his marksmanship. He then offers the pistol to Quentin [but Quentin faints] . . . . . . Later, sick and ashamed, Quentin thinks, 'I knew that he hadnt hit me that he had lied about that for her sake too and that I had just passed out like a girl' (p. 161). Quentin, by rejecting the use of the pistol with its phallic significance and thus avoiding the necessity of risking his life to back up his words, relinquishes the masculine role of avenging brother and finds suddenly that in relation to the seducer he has shifted to a feminine role. Struggling in Ames's grasp, Quentin faints 'like a girl', and Ames, because he sees the sister in the brother, refuses to hurt Quentin and even lies to keep from humiliating him.

Quentin's failure of potency in the role of avenging brother is a repetition of an earlier failure in the role of brother seducer. On that occasion, Quentin had gone looking for Candace, suspecting that she had slipped away to meet Dalton Ames, and he found her lying on her back in the stream . . . Forcing Candace to get out of the water, Quentin begins to question her about Ames, only to find that the questioning suddenly turns to the subject of his own virginity . . . . . . Candace says that she has died for her lover many times ['I would die for him Ive already died for him I die for him over and over again every time this goes' (p. 150)], but for the narcissistic Quentin the mention of sexual death evokes the threat of real death, the feared dissolution of the ego through sexual union with another, the swallowing up of the ego in the instinctual ocean of the unconscious. And Quentin, tormented by his virginity, by his impotence ('poor Quentin . . . youve never done that have you' (p. 150)), can only reply to Candace's sexual death by offering a real *liebestod* [lovers' suicide]. He puts his knife to his sister's throat and proposes that they be joined forever in a murder/suicide – a double killing that represents the equivalent, on the level of brother/sister incest, of the suicidal murder of the brother seducer by the brother avenger. For if the brother-seducer/brother-avenger relationship represents doubling and the brother/sister relationship incest, then the brother/brother relationship is also a kind of incest and the brother/sister relationship a kind of doubling. In at least one version of the Narcissus myth (Pausanius 9.31.6[28]), Narcissus is rendered inconsolable by the death of his identical twin sister, and when he sees himself reflected in the water he transfers to his own image the love that he felt for his dead twin. In this light, consider once again the image that begins the scene [where Quentin finds Caddy in the water]: 'I ran down the hill in that vacuum of crickets like a breath travelling across a mirror she was lying in the water' (p. 148). The narcissistic implication is that his sister lying on her back in the stream is like a mirror image of himself, and indeed, one of the recurring motifs in Quentin's internal narrative is the image of his sister in her wedding dress running toward him out of a mirror (pp. 75, 79). Further, Quentin says that Ames was always 'looking at me through her like through a piece of coloured glass' (p. 174).

It would appear that for Quentin the double as a male figure is associated with the shadow and the double as a female figure is associated with the mirror image. If so, then his suicide represents the attempt to merge those two images. During his walk in the country on the afternoon of his death, Quentin senses the nearness of a river and suddenly the smell of water evokes a memory of his desire for his sister and his desire for death:

> The draught in the door smelled of water, a damp steady breath. Sometimes I could put myself to sleep saying that over and over until after the honeysuckle got all mixed up in it the whole thing came to symbolize night and unrest I seemed to be lying neither asleep nor awake looking down a long corridor of grey half-light where all stable things had become shadowy paradoxical all I had done shadows all I had felt suffered taking visible form antic and perverse mocking without relevance inherent themselves with the denial of the significance they should have affirmed thinking I was I was not who was not was not who.

> I could smell the curves of the river beyond the dusk and I saw the last light supine and tranquil upon tide-flats like pieces of broken mirror . . . Benjamin the child of. How he used to sit before that mirror. Refuge unfailing in which conflict tempered silenced reconciled. (pp. 168–69)

The image of Benjamin, Quentin's idiot younger brother, staring at himself in a mirror, locked forever in mental childhood, is a forceful evocation of the infantile, regressive character of narcissism, and it is in light of that infantile, regressive character that we can understand Quentin's drowning of himself in the river as an attempt to merge the shadow and the mirror image. Quentin's narcissism is, in Freudian terms, a fixation in secondary narcissism, a repetition during a later period of life (usually adolescence) of that primary narcissism that occurs between the sixth and the eighteenth months, wherein the child first learns to identify with its image and thus begins the work that will lead to the constitution of the ego as the image of the self and the object of love. The fixation in secondary narcissism in which the ego at a later period is recathected as the *sole* object of love condemns the individual to an endless repetition of an infantile state. This attempt to make the subject the sole object of its own love, to merge the subject and the object in an internal love union, reveals the ultimate goal of all infantile, regressive tendencies, narcissism included: it is the attempt to return to a state in which subject and object did not yet exist, to a time before that division occurred out of which the ego sprang – in short, to return to the womb, to reenter the waters of birth. But the desire to return to the womb is the desire for incest. Thus, Quentin's narcissism is necessarily linked with his incestuous desire for his sister, for as Otto Rank points out, brother-sister incest is a substitute for child-parent incest – what the brother seeks in his sister is his mother.[29] And we see that the triangle of sister/brother avenger/brother seducer is a substitute for the Oedipal triangle of mother/father/son. Quentin's drowning of his shadow, then, is not only the punishment, upon his own person, of the brother seducer by the brother avenger, it is as well the union of the brother seducer with the sister, the union of Quentin's shadow with his mirror image in the water, the mirror image of himself that evokes his sister lying on her back in the stream. The punishment of the brother seducer by the brother avenger is death, but the union of the brother seducer and the sister is also death, for the attempt to merge the shadow and the mirror image results in the total immersion of both in the water on which they are reflected, the immersion of the masculine ego consciousness in the waters of its birth, in the womb of the feminine unconscious from which it was originally differentiated. By drowning his shadow, Quentin is able simultaneously to satisfy his incestuous desire and to punish it, and . . . it is precisely this simultaneous satisfaction and punishment of a repressed desire that is at the core of doubling. For Quentin, the incestuous union and the punishment of that union upon his own person can be accomplished by a single act because both the union and its punishment are a *liebestod*, a dying of the ego into the other.

In the confrontation between Quentin and Candace at the stream, this linking of sexual desire and death centers for Quentin around the image of Candace's muddy drawers and the death of their grandmother, 'Damuddy'. The image recalls an incident in their childhood when, during their grandmother's funeral, they had been sent away from the house to play. Candace goes wading in the stream, and when Quentin and Versh tell her that she'll get a whipping for getting her dress wet, she says that she'll take it off to let it dry, and she asks the black boy Versh to unbutton the back:

'Dont you do it, Versh.' Quentin said.

'Tain't none of my dress.' Versh said.

'You unbutton it, Versh.' Caddy said, 'Or I'll tell Dilsey what you did yesterday.' So Versh unbuttoned it.

'You just take your dress off,' Quentin said. Caddy took her dress off and threw it on the bank. Then she didn't have on anything but her bodice and drawers, and Quentin slapped her and she slipped and fell down in the water. (p.16)

Candace splashes water on Quentin, an act that in retrospect is sexually symbolic, and Quentin's fear that now they will both get a whipping destroys his attempt to play the role of the protective brother. Shifting from an active to a passive role, Quentin sees Caddy take charge and lead the children back to the house while he lags behind, taunted by Caddy. When they reach the house, Caddy climbs the tree outside the parlor window to see the funeral, and at that point the image of her muddy drawers seen by the children below is fused with the image of Damuddy's death. It is significant that Quentin's obsessive linking of these two images (his sexual desire for his sister and death) involves the repetition, in each case, of the same word – the word 'muddy' in Candace's 'muddy drawers' and 'Damuddy's' funeral', for the threat that sexual union poses to the bright, narcissistic ego is, in Quentin's mind, associated with the image of mud – soft, dark, corrupt, enveloping – the image of being swallowed up by the earth. In the scene where Candace interrupts an abortive sexual encounter in the barn between Quentin and a girl named Natalie ('*a dirty girl like Natalie*' (p.133), as Candace says), Quentin retaliates by jumping into the hog wallow and then smearing his sister with mud . . . . Later, when Quentin identifies with his sister's lover Dalton Ames and imagines Ames and Candace making '*the beast with two backs*' (p.147), the image of Quentin and Candace smeared with mud from the hog wallow metamorphoses into the image of the swine of Eub[oe]leus – the swine that are swallowed up into the earth when Hades carries Persephone down to be the queen of the dead. And a variant of this image occurs in Quentin's last internal monologue before he drowns himself when he imagines the clump of cedars where Candace used to meet her lovers: 'Just by imagining the clump it seemed to me that I could hear whispers secret surges smell the beating of hot blood under wild unsecret flesh watching against red eyelids the swine untethered in pairs rushing coupled into the sea' (p.175).

Since Quentin's incestuous desire for his sister is synonymous with death, it is no surprise that in the scene by the branch, where

Quentin puts his knife to his sister's throat and offers to kill her and then himself, their conversation parodies that of sexual intercourse:

> will you close your eyes
>
> no like this you'll have to push it harder
>
> touch your hand to it . . . . . .
>
> push it are you going to
>
> do you want me to
>
> yes push it
> touch your hand to it (p. 151)

It is a mark of the brilliance and centrality of this scene that its imagery evokes as well the reason for that fear which continually unmans Quentin whenever he tries to assume the masculine role. When Quentin puts his knife to his sister's throat, he is placing his knife at the throat of someone who is an image of himself, thereby evoking the threat of castration – the traditional punishment for incest. The brother seducer with the phallic knife at his sister's throat is as well the brother avenger with the castrating knife at the brother seducer's throat – the father with the castrating knife at the son's penis. The fear of castration fixes Quentin in secondary narcissism, for by making sexual union with a woman synonymous with death, the castration fear prevents the establishment of a love object outside the ego. Quentin's fear of castration is projected onto the figure of his sister, incest with whom would be punished by castration. Thus in her encounters with Quentin, Candace becomes the castrator. When Candace tells him to go ahead and use the knife, his fear unmans him; he drops the phallic knife and loses it, and when he tells Candace that he will find it in a moment, she asks, '[a]re you afraid to?' (p. 152). Recall as well that in the scene at the hog wallow Candace says that she tried to scratch Quentin's eyes out. Having failed in the masculine role of brother seducer in relation to Candace, Quentin shifts to a passive, feminine role, and Candace assumes the active, masculine role. It is a shift like the one that Quentin undergoes when he fails in the masculine role of brother avenger in relation to the seducer Dalton Ames; Quentin immediately assumes a feminine role, fainting like a girl in Ames's grasp. Indeed, brooding on that fear of risking his life that caused him to reject Ames's offer of the phallic pistol, Quentin thinks:

> And when he put Dalton Ames. Dalton Ames. Dalton Ames. When he put the pistol in my hand I didn't (p. 77) . . . Dalton Ames.

Dalton Ames. Dalton Ames. If I could have been his mother lying
with open body lifted laughing, holding his father with my hand
refraining, seeing, watching him die before he lived. (p. 78)

. . . the characteristic doubling scenario of madness leading to suicide
often includes incidents of self-mutilation, for self-mutilation is simply a partial form of self-destruction. During the walk in the country
that Quentin takes on the day of his suicide, he stops on a bridge and
looks down at his shadow in the water and remembers[:]

> Versh told me about a man mutilated himself. He went into the
> woods and did it with a razor, sitting in a ditch. A broken razor
> flinging them backward over his shoulder the same motion com-
> plete the jerked skein of blood backward not looping. But that's
> not it. It's not not having them. It's never to have had them then I
> could say O That That's Chinese I don't know Chinese. And Father
> said it's because you are a virgin: don't you see? Women are never
> virgins. Purity is a negative state and therefore contrary to nature.
> It's nature is hurting you not Caddy and I said That's just words
> and he said So is virginity and I said you dont know. You can't
> know and he said Yes. On the instant when we come to realize that
> tragedy is second-hand.
>
> Where the shadow of the bridge fell I could see down for a long
> way, but not as far as the bottom. (pp. 114–15)

In a real or imagined conversation with his father, bits of which recur
during his internal narrative, Quentin confesses that he and Candace
have committed incest, and he seeks a punishment, he says, that will
isolate himself and his sister from the loud world. When his father
asks him if he tried to force Candace to commit incest, Quentin replies,
'i was afraid to i was afraid she might' (p. 176). It is as if in seeking to
be punished for incest, to be castrated, Quentin would have proof that
his masculinity had ever been potent enough to constitute a threat to
the father; castration would constitute the father's acknowledgment of
the son's manhood . . . . . .

. . . Quentin's brother Benjy is in certain respects a double of
Quentin – in his arrested, infantile state, in his obsessive attachment
to Candace, in his efforts to keep Candace from becoming involved
with anyone outside the family, Benjy is a copy of Quentin, and when
their brother Jason has Benjy gelded for attempting to molest a little
girl, Benjy's physical condition doubles Quentin's psychological impotence, acting out the fate of the brother seducer at the hands of the
brother avenger. Jason is, of course, named after his and Quentin's father.

. . . when Quentin kills himself by descending into the river to join his shadow, there is in his internal narrative a religious significance attached to the act. Quentin wonders whether his bones will rise from the water at the general resurrection, a resurrection for which baptism makes one a member of the elect. Quentin thinks[:]

> And I will look down and see my murmuring bones and the deep water like wind, like a roof of wind, and after a long time they cannot distinguish even bones upon the lonely and inviolate sand. Until on the Day when He says Rise only the flat-iron would come floating up. (p. 78)

And again later: 'And maybe when He says Rise the eyes will come floating up too, out of the deep quiet and the sleep, to look on glory' (p. 115). The date of Quentin's section of *The Sound and the Fury* is June 2, 1910, while the dates of the other three sections of the novel are April 6, 7, and 8, 1928, that is, Good Friday, Holy Saturday, and Easter Sunday. As Quentin's suicide is associated in his mind with the image of the general resurrection, so the dating of the other sections in the novel associates Quentin's death with Christ's death and resurrection, establishing for Quentin's suicidal murder of the brother seducer by the father-surrogate a religious context in which the archetypal son sacrifices his life to appease the anger of the archetypal father. As the dates of the three sections have a liturgical significance [that is, they are dates of public worship for Christian churches], so too does the date of the fourth section: June 2, the day of Quentin's drowning, is the feast day of St. Erasmus (also known as St. Elmo), who is the patron saint of sailors, particularly of sailors caught in a storm, and thus the saint whose special care it is to prevent drownings.[30] □

After this richly suggestive account, Irwin draws a fascinating comparison between *The Sound and the Fury* and *As I Lay Dying*:

■ In *As I Lay Dying* . . . , the novel that Faulkner published immediately after *The Sound and the Fury*, the triangle of a mentally unbalanced brother, a promiscuous sister, and a seducer recurs. Darl Bundren discovers that his sister Dewey Dell has made love to her boyfriend Lafe, and Dewey Dell thinks[:]

> . . . then I saw Darl and he knew . . . and I said 'Are you going to tell pa are you going to kill him?' without the words I said it and he said 'Why?' without the words. And that's why I can talk to him with knowing with hating because he knows. (p. 25)

Dewey Dell is pregnant, and when Doc Peabody comes out to be at her mother's deathbed, Dewey Dell tells herself that the doctor could help her out of trouble if he only knew: 'I would let him come in between me and Lafe, like Darl came in between me and Lafe' (p. 52). The implication at various points in the novel is that there exists, at least on Darl's part, an incestuous attachment between brother and sister, an attachment that represents for Darl a displacement of his love for his mother Addie. In a fantasy that is the reverse of the scene in which Quentin puts the knife to Candace's throat, Dewey Dell, riding into town with Darl, thinks[:]

The land runs out of Darl's eyes; they swim to pin-points. They begin at my feet and rise along my body to my face, and then my dress is gone: I sit naked on the seat above the unhurrying mules, above the travail. *Suppose I tell him to turn. He will do what I say. Don't you know he will do what I say.* Once I waked with a black void rushing under me. I could not see. I saw Vardaman rise and go to the window and strike the knife into the fish, the blood gushing, hissing like steam but I could not see. *He'll do as I say. He always does. I can persuade him to anything. You know I can. Suppose I say Turn here.* That was when I died that time. *Suppose I do. We'll go to New Hope. We won't have to go to town.* I rose and took the knife from the streaming fish still hissing and I killed Darl. (pp. 107–8)

When at the end of the novel Darl is being taken to the state asylum, one of the two guards accompanying him must ride backwards in the railroad coach (so that the guards are facing each other), and Darl thinks[:]

One of them had to ride backward because the state's money had a face to each backside and a backside to each face, and they are riding on the state's money which is incest. A nickel has a woman on one side and a buffalo on the other; two faces and no back. I don't know what that is. Darl had a little spy-glass he got in France at the war. In it it had a woman and a pig with two backs and no face. I know what that is. (p. 241)

The image of 'a woman and a pig with two backs and no face' recalls Quentin's fantasy of Candace and Ames making love:

running the beast with two backs and she blurred in the winking oars running the swine of Euboeleus running coupled within how many Caddy (p. 147)

And the image of the coin with 'two faces and no back' balanced against the image of the two guards facing each other evokes the psychic splitting, the doubling, that has taken place in Darl's personality. This doubling is clear from the very start of the section in which Darl describes his departure for the asylum, for Darl talks about himself in the third person, and then the first-person Darl carries on a dialogue with this other self (p. 202) . . . [31] □

The compelling readings of Irwin and Bleikasten in the 1970s demonstrated that *The Sound and the Fury* and *As I Lay Dying* could not be safely contained within the interpretative modes of the two previous decades. The major critics of those decades who were considered in chapter two of this Guide – Howe, Vickery, Brooks and Millgate – performed an invaluable service by amply rebutting the charges of chaotic unintelligibility and unremitting cruelty laid against Faulkner in the 1930s; and their copious critiques still offer many insights, as the extracts in the previous chapter illustrate. Like much criticism of that period, however, they ran the risk of taming their chosen texts too fully, of turning them into intricate but orderly artefacts, well-wrought urns that would grace the house of fiction and please the presiding spirit of Henry James. Bleikasten himself, in one of the above extracts, pays due tribute to James (pp. 92, 93); but his explorations of Faulkner, like Irwin's, show that the house of fiction has many more rooms than were dreamt of in James's philosophy, and that it is possible – and indeed, with Faulkner, necessary – to descend into the cellars, and to get out into the streets and down to the river. And in the streets and the landscapes of Yoknapatawpha County, one will find that the wounds of the psyche are also the wounds of history and of racial division. As the next chapter of this Guide will show, the most powerful criticism of the 1980s would bring together the analysis of psyche, race, history and fiction, and reshape the contours of Faulkner studies.

CHAPTER FOUR

Division, Death and Desire: Race and Form in Faulkner in the 1980s

THE 1980S saw the radical transformation of literary studies in the UK and USA.[1] There were two major aspects to the change. One was the application of complex but illuminating structuralist, post-structuralist and deconstructionist theories to the interpretation of literary texts; the other was the reawakening of a concern for the political and historical contexts of those texts, a concern that once seemed to have been buried with the 1930s but which now re-emerged in a far more sophisticated form, often forming powerful if unstable alliances with the new theories. As the transformation gathered force, the literary canon was challenged, and revered texts received rough rides; but Faulkner weathered the storm rather well. A critic could cause quite a stir by deconstructing Dickens's novels[2] – but as Donald M. Kartiganer pointed out, Faulkner's novels deconstructed themselves.[3] A Chinua Achebe could send shock-waves round the world by denouncing Joseph Conrad as a racist;[4] but Faulkner's attitudes to race had long been a source of controversy. Nonetheless, it was the case that, in the 1980s, the deconstructive aspects of Faulkner's novels, and their representations of race, came under closer scrutiny than ever before and new mappings of his work began to emerge.

As Eric Sundquist pointed out in his major study, *Faulkner: The House Divided* (1983), Faulkner had, 'on the basis of his fiction and his public statements alike, been variously denounced as a racist and admired as a civil rights advocate', and his 'treatment of difficult racial issues' could not be, and had not been, ignored; nonetheless, there was 'surprisingly little in the critical literature about him that has suggested the complexity, in both emotional and social terms, of his imaginative commitment or examined it within the relevant historical contexts'.[5] Sundquist's book sets out to remedy this state of affairs, to historicise Faulkner and suggest the complexity of his treatment of race; and he starts by providing rich and thought-provoking accounts of *The Sound and the Fury* and *As I Lay Dying*. Discussing *The Sound and the Fury*, he quickly springs a surprise; in contrast to so many other critics, he does not regard it as Faulkner's best work, even though 'his whole fictional effort . . . must nevertheless be judged in relation to it for reasons both formal and thematic'.[6] Sundquist mounts a bracing challenge to the critical 'myth' of *The Sound and the Fury* and some of the interpretations it has generated:

■ . . . the most perplexing thing about [*The Sound and the Fury*] is the discrepancy between its merits and the burdensome interpretations it has inevitably had to support. It is read as an allegory of the South, an exposition of the Oedipal complex, an ironic enactment of Christ's agony, and a sustained philosophical meditation on Time. While it engages all of these issues, it illuminates none of them very exactly; rather – and here lies part of its strange magnificence – it engages these issues, allows them to invade the domain of the novel's arcane family drama, and disavows their capacity to bring the novel out of its own self-enclosing darkness. The 'psychology' that is of most interest in the novel is not Benjy's or Quentin's or Jason's or Dilsey's, but the psychology of the novel as a form of containing consciousness, one that is self-contained and at the same time contains, by defining in subliminal projection, Faulkner's most significant accomplishments and their ultimate derangement . . . the 'mind' the novel does not have – and will not have until Faulkner's career develops – the mind of 'the South,' [the allusion here is partly to W.J. Cash's book *The Mind of the South* (1941), which, as Sundquist has earlier pointed out, 'set out to define ['the mind of the South'] as a romantic continuum'[7]] is paradoxically the only one that fully explains Quentin's incestuous fascination with Caddy's purity and the novel's strange obsession with her.[8] □

Later in his analysis, Sundquist develops the link between incest and the condition of 'the South'; like Irwin in the previous chapter of this Guide (p. 108), Sundquist sees analogies between incest and miscegenation:

■ In *The Sound and the Fury* . . . incest is made to stand for something larger than itself, something having to do with the doom of 'the South' . . . Quentin's incestuous desires do, no doubt, define a libidinal Oedipal drama played out among the Compsons, father and son and preceding generations (we may later propose on the basis of the appendix), but this drama is argued and not acted by the novel; as of yet it has not completely engaged the central tragedy of the South . . .
. . . The black characters in *The Sound and the Fury* do provide a context for the social and psychic decay of the Compsons, and that context is crucial; but as the marginal attention given to them in the appendix

suggests, it would not be evident until *Light in August* why, as Quentin observes to himself, a 'nigger' is not a person but 'a form of behaviour; a sort of obverse reflection of the white people he lives among' (p. 84). At that point Quentin's obsession with Caddy's purity acquires a more subtle and provocative coherence, for the introduction of the theme of miscegenation reveals the absolute paradox in his obsession. Because the etymology and received meaning of *incest* suggest precisely the opposite, such purity is blasphemous by definition: incest is *impure*. To recognize this does not significantly change our perspective on Quentin's fantasy in Oedipal terms. It does, however, begin to alter Caddy's position as representative embodiment of Southern virtue and as ghostly echo of an honored ideal under severe contemporary pressures; and it begins to clarify why Quentin, as the appendix would put it, 'thought he loved, but really hated, in her what he considered the frail doomed vessel of [his family's] pride and the foul instrument of its disgrace'.[9]

Quentin's madness, as Faulkner came to depict it and as the retrospective vantage of the appendix could more justly assume, is primarily the South's, whose intense fascination with gynealotry [worship of women] increased in proportion to threats against it and created the peculiar situation in which the period of Southern history that came mythically to embody extreme virtue and honor, however they may have been manifested, were built on the most hideous corruptions of the human spirit imaginable. Like Quentin's conception of incest, such nostalgic conjuring makes 'pure' what is thoroughly 'impure' – though with this important complication: because incest defines a violation of purity or caste (*in* + *castus*), the integrity of the antebellum South, since it was projected in direct opposition *against* the violent threat of miscegenation that abolition and emancipation were said to entail, might well seem a clean, pure space of remembered innocence. Mr. Compson's contention that Caddy's purity is a 'negative state' (p. 115) defined only by violation . . . or that it is 'like death: only a state in which the others are left' (p. 76) . . . is thus to the point: Caddy's purity and that of the South are defined by a transgression or violation of moral limits that virtually brings them into being, that define what is just as irrevocably lost, past, and 'dead' as Caddy herself. Quentin's dilemma is to imagine that by committing the act himself he can preserve that purity by defining it in violation . . .

If it is to act thus in counterpoint to Quentin's obsessions, Caddy's moral fragility, like her near invisibility as a character, must be seen to portray the violent paradox upon which such conceptions of Southern innocence were built. This paradox would seem irrelevant to (or entirely at odds with) the issue of miscegenation if the contemporary fear of sexual mixing between blacks and whites did not entail a willful denial that Southern innocence, symbolized by its essential purity of white blood, had not already been irrevocably lost . . .

By the time Faulkner began his literary career, the 'lost' but feverishly maintained innocence of the South, so like Quentin's paradoxically puritanical concept of Caddy's purity, had become nothing less than the entire burden of white identity, and the threat against it was more and more obviously constituted, as Joel Williamson has noted, by the failure of 'the myth of the mulatto demise'. The historically prevalent Southern view that mulattoes were a dying breed, both biologically and culturally, and that the sins of the antebellum fathers were therefore passing from view, had begun to be exposed as a myth in its own right by the early twentieth century, with the result that miscegenation, whether instigated by whites or blacks, came to seem more heinous and the purity of white women more crucial than ever. 'To merge white and black would have been the ultimate holocaust, the absolute damnation of Southern civilization,' Williamson writes, and yet the mulatto made apparent 'that white and black had interpenetrated in a graphic and appalling way', that 'life in the Southern world was not [as] pure, clean, and clear as white people needed to believe'.[10]

This interpenetration of the races need not, of course, require us to believe in the thorough interpenetration of either the twin themes of incest and miscegenation or the two novels those themes bring into troubled union. At this point they do not, in Faulkner's imagination, belong together as explicitly as *Absalom, Absalom!* will insist, and one need not believe that the threat of miscegenation is the repressed fear generating Quentin's incestuous desire in order to witness, as Faulkner's career unfolds, the absorption of a private, aesthetic neurosis by a potentially more volatile, comprehensive cultural disorder. That disorder, the threat to the fragile innocence of the white South, along with the historical dimension of tragic action it implies, is latent in *The Sound and the Fury* in the same way that the entirety of Quentin's tormented involvement in the conclusion of the Sutpen saga may be said to be latent, as if by imaginary projection, in the events of June 2, 1910. Miscegenation promised the slow but eventual extinction of the white race (few bothered to notice that the contrary might also be true); like incest, its exact opposite in the operation of prohibitions, it meant the suicidal failure of families and their caste to be perpetuated. It also meant the lasting extinction of a memory, a dream, in which half the South (and the nation) lived in an illusion, the other half in the long shadow it cast.

This complex situation, which Faulkner came to see as the heart of the South's damnation, in all its related mythical and contemporary extenuations, is left broodingly unconscious in *The Sound and the Fury*, which we only recognize at all in the larger context of later novels,

where its shadow looms up in monstrous proportions. There is virtually no way to read it out of the novel itself, even though it adds a
dimension of exceptional power to Quentin's theatrical agony; it is, so
to speak, one of the novel's myths – paradoxically its most crucial and
speechless. It is surely no mistake, however, that Faulkner some years
later would burlesque Quentin's obsession with Caddy by describing
his concept of honor as 'the minute fragile membrane of her maidenhead', as precariously balanced as 'a miniature replica of all the whole
vast globy earth may be poised on the nose of a trained seal', and then
in the same vein of wretched prose describe Jefferson itself, and the
anecdote it here produced, circa 1864, as 'a bubble, a minute globule
which has its own impunity' but which was also 'too weightless to
give resistance for destruction to function against . . . having no part in
rationality and being contemptuous of fact'.[11] The myth at the heart of
The Sound and the Fury was as weightless and intangible (and as subject
to grotesque caricature) as the lost dream it depended on. Nothing that
Faulkner was to write would prove it otherwise, but he would certainly find better and more dramatically exacting ways to say it.[12] □

Moving on to *As I Lay Dying*, Sundquist observes, as other critics have
done, that the novel is different from Faulkner's other major works; it
'seems curiously detached' from them, it is the most capable of being
read independently, and it stands as 'his most perfect and finished piece
of fiction'. But, possibly because of this, Sundquist suggests, 'it is nearly a
compendium of the problematic techniques that Faulkner had discovered in the sudden creative illumination of *The Sound and the Fury* and
would relentlessly pursue throughout the remainder of his career'. A
'virtual textbook of technique', it 'displays all [Faulkner's] talents and
their inevitable risks as they support and drive one another to the per-
ilous limits of narrative form Faulkner would require for his great novels
on the prolonged tragedy and grief of the South'.[13]

Sundquist looks closely at the relationships between theme, technique and form in *As I Lay Dying*, taking up some of the critical issues that
had been debated since its first appearance in 1930. It should be said that
his primary focus here is not on the novel's relation to racism and the
fear of miscegenation, but on the way in which its formal qualities can
be seen as analogous to its themes – and here Sundquist produces a subtle
and striking analysis that has already acquired classic status. Invoking the
many objections that have been made to Faulkner's rhetoric, he identifies two main grounds for complaint: 'that the author or narrator (the
two are easily confused) has fallen victim to his own fantasies of technique; or that a character or speaker (these two are also easily confused)
has been allowed a command of language utterly incommensurate with
his place in the novel's realistic or representational scheme'. Sundquist

proposes, however, that 'the form of *As I Lay Dying* . . . astutely challenges [the assumption of] a narrative consciousness formed by a supposed union between the author and his language, a union formalized and made conventional by the standard device of omniscient, or at least partly omniscient, narration, which the novel explicitly discards and disavows'. The disjunctions between the language, or languages of *As I Lay Dying*, and the characters and/or author relate to the theme of the novel 'insofar as [it] is obsessively concerned with problems of disembodiment, with disjunctive relationships between character and narration or between bodily self and conscious identity'.[14] The extract below begins with Sundquist's exploration of the significance of Addie Bundren in relation to these disjunctions:

■ [It can be suggested that there is] an intimate analogy between the absence of an omniscient narrator, a controlling point of view, and the central event of the book: the death of Addie Bundren, with respect to which each character defines his own identity. The relationship between absent omniscient narrator (or author) and dead mother does not, of course, consist of an exact parallel. Addie Bundren appears in the book, not only dying but speaking her own story in one chapter that appears more than a hundred pages after her literal death . . . . . . the dying maintains a figurative power far succeeding the literal event of Addie's death; and the chronological displacement of her single monologue alerts us to the possibility not only that we must understand the death itself to function as an act of temporal and spatial disembodiment, but that Addie's speech, as it were logically disengaged [from[15]] the corporeal self that could have uttered it, is an extreme example of the way in which the novel's other acts of speech should be interpreted – as partially or wholly detached from the bodily selves that appear to utter them . . . the voices of *As I Lay Dying*, because they are detached . . . from a bounded authorial self, raise doubts about the propriety of referring to the novel's narrative acts as monologues. Such doubts are readily apparent in the example of Vardaman's encounter with Jewel's horse, where the utterance seems disembodied from the conscious identity of author and narrator alike. Yet it also works to enforce our understanding of Vardaman's traumatic reaction to his mother's death and by doing so provides an analogy for the narrative form of the entire novel. The horse that is resolved 'out of his integrity, into an unrelated scattering of components . . . an illusion of a co-ordinated whole of splotched hide and strong bones within which, detached and secret and familiar, [there is] an *is* different from my *is*' (p. 51), is emblematic, even symptomatic, of the 'body' of Addie, in process of being resolved out of her integrity, the '*is*' of her self-contained identity; and it is emblematic of the 'body' of the novel, itself disintegrated and yet carefully producing the 'illusion of a co-ordinated whole'.

Because the relationship between the bodily self and the conscious identity of Addie remains an issue throughout the book, because the self must continue both *to be* and *not to be* the corpse carried along on its self-imposed journey to Jefferson (a possibility disturbingly underscored by Anse's comic refrain '"[h]er mind is set on it"' (pp. 24, 28, 102 ['"Her mind is sot on hit"' (p. 40)])), one is tempted to speak of the body of the book as existing in an analogously fragile state and maintaining its narrative form despite the apparent absence of that substance one might compare to, or identify with, a central point of view embodied in an omniscient narrator. The horse's phenomenal dissolution and 'float[ing] upon the dark' (p. 51) recalls other instances in the novel in which objects as experienced are detached from their fixed physical limits: for example, Addie's face in death, which 'seems to float detached upon [darkness], lightly as the reflection of a dead leaf' (p. 45), or the flooded ford, where the road appears to have 'been soaked free of earth and floated upward, to leave in its spectral tracing a monument to a still more profound desolation' (p. 130) – all of which contribute to our experience of the novel itself as an object whose uttered parts are radically detached from fixed limits and fully identifiable sources. The novel, like the family whose story it tells, is held together in the most precarious fashion, its narrative components adhering and referring to an act that is simultaneously literal and figurative, just as the body of Addie is neither exactly corpse nor conscious self. The logic thus presents itself of speaking of the novel too as a corpse, as a narrative whose form is continually on the verge of decomposition and whose integrity is retained only by heroic imaginative effort.

. . . for all members of the novel's family . . . Addie, at least in the portion of their history presented in the novel (the portion detached, as it were, from the fuller one we imagine by interpretive projection), is the center that no longer holds, that is defunct and yet lingers in stages of tenuous attachment. Vardaman's confusions between his mother and the fish, and between her seeming imprisonment in the coffin and his own recollection of being momentarily trapped in the corn crib . . . . . . provide the most moving instances of the psychological disorientation that affects each of the Bundrens in his or her own way. And they bring into focus the two central problems of bodily integrity and conscious identity with which the novel is concerned: [h]ow can a body that still *is* be thought of as *was*? How can I, whose self has depended upon, and been defined in relation to, another self, now understand the integrity of my own identity? . . . . . . In speaking of a corpse like Addie's that continues to seem both dead and alive, the difficulty of choosing between grammatical forms – *she* and *it*, *is* and *was* – keeps in view the central problem of bodily integrity, a problem explored insistently by the novel's blurring of boundaries between the animate and the inanimate, as in Anse's monologue on roads, Darl's on the river and the wagon, or Dewey Dell's on the dead earth. There are other examples we must turn to, but in all cases such blurrings increase our dependence on the rhetorical terms of the novel, preventing us from doubting the legitimacy of the absurd ritual journey as it unfolds and keeping us attached to the startling possibility of Addie's continued integral power. In this respect the most unnerving yet effective device is the sudden appearance more than halfway through the book, and chronologically (though it makes little sense to speak of it so) some four days after her death, of Addie's single monologue, one of the most emotionally charged pieces of writing in the novel and perhaps the one that comes closest to stating internally a theory of its narrative form.

The importance of Addie's diatribe against 'words' – and particularly the word *love* – lies not simply in her belief that 'words don't ever fit even what they are trying to say at' (p. 159), that we have 'to use one another by words like spiders dangling by their mouths from a beam, swinging and twisting and never touching' (p. 160), for these remarks add virtually nothing to the overwhelming effect already generated by the novel that this is the case. Nor does Addie's enumeration of her pregnancies and the manner in which each balances out or revenges another accomplish much more than providing a partial key to the various relationships of antagonism and devotion that exist among her children. While these relationships are important and finally have much to do with analogies one might draw between the family and the book as integrated forms, the instrumental significance of Addie's monologue arises rather in those sections of her utterance that may be said most to resemble the brooding, silenced voice of the narrator (or author) and are therefore most likely to be misread as moments of sheer invention for the sake of invention on Faulkner's part. The implied or explicit correlation between words and bodies that appears throughout Addie's monologue recalls similar dramatizations of Faulkner's authorial agony in *The Sound and the Fury*, dramatizations that in each case also prefigure the intimate analogy between creation and grief in Faulkner's most passionate explorations of wasted love and historical loss, *Absalom, Absalom!* and *Go Down, Moses*.

The technical wonder of *As I Lay Dying* and its relative thematic isolation among Faulkner's major novels may obscure its place in the development of his handling of loss and grief. The book elaborates those intimacies of loss that *The Sound and the Fury* had broached, but here the simultaneous rage and sentimental indulgence that unbalance the Compson[s'] story are modified and merged; and the emotion spent in the sublimation of erotic passion in the earlier book, and later spent in the sublimation of the equally passionate tragedies of race, is brought to focus and distanced in the novel's extraordinary technique. This technique, fracturing that universal presence by and in which we constitute the essence of a story, defines grief as a characteristic of Faulkner's narrative form itself, a characteristic, that is to say, in which his forms find their fullest expressive power – that of articulating what is lost but lingering on the verge of memory, what will never be but *might have been*, what passionate word or act is harbored in that which remains, for fear or shame, unspoken or unactualized. While suggesting that the decaying corpse of Addie is emblematic of the burden of the Southern past, Faulkner at the same time comes closer to a full evocation of that feminine presence he everywhere associates with creative desire, its failure, and the resulting grief; identifying himself with that presence and yet barely screening his apparent hatred of it, he portrays in Addie the figure of *mothering* conspicuously absent in *Sartoris*, *The Sound and the Fury*, and *Sanctuary* – the figure his later novels will seek to actualize in a crossing of races and whose essence is the literal embodiment of the loss, the separation, and the grief Faulkner finds at the heart of cultural and familial history and acts out in the lives and form of fictional narrative.

Words like *motherhood, love, pride, sin,* and *fear*, Addie suggests, are just 'shape[s] to fill a lack', shapes that, when the need for them arises, cannot adequately fill the void left by an accomplished act or a past event. Words 'fumbl[e]' at deeds 'like orphans to whom are pointed out in a crowd two faces and told, That is your father, your mother' (p.168), and they resemble, in Addie's mind, the names of her husband and children, whose names and bodies imperfectly fill the lack in her bodily self they have caused:

> I would think: The shape of my body where I used to be a virgin is in the shape of a   and I couldn't think *Anse*, couldn't remember *Anse*. It was not that I could think of myself as no longer unvirgin, because I was three now. And when I would think *Cash* and *Darl* that way until their names would die and solidify into a shape and then fade away, I would say, All right. It doesn't matter. It doesn't matter what they call them. (pp. 161–62)

Although it might be too much to claim that the confused and sometimes contradictory remarks of Addie's monologue immediately explain anything, they do reveal that the novel, as John K. Simon has pointed out, is 'the story of a body, Addie's, both in its existence as an unembalmed corpse and as it was – at least partly – conceived for passion'.[16] That is, her remarks clarify what Addie implies and what

Dewey Dell, in her own first pregnancy, has begun to discover – that the connection between sexual 'lying' and lying dying is an intimate one, and that the violation is not simply sexual but generational, as Dewey Dell understands: 'I feel my body, my bones and flesh beginning to part and open upon the alone, and the process of coming unalone is terrible' (p. 55).

Pregnancy for Dewey Dell and for Addie involves a confusion of identity that inverts the one expressed in the process of death, in which the impossibility of conceiving of the self as a singular entity is made paradoxically conspicuous in the sudden need to preserve those connections that define the self even as they pass away. Standing at the other end of death, as it were, 'the process of coming unalone' initiates in their most apparent physical form the connections without which one cannot fully imagine ever having been a lone, identical self existing apart from conscious and bodily ties to others. In extremity, the 'coming unalone', the becoming more than one 'I', leads to a threat of utter extinction through saturation, as in the case of Darl, whom we might think of as figuratively invaded by, and thus consciously 'bearing' in distorted shape, all the novel's characters and events; or it leads to an extinction in which consciousness is completely severed from its own 'I', as in Darl's meditation on sleep and in the nightmare that Dewey Dell's pregnancy, in conjunction with her mother's death, leads her to recall:

> When I used to sleep with Vardaman I had a nightmare once I thought I was awake but I couldn't see and couldn't feel I couldn't feel the bed under me and I couldn't think what I was I couldn't think of my name I couldn't even think I am a girl I couldn't even think I nor even think I want to wake up nor remember what was opposite to awake so I could do that ... (p. 108)

It is this predicament that Addie speaks of metaphorically when she cannot remember the shape of her body when virgin, cannot even articulate the word that might describe it. Words, that is, are inadequate not so much because they fail to 'fit even what they are trying to say at' (p. 159), but because they fail to describe or fill the blank space that only the act of conceiving the need for a word can make manifest as irreparably lost or passed. Words are for something we are not or can no longer be: or as Peabody remarks, in a humorous variation on this potent analogy, when it 'finally occurred to Anse himself that [Addie] needed [a doctor], it was already too late' (p. 36).

As I Lay Dying speaks pointedly to the need for establishing and maintaining conscious attachments symbolically incorporated in bodily ties by constant reference, in both actual and formal terms, to the loss of the originating mother. Darl's claim that he has no mother and that the illegitimate Jewel has a horse for a mother; Dewey Dell's psychological merging of death and childbearing (both in her rhetorical association with Addie as mother and in her conceiving of the funeral journey as a means to get an abortion); Cash's obsession with Addie's coffin, as though its perfection and preservation will somehow save the bodily integrity of Addie; Jewel's heroic actions to save that coffin and its body from flood and fire; and Vardaman's transfiguration of mother into fish[17] – all of these reactions identify grieving as foremost a process of detachment, of disembodiment, in which the act of *expression* is central. Supported by the chaotic chronology of the novel, which prevents us from knowing 'where' the characters are speaking from, the community of voices itself participates in the paradoxical action that grieving is, an action that expresses connections in order both to make them and let them go. Like the voices of the women singing at the wake described by Tull, the voices of the novel that tell Addie's story (including her own) seem to 'come out of the air, flowing together and on in the sad, comforting tunes. When they cease it's like they hadn't gone away. It's like they had just disappeared into the air and when we moved we would loose them again out of the air around us, sad and comforting' (p. 84).

This is true whether we conceive of the characters as talking, as thinking, or – in some instances – even as writing their stories; and the confusion as to which is the more appropriate conception makes it clear that grief seldom has an appropriate form or a distinct chronology. What Faulkner once spoke of as characteristic of his entire work is particularly relevant to *As I Lay Dying*: 'The fact that I have moved my characters around in time successfully, at least in my own estimation, proves to me my own theory that time is a fluid condition which has no existence except in the momentary avatars [incarnations, manifestations] of individual people. There is no such thing as *was* – only *is*. If *was* existed, there would be no grief or sorrow'.[18] The form of the novel keeps *is* from becoming *was* as Addie's corpse is kept dying beyond the physical death and – because the stories have no fixed temporal origins but rather are desperately detached from them – even beyond the supposed chronological end of the action, Addie's burial and Anse's remarriage. Grief itself seems disembodied from its object precisely because the boundaries of that object have ceased to have specific meaning and now receive abnormally deliberate, if displaced, attention. The dislocation of conscious attention that grief can produce makes Vardaman's psychological transferences from mother to fish, for example, or Cash's from body to coffin plausible and even necessary, and helps explain what André Bleikasten has referred to as Faulkner's possession by the 'demon of analogy' in the novel.[19] The action of grief responds to and reflects the demand for analogy, for the possibility of relocating the lost integrity of one object in another as a way of expressing the maintenance of emotional connections that are threatening to disappear.

Because the novel refuses to settle on a point of view, a narrative focus that gives immediate coherence to the story, but on the contrary forces us to develop that coherent identity by an act of imaginative identification, piecing it together from disparate parts, it too might well be regarded as a family without a mother, as it were, without a single source from which we can clearly say the parts have sprung. And yet of course we do say just that: we say Faulkner is the author, these all are parts of him, products of his creation. To say this, however, is both necessary and speculative, for the parts – disembodied from the act that apparently produced them – are in their own way as much orphaned as Addie's own children or the words that she speaks of as filling a lack left by a deed that has passed. The self that produced them, or the integral point of view that we imagine as controlling them, has 'come unalone' in that act, which is now a lack filled by shapes. We know and need it only in retrospect; because this is the case, the process of grieving that the Bundrens undergo – a process in which their breaking of connections with Addie at once defines her self as composed of them yet requires each of them to lie dying along with her – is analogous to the narrative unfolding of 'Faulkner's story', a process in which the shape of the book is built up by accumulation and connection but paradoxically participates in the disintegration of that imagined single form, leaving each episode in isolation, tenuously attached to the others and at the same time orphaned – referring to, yet failing properly to 'fill' and complete, the lack that they make manifest. Because they exist in the novel's form as disembodied both from the bodies that utter them *and* from the one body that we must understand as having once produced them, the narrative episodes do indeed seem a collection of voices in the air.

As I Lay Dying is best understood, then, as a book in which death is the story and the story is a death, a book in which the authorial 'I' also lies dying; that is, he is dead as Addie is dead, dead as a single identity but still alive in the episodes that continue to refer themselves to that identity and continue to constitute it even more emphatically in our desire to locate Faulkner's own 'language', his own 'story', in the voices of his characters. To speak of the book as a corpse is to recognize that such an expression is at once appropriate and inadequate, for just as Addie's corpse is not what dies (except on one occasion) in the book, the words that fill the book, like the family that continues to fill and be filled by Addie Bundren, are alive, however disembodied, fragmented, and comically bereaved. The expressions of grief that work out their own disembodiment from a lost, decomposing object by the insistent desire for analogous experience find analogy in the novel's form, which, like the action of grief, relocates the limits and power of that object in the stories of which it is now composed. Those expressions continue to have and to acquire meaning, and continue to make connections, despite the absurdity of doing so and appearing to act, as Faulkner recognized, in a virtual vacuum.[20] □

Sundquist's powerful analyses demonstrate the fruitfulness of a critical approach that combines a close attention to the formal qualities of a novel with a concern for content and historical context. This is also true of the interpretations of James A. Snead in his book *Figures of Division: William Faulkner's Major Novels* (1986). Snead, an African American critic of formidable erudition who died too young,[21] focuses on the relation between rhetoric and racism in Faulkner's novels, the way in which they 'self-consciously analyze' the 'figures of racial division' that are 'the linguistic supports of an immoral social system'.[22] According to Snead, '[f]igures of division fail on two counts': first, 'they are binary and as such require an opposite term in order to signify anything' – for example, 'white' depends for its meaning on its posited opposite, 'black', and must thus invoke blackness even as it attempts wholly to exclude it; and 'absolute segregation, in trying to enforce an unreal polarity, only further agitates the psychic desire to exceed its artificial boundaries'[23] – in other words, the attempt rigidly to enforce an ultimately unsustainable total division between black and white arouses the wish, consciously and/or unconsciously, to go beyond that false division, to mix the races. Like Sundquist, Snead focuses on the matter of the mixing of races, of miscegenation, in Faulkner's fiction:

■ Since figures of division are at the same time social and linguistic, Faulkner's novels, as literary texts, can examine their invention and demise on both thematic and stylistic levels of analysis. Particularly germane to Faulkner's novels as an instance of actual and stylistic merging is the issue of *miscegenation*. The system of racial division elicits the desire for racial mixing or miscegenation, the South's feared, forbidden, denied, yet pervasive release from societal division. Notions such as 'white racial purity', aimed at underpinning the economic order, underlie figures of division. Southern society typically and publicly abhorred racial mergings by integration, cohabitation, and miscegenation. Yet Faulkner's narratives repeatedly present a world in which blacks and whites eat, live, and often sleep together, despite written Jim Crow laws and spoken categories of racial differentiation. [The name 'Jim Crow' comes from a popular 'minstrel' song first introduced in Louisville in 1828. 'Jim Crow' legislation referred to any law that prohibited African Americans from mixing with or having the same privileges as white Americans.[24]] Faulkner's narratives dismember figures of division at their weakest joint, the 'purity' notion that seems the requirement for white supremacist logic. White skin could never be the certain signifier of the absence of 'black' blood (white racial purity), because white skin, as Faulkner amply demonstrates, can also signify 'mixed' blood.

Faulkner's most compelling protagonists do not seek division, but rather its often non-conventional remedies: miscegenation, incest, Edenic refuge in the Big Woods, or schizoid mental mergings. Absolutisms, facing the test of experience, break down under the pressure of the unsystematic real. Faulkner's major novels, *The Sound and the Fury, As I Lay Dying, Light in August, Absalom, Absalom!, The Hamlet*, and *Go Down, Moses*, primarily concern the white mind and its struggles with the systems of division it has created. The stylistic strangeness of Faulkner's novels is not purely post-Joycean experimentalism, as often suggested, nor even a residue of his infatuation with Romanticism and French symbolism. Instead, Faulkner's narratives are accurate reconstructions and dismantlings of linguistic and social classifications, proving that some extraordinary human beings struggle, against overwhelming odds, to reverse a separation that rhetoric has tried to make into a permanent reality.[25] □

Snead then focuses on *The Sound and the Fury*, in a lucid, compelling and wide-ranging analysis:

■ [*The Sound and the Fury*] deviates in many ways from standard fictional treatments of the white, and also of the black, for the main narrative conflict is not any putative [supposed] 'negro' problem. The problem, in fact, is white; we here inquire into the deleterious effects of racial division upon the *nous*, the 'white mind' ['nous' is a classical Greek term for mind, or intellect]. The white Compsons' perceptions are askew, each in its own way. A narrative of Negro suffering, ignorance, or endurance is not forthcoming. Whether by its unusual syntax or by its skewed social relations, *The Sound and the Fury* features a discourse that puts its readers *somewhere else* . . . Many readers have confused their own displacement with a suspicion that the author was unskilled or fuzzy in his aesthetic aims . . . *The Sound and the Fury's* mergings indeed begin, within ten pages, to seem a kind of chaos.

Benjy's chaos

[The section headings throughout this extract are Snead's]

. . . Benjy's prose gives a disjointed impression because it does not assemble events in a causal fashion or manipulate large-scale analytic propositions any more complex than the simple connective 'and'. His discourse signifies by non-linear association rather than syntactical and causal linearity. His prose, then, is the kind of chaos 'whose ill-assorted elements [are] indiscriminately heaped together in one place', to quote Ovid.[26] 'Mind' [*nous*] has given way to metaphor, with its unpredictable, seemingly random connections:

> Mrs Patterson came to the door and opened it and stood there.
> *Mr Patterson was chopping in the green flowers. He stopped chopping and looked at me. Mrs Patterson came across the garden, running.* (pp. 11–12)

> 'Stay on your side now.' Dilsey said. 'Luster little, and you don't want to hurt him.'
> *You can't go yet, T.P. said. Wait.* (p. 30)

In the first example, Benjy connects Mrs Patterson in the present with an incident in which, while taking his Uncle Maury's adulterous messages to Mrs Patterson, he was caught by her jealous husband. In the second example, Benjy connects two examples of physical separation. Such abstract notions as 'separation' or 'absence' remain the crucial abstractions in Benjy's consciousness, since he constantly wonders whether he is about to lose or regain a beloved object.[27] Faulkner has created in Benjy a highly unusual and even risky exception to Jefferson, Mississippi's rule of division: since Benjy cannot 'order' chaos, he represents Faulkner's first experiment in creating a character who has no capacity to discriminate racially. Benjy knows fire and darkness, presence and absence, but not hierarchy. *Nous* has given way, and Benjy sees color as color, not as an index of power and privilege. Indeed, Benjy, as we shall see, enjoys one privilege denied any other white man: he travels to the church service in 'Nigger Hollow'.

In *Beyond the Pleasure Principle,* Freud reports the *'fort/da'* ('gone/here') game wherein his grandson gets pleasure from making a toy vanish and reappear. Similarly, Luster toys with the childlike Benjy's automatic reactions to presence and absence:

> A long piece of wire came across my shoulder. It went to the door, and then *the fire went away.* I began to cry.
> 'What you howling for now.' Luster said. 'Look there.' *The fire was there.* I hushed. (p. 55; [Snead's] italics)

'Whyn't you hush?' Luster said, 'You want me to give you somethin' to sho nough moan about? Sposin I does dis.' He knelt and swept the bottle suddenly up and behind him. Ben ceased moaning. He squatted, looking at *the small depression where the bottle had sat,* then as he drew his lungs full *Luster brought the bottle back into view.* 'Hush!' he hissed, 'Don't you dast to beller! Don't you. Dar hit is. See?' (p. 315; [Snead's] italics)

Benjy reacts to absence by crying; white Southern customs react to the absence or presence of white skin by classifying. Perhaps now the novel's underlying irony becomes clear, and the 'initial obscurity' as well.

Benjy's odd syntax manifests his underlying inability to handle extended figures of racial designation. As Ferdinand de Saussure says in discussing the basic nature of linguistic signification, so-called 'metonymic' relations concern how any message is spoken or written in a linear connecting chain [that is, how words are associated together, one after the other, in phrases and sentences – metonymic relations are relations of contiguity, of words being next to each other]. 'Metaphoric' relations, in their turn, are virtual, not combinational, and concern the pool from which a particular message's elements are selected [that is, how a word is similar to (and also, by implication, different from) other words – metaphoric relations are relations of similarity, of words being like (or unlike) each other]. Applied to social groups, racial hierarchies would employ the rule of metonymy. Metaphor, for its part, would determine the 'natural' marks of generic similarity by which these groups would be identified and discriminated against.[28] Benjy seems to have the metaphoric but not the metonymic capacity. Benjy cannot despise blacks, being fully unaware of their metonymic positions in the social array. He might associate their skins with night or soil, but never with enslavement or debasement. Roman Jakobson invented a term that seems quite apt for Benjy's utterances – 'contiguity disorder', wherein 'word order becomes chaotic; the ties of grammatical coordination and subordination, whether concord or government, are dissolved'.[29] For their part, readers are not immediately aware of Luster's color exactly because the narrative is in the first place from Benjy's point of view. Through the manipulations of style early on, the reader's sense of familiarity with racial categories is fundamentally questioned. Benjy's section engages our talent, or rather our dire necessity, to *classify*, precisely because he cannot. [As Irving Howe says,] '[t]he Benjy section forces the reader to participate in the novel, to become, as it were, a surreptitious narrator; otherwise he cannot read it at all'.[30] But the reader must be extremely careful to mark what type of narrator he or she becomes, and with what types of prejudices.

The Compson family, particularly Mrs Compson, has had to face the trauma of not knowing whether their youngest son was one of *us* ('Maury') or one of *them* ('Benjy'). But Benjy's chaotic otherness only continues the larger collapse of definition that the Confederate Army's losses began, given that the Civil War was largely fought over definitions: who is a 'free man' and who a 'slave'? What does 'white' mean in terms of civil and social rights? The disarray of Lee's fighting machine was a 'chaos' which ended the privilege of the Southern male to define social relations: master/slave, husband/wife, and so on. Jim

Crow legislation, written to curb heretical whites as much as uppity blacks, sought a definitional consensus, but the unwritten history of racial mixing, inscribed into the skin of the mixed-race progeny, gave it the lie.

The tensions within the Compson family only underscore public tensions. Yet the notion that the substance of racial politics in America is not primarily a 'Negro problem' but rather a problem of white psychic, economic, and family structure would not have gone down terribly well in 1929. In effect, the complexity of the novel's first page and its jumbled 'chaos' repeats and reverses the South's distorted legacy of white racial superiority, exposing the manner of both its construction and its eventual self-destruction.

Plots of exchange: Benjy, Quentin, Jason

Traces of unequal relations occur and recur in the speech of the main narrators of *The Sound and the Fury* (Benjy, Quentin, and Jason), mitigated by a countervailing prose that, often against the speaker's wishes, dissolves these relations. Such dissolution even extends to the unexpected and often uncanny relationships between the three brothers' narratives. Links between Benjy's and Quentin's sections abound: Benjy ends his chapter by falling asleep, and Quentin wakes up to begin his. [As Cleanth Brooks says] Benjy 'is filled with a kind of primitive poetry'; Quentin's poetry is 'essentially decadent'.[31] Benjy is castrated, and Quentin wishes to be castrated. But physical castration is only part of the story. Quentin perhaps wishes to destroy not merely his own sexual organs but all other evidence of separations as well. But, even here, the matter is not so clear-cut. Consider for a moment Quentin's seeming hatred of time. First he hides the watch face, then he twists off its hands. He does not destroy the watch; he merely defaces it. It seems, then, that Quentin wants to reject conventional measures of time, but not time itself, which relies on the less arbitrary measure of planetary movement. Indeed, Quentin spends much of the day telling time by the length of his sun-cast shadow. To tear off watch hands removes only the signifiers of real time. Such a separation, generalized, between thing and signifier would kill language, but would also allow Quentin an ideal realm in which the tabooed 'other' would no longer be other. Quentin tears off the watch hands because he wants to 'castrate' conventional division, render separation impotent by means of separation – an impossible, because contradictory, goal. Failing in this attempt, he stages his own final separation in search of oneness, a separation from life itself . . . . . .

Although he is subject to various exchanges, Quentin none the less bemoans his entrapment within fixed categories. Quentin has a primal and ineluctable [inescapable] question: '[w]hy couldn't it have been me and not her who is unvirgin' (p. 76). The negative prefix to 'unvirgin' denotes the overall impossibility of an exchange between Quentin and his sister ('me and not her'). Quentin repeatedly finds himself on the wrong side of division. In fact, he should be the one who has had sex before marriage; he should be able to 'protect' his sister from that experience – but this time roles, though fixed, have reversed: Caddy is more like a man than he is. Quentin tries to reverse in so many words the unhappy exchanges of his life. But exchange does not lead to change . . .

Neither Quentin nor Benjy can be defined according to convention. The division Quentin insists upon seems to bring about a racial and sexual mixing he both desires and fears. Whether Quentin likes it or not, people consider him at times 'black' and at times a 'woman'. The New Englanders he meets are not particularly helpful, saying '"he talks like a coloured man"' (p. 119), or that his hand is feminine, as if 'just out of convent' (p. 108). He confronts Dalton Ames, but cannot defend his sister, and 'just passe[s] out like a girl' (p. 161). Spoade repeatedly taunts him by saying that Shreve is Quentin's 'husband' (p. 170). Caddy names a daughter after him, so that not even his name, 'Quentin', is unequivocally male . . .

Yet Quentin at times wishes to unite with his antithetical counterparts. He tries to reverse separation to re-create an original wholeness . . . The compulsion to merge, reducing distance and difference, seems only human, but so is its opposite compulsion, to separate and divide, as facilitated by analytical thought. Quentin has settled upon an almost unimaginably difficult ambition. Whereas the plot of *The Sound and the Fury* consists of its characters' errors, its greatest challenge is to ask whether alternatives to error are possible. Such alternatives would have to overcome formidable conflicts between desire and large-scale barriers.

Time and space are also a kind of barrier. The phrase 'Tomorrow, and tomorrow' begins the *Macbeth* soliloquy (Act 5, Scene 5, line 18[32]) that suggested *The Sound and the Fury* as a title. Separations brought about by time and space are the chief causes of desire. 'Tomorrow' postpones satisfaction, for 'today' is never the end of the line . . . Quentin intuitively knows he is fighting a losing battle, against, above all, time. His suicide letter says '"[n]ot good until tomorrow"' (p. 97). Thoughts need articulation and dissemination – they are not 'good' until they become 'later'. But articulation makes language, distanced from the point of conception, only a 'bad' secondary version of things. Quentin will not be 'good' until 'tomorrow' – when he will no longer be torn between antagonisms, because he will be dead. Indeed, in this novel, the unfulfilled state of being constantly *before*, the state of the *not yet*, intrigues Faulkner. There seems to be a 'day before' pattern through-out this novel, in which crucial plot events occur one day before a religious or historical, usually Confederate, commemoration. Historical myths, no less than literary plots, seem to require varieties of temporal separation – usually delay, retrospection [looking back], or anticipation – in order to function at all.[33] Quentin's suicide letter is also the literal letter, for a written narrative really comes into its own when separated by space or time from its producer – indeed, as [Roland] Barthes reminds us, with the death of the author comes the birth of the book.[34]

Barriers of society and time often appear in the form of spatial barriers in *The Sound and the Fury*. For instance, in the seminal image of the novel, Caddy disobediently peers at her grandmother's corpse through a window. Her daughter Quentin later escapes by climbing through a window and down a pear tree (or rainpipe, as in the 'Appendix'[35]). Her brother, also a Quentin, tries to shoot her and Herbert Head's voices 'through the floor'. The theme of 'barriers' comes up most tellingly in the opening words [of the novel]: '[t]hrough the fence, between the curling flower spaces, I could see them hitting' (p.1). Fences separate ('crossing the fence' is a standard term for black-white miscegenation) and enclose a normative space – the ironic reader of the novel might actually question which side of the Compson fence constitutes normality. Benjy keeps peering through the fence at a plot of earth once his, now sold. Were Benjy to go '[t]hrough the fence', he would violate the contract that exchanged his precious land for money, but he does not know this, and breaks through the barrier. The first time he tries actually to cross the fence, he also tries to speak – 'I opened the gate and they stopped, turning. I was trying to say and I caught her, trying to say, and she screamed and I was trying to say and trying' (p.51). Benjy has spotted a girl who presumably resembles Caddy. He really wants Caddy, as signified by the girl. If he could speak, he would probably tell the girl 'My name is Benjy' or say 'Hello'. But he cannot say 'Hello' because he is congenitally mute, and, even were he not, he could not know his real name ('Maury') because his family has exchanged it for a substitute ('Benjy'). The family at first names Benjy after his alcoholic uncle Maury. But once Benjy's condition manifests itself they change his name. Versh tells Benjy: '"[y]our mamma too proud for you"' (p.68). Quentin, appropriately, invents the new name: 'rechristened Benjamin by his brother Quentin (Benjamin, our lastborn, sold into Egypt)';[36] 'Benjamin the child of mine old age held hostage into Egypt' (p.169); *'Benjamin came out of the bible, Caddy said. It's a better name for him than Maury was'*. Then the family makes the name fixed: challenged to say why Benjy is a *'better name'*, Caddy simply replies, *'Mother says it is'* (p.56). Benjy, then, succumbs to a form of division by the exchange of names (only Dilsey protests at the substitution – she has seen its like before), a separation perpetuated by family custom. Benjy cannot speak a name that, even if he could speak, he would not actually know. By 'trying to say' a lost name without actually uttering it, he loses his testicles, whose pale replicas he later seeks 'through the fence' in the first lines of the novel.

Benjy's frustration with words, his 'trying to say', resembles a more general insufficiency. In accosting the girls, he cannot speak, he cannot attain his desire. Even were he to speak, he would be giving out a false name, *'a better name for him'* (p. 56). He tries to speak and is castrated for it. After the operation, he sees lost golf balls '[t]hrough the fence, between the curling flower spaces' (p. 1). These events have already occurred before we peer with him 'through the fence . . . spaces'. So the opening of the novel reveals an already irremediable loss, and further loss follows any attempt to recapture what was lost. In this way, *The Sound and the Fury* forces the reader to participate in the novel not merely as a white under the dominance of chaotic language and a canny black [as Benjy, at the start of the novel, is under Luster's dominance], but also as an already castrated viewer. We assume Benjy's point of view here; language has already undone our efforts to stave off its amputative effects. . . . Interestingly, Quentin equates sexlessness with a linguistic exclusion: 'But that's not it. It's not not having them [genitals]. It's never to have had them then I could O That That's Chinese I dont know Chinese' (p. 114). Benjy gazes into 'spaces' that 'signify nothing'. Yet, unlike Benjy, the 'sane' mind does not react to verbal impotence with silence and tears but rather with *nous*, which manipulates language to simulate facts, and constructs 'reality' from the simulations . . . Society and language become 'rhetorical'; they are the chief ways in which *nous* tries to fend off chaos and hide all consequent deprivations.

. . . Signification may be a form of conceptual violence, but the Yoknapatawpha enforcers of specious division often have recourse to actual, less indirect, forms of coercion. Quentin's cerebral bent does not keep him from sharing his brother Jason's tendency towards violence; he provokes at least two fights during the course of the day. Public tensions, created by the need to rank diverse entities, are now Quentin's 'private' agonies. Illicit attempts at sexual coupling, failure, and guilt over trying now comprise a palpable shadow that hovers about Quentin. Quentin perhaps never grasps what his father means when he says that 'it was men invented virginity not women' (p. 76): the very concept of 'virginity', like the idea of 'nigger', is a mask covering the urge to violate these categories. Neither term has much to do with what it presumably describes. Black skin only signifies for the white eye: 'there was a nigger on a mule . . . like a sign put there saying You are home again' (pp. 84, 85). The black face is a *sign* to

Quentin, not a personality, and the 'shadow' that tracks him all day long is a certain ideational impurity he cannot countenance. The sign of the 'nigger on a mule' must be taken together with Benjy's carriage ride at the end of the novel, when Benjy sees 'post and tree, window and doorway, and signboard, each in its ordered place' (p. 321). Quentin wants to kill a black sign of his own mental chaos, even as Benjy wants to cling to his white 'signboard' of order. Quentin would kill the black other in himself, the shadow that must be separated from his 'I', either by violence or by the threat thereof . . . . . .

Skin color is a biological characteristic that can separate for a probing, classifying eye. One reduces the visual sign of color as under a microscope's objective. Yet, unlike a dead specimen, race examines the examiner . . . [As Quentin thinks,] 'a nigger is not a person so much as a form of behaviour; a sort of obverse reflection of the white people he lives among' (p. 84). The semiotic black exists in order to redress a prior white loss of meaning and authority: 'They [blacks] come into white people's lives like that in sudden sharp black trickles that isolate white facts for an instant in unarguable truth like under a microscope' (p. 169). Even if isolation and objectification distort both viewer and object, Quentin needs these defenses against what he considers to be chaos. He yearns for separating . . . figures; his prose is discrete [discontinuous], fragmentary, lacking any synthesis.[37] He spends most of his day trying to prove to himself that he is white and not black, male and not female. For instance, his black/white and female/male confusion comes up in a memory shortly after he confesses his incestuous urges to Caddy. He suggests that they perform a *Liebestod* [a lovers' suicide] so that Caddy will never love another man. She rejects his advances. In the end, they stand, 'their shadows one shadow her head . . . . . . her shadow high against his shadow one shadow' (p. 153).

Quentin is the gnomon of a sundial that is himself [a 'gnomon' is a pillar, rod, pin, or plate on a sundial, showing time by where its shadow falls on the marked surface of the sundial] . . . his shadow conveys a sense of antithesis dying. Quentin walks both inside and outside his shadow. He wishes both to integrate himself with the black and to punish the color that stands for his tabooed wishes, particularly the wish to sleep with his sister: 'I stood in the belly of my shadow . . . I went back to the post office, treading my shadow into pavement' (p. 99). The empty signifier of black skin can support Quentin's paradoxical handling, and can be for others a 'sign' (p. 85) for 'white facts' (p. 169), an 'obverse reflection of . . . white people' (p. 84). Shadows, as we have seen, represent Quentin's frustrated wish to merge with what the law says he must be separate from. Merging takes place, but under penalty of law: Quentin carries out the sentence upon himself – he jumps.[38] Through one monumental action, Quentin ends separation

from blackness exactly where he had hoped to assert his white unique-
ness: he jumps into 'my shadow leaning flat upon the water' (p. 88).

Jason's ploys of exchange are less psychological in nature than
Quentin's ['ploys' may be a misprint for 'plots' here, as 'Plots of exchange
. . .' is the title of this section]. Jason, unlike his brothers, is a pragma-
tist who tries to cope with the 'real' world. None the less, his exchange
transactions also go awry. Jason's section seems accessible, delivered
in first-person, conversational style, recalling [J.D. Salinger's] *Catcher
in the Rye* (1951) or [Sinclair Lewis's] *Babbitt* (1922). His colloquial tone
presents a discourse whose main topic seems to be *exchange*, and
whose basic tonalities view life as equitable or disequitable exchange.
Jason, more than either his older or his younger brother, seems to
know how society sets its values.[39] Indeed, Jason's 'sanity' is all too
close to our own obsession with economic value. Perhaps for this
reason more than any other, Jason's motives seem less complex than
those of his brothers. Yet, ironically, Jason cannot control any of the
exchange systems to which he belongs . . . Jason's life in the community effectively separates him from it. Jason has little to say to Earl or
the cotton traders. One feels that, even in a third-person narration,
Jason would always wish to be the first.

Jason encounters a series of ambiguous exchanges. He seeks
redemption through a 'cotton exchange', but its true activity and
power is absent, and Jason has a substitute, the 'telegraph wire' that
gives him deferred reports of the market events. He pays ten dollars a
month for a broker's advice, yet ends up losing 200 dollars in one day.
He has exchanged his mother's thousand dollars for a car, but he cannot drive the car because he is allergic to its gasoline fumes. His sister
Caddy's husband-to-be promises him a bank job in exchange for his
consent to their marriage, but soon he reneges on his promises. Jason
takes revenge, stealing the money that Caddy sends her illegitimate
daughter Quentin. He does it by exchanging a false check for the real
one that Caddy sends every month, and banking the sum while their
mother burns the substitute check. He deposits his salary under his
mother's name as a bogus gesture of faith, but withdraws Caddy's
money and spends it. His niece Quentin ultimately steals from him the
money he has stolen from her. All these exchanges are symbolic acts
that paradoxically act against their agent . . .

Mrs Compson calls Jason '"the only one who had any business
sense"' (p. 221) but Jason cannot keep his dominant position in the
marketplace, in the town, or in the family, because exchange, by definition, both encourages and disallows fixed positions. Even though
markets require traders to 'take positions', these positions are in
constant flux. Jason does not acknowledge the reciprocity that rules economic (and ultimately social) interaction: his loss of 200 dollars is

someone else's (he suspects a 'damn New York jew' (p.264)) gain . . . . . .

Jason was a small-scale tattletale and bully as a child, as we recall from the short story 'That Evening Sun'.[40] Now he has graduated to more widely sanctioned forms of brutality. Jason, whom the 'Appendix' calls the ['first] sane'[41] Compson, is also the most violent. For violence of every sort, from the whip to the KKK [Ku Klux Klan] lynch mob, underpins the so-called 'sanity' of Faulkner's Yoknapatawpha. In the 'Appendix' we learn of Jason's violent wish to catch his niece Quentin 'without warning, springing on her out of the dark, before she had spent all the money, and murdering her before she had time to open her mouth'.[42] In the novel's last scene, Jason, beating Luster for a minor infraction, apes other symbolic acts of violence against blacks, trying, in a forceful symmetry, to restore in the end, at Luster's expense, the 'order' of white authority that was lost to Luster in the beginning on account of Benjy's 'chaos'. 'Then he struck Luster over the head with his fist' (p.320).

Jason's section continues the novel's inquiry into rhetoric. The novel's various narrators journey 'from the sensory to the interpretive'; the 'progression from Benjy's section through Quentin's to Jason's is accompanied by an increasing sense of reality'; a 'progression from murkiness to increasing enlightenment'. Indeed, more than half of the interest in the novel comes from its style and not its narrative development. So critics' elaborate plot summaries and charts of time levels (as in Stewart and Backus or Volpe), while helpful, cannot properly illustrate the aims of the novel.[43]

The hollow heart

The Sound and the Fury's most remarkable section, 'April 8, 1928', contrasts Jason with Dilsey, the one divisive and irascible, the other conciliatory and level-headed. Jason ranges over a thirty-mile radius in his mad car-chase after his niece Quentin, who has stolen his money. He journeys the most widely, but the least successfully; Dilsey simply walks to church and back. We are less in the dark than ever before – the narrative is comprehensible, taking up a single day, not thirty years, as in Benjy's section. There are few flashbacks; events are linear. One expects a conclusion, a moral, a statement of some kind, for there is no 'tomorrow, and tomorrow, and tomorrow'; April 8, 1928 is the final day.

More so than the ludic [playful] narrators of previous chapters, the lucid one of the fourth seems fully reliable. Yet the narrator is still questionable; critical opinion has not yet decided whose voice informs the final chapter. Millgate says that Dilsey is the 'immensely positive figure' who centers the last section;[44] Kinney agrees that we see Dilsey 'directly' here for the first time;[45] Waggoner claims that the last section is 'effectively hers [Dilsey's] even though told from the narrative point of view of [an] omniscient author'.[46] Others differ about the degree of 'omniscience'. Matthews, hedging his bets, calls the last section 'Faulkner's';[47] Reed claims that 'Faulkner turns to the third person to finish the novel' with 'absolute objectivity';[48] Slatoff agrees that the last section is 'narrated from an omniscient and objective point of view'.[49] Whether the section is 'Faulkner's' ([a]s Faulkner himself once claimed) or 'Dilsey's' (by analogy with the other three sections) is important, since one might read its events differently in either case. If Dilsey, as important as she is to the plot and to the household, cannot narrate her own section, then the novel contains a peculiar imbalance: why should Dilsey, the most sympathetic character, be denied a privilege granted to Jason, the least sympathetic? If Dilsey is not the narrator, then this chapter deviates from the novel's typical practice, not just by being relatively readable and coherent, but by separating Dilsey from the narrative's habitual mode of expressing consciousness.

The chapter's highpoint comes in a scene that is almost theatrical in its location and impact. 'Highpoint' perhaps misnames the actual location – a deep hollow, 'the section known as Nigger Hollow' (p. 302).[50] This black world is a 'scene like a painted backdrop . . . the whole scene was as flat and without perspective as a painted cardboard set upon the ultimate edge of the flat earth' (p.292). Dilsey's and Benjy's spiritual migration takes them to the most separate place possible. They travel (in an unmistakable reference to Odysseus'[s] journey to the Underworld in Book XI of *The Odyssey*) to 'the ultimate edge of the flat earth'.[51] What could be more remote than 'the ultimate edge of the flat earth'? They find what they must know only after tracing a depression or hollow in the ground to attract the shades and spirits of the supernatural.

The trip to Nigger Hollow takes the reader through a fence that is both linguistic and racial. Benjy, a white separated from whites, is well qualified to be the reader's *psychpomp* [guide] through the Underworld. *The Sound and the Fury* from the first to last is Benjy's book: 'Benjy's fusion of life and death correlates to what seeing the first and last means to Dilsey, and, finally, to us'.[52] He is the only white in Nigger Hollow. He may never speak, castrated in the first place as a result of his wish to speak. He therefore perceives the otherworldly events with inarticulate and 'slackjawed' wonder, but the price of his ticket to Nigger Hollow is that he cannot reveal a black language that Faulkner calls 'ejaculant' – a language sexually potent, delivering meaning. Benjy is privileged above the whites who have excluded him, privileged exactly by that exclusion. Not incidentally, his censored actual name, 'Maury', comes from the Latin *Maurus*, 'a Moor'. This 'white Moor', then, hears black language using the password of his suppressed name, a name that, like the vibrant black tongue itself, is to be neither known nor uttered within the conventional discourse of white society. Yet Benjy is not the only white who 'crosses the fence' of race and language, because, miraculously, the white reader has also come along.

The first three sections of the novel have shown the failures of white society and its discourses. By the end of *The Sound and the Fury*, the choice seems to be either to admit that language is a castrated compromise (to be content with passive left-to-right orderings) or to annihilate the self in a final suicidal revenge against the letter. Neither of these choices seems really satisfactory. The fourth section tests whether non-whites can negate such a white language with a non-denotative [non-signifying] language of otherness. In the last chapter we seek answers in that place most marginal to white society – Nigger Hollow. The novel's Easter Sunday project is to descend into Nigger Hollow, yet still ascend to tell the tale to a thirsting white world. The narrator wants to 'cross the fence' of language and race, possibly taking the reader there too. To write differently, to write in 'black language', might be to read and to experience differently. Only a person who straddles both worlds can eavesdrop on the language of blacks speaking *for themselves*. Benjy witnesses it, but cannot speak of it. Dilsey witnesses it, but she is not the narrator. So who narrates? One would not necessarily need to be black in order to know. Here, the consistent point of view, such as it is, is neither Dilsey's nor Faulkner's, but both: an integrated audience, and an integrated narrative voice.

In '*The Sound and the Fury* and *As I Lay Dying* everything is subordinated to the voices of the characters – the voices are the characters'.[53] Hearts speak: 'the voice consumed him, until he was nothing and they were nothing and there was not even a voice' (p. 295). The voice engulfs both source and listener, seeming the sort of language that black worshippers share. Within this voice, identities melt into the chaos of unity, like a suicide note that would self-destruct with its author in a pure blue flame, or even like *The Sound and the Fury* itself, a novel that consumes us and our reading.[54] Black words are hardly language at all. Benjy's speech, like blacks' language, seem 'just sound' (p. 320), and both transcend words 'like an alto horn, sinking into their hearts and speaking there . . . beyond the need for words' (pp. 294, 295).

Aside from the black congregation and the one white, Benjy, we have the preacher himself, the heart at the heart of the voice, Reverend Shegog. But not only Shegog. His description gives us the major clues:

> The visitor was undersized, in a shabby alpaca coat. He had a
> wizened black face like a small, aged monkey . . . . . . When the
> visitor rose to speak he sounded like a white man (p. 293) . . . . . .
> They did not mark just when his intonation, his pronunciation,
> became negroid, they just sat swaying a little in their seats as the
> voice took them into itself. (p. 295)

[The visitor] is, as André Bleikasten was the first to point out, an
analogue of the novelist himself, 'reaching the point of inspired dis-
possession where his individuality gives way to the "voice"'.[55] And
the mystical vision granted to the preacher may likewise be said to
metaphorize the poetic vision sought after by the writer. Note
Faulkner's self-portrait as a black-white composite, a voice 'crossing
the fence' of race and language, transcending opposition in its imaginary journey to 'Nigger Hollow'. The white narrator places himself
here into that lost black language 'for itself' that he had only conjec-
tured about before, and into the communality of voice that enwraps
the congregation with invisible bonds.

The Easter Sunday scene is refreshing in contrast to earlier scenes.
Bleikasten captures its tone of hopeful ending, but also indirectly
names its greatest failure:

> The orderly discourse of cold reason . . . has given way to the spon-
> taneous language of the heart, which alone can break down the
> barriers of individual isolation . . . [a]ll that 'white' rhetoric could
> achieve was 'a collective dream' (p. 294); what is accomplished
> now is a truly collective experience, a welding of many into one.
> For the first time in the novel, separation and fragmentation are at
> least temporarily transcended . . . . . . Another language is heard,
> unprecedented in the novel, signaled at once by the cultural-ethnic
> shift from 'white' to 'black', the emotional shift from rational cold-
> ness to spiritual fervor, and lastly by the stylistic shift from the
> mechanical cadences of shallow rhetoric to the entrancing rhythms
> of inspired speech.[56]

Shegog's emancipatory speech seems to satisfy the novel's overall
hope of ending 'separation and fragmentation'. Bleikasten seems to
have followed Faulkner down this path of hope. But on second view
this path seems too 'ordered' to be entirely trustworthy . . .

Reverend Shegog gives us a way out of language, and perhaps of
racial politics, but does so on the 'edge of the flat earth'. The black
ecstatic concord might be 'collective', but it is figuratively post-
humous.[57] Let us not forget that, for Homer, Hades – the land of the
dead – was at the 'edge of the flat earth'; to be resurrected, you first

need to have been crucified. The Shegog unification is *non-temporal*. Without time, there is no separation and frustration, but also no articulation; 'the language of the heart' can alter nothing – particularly not Southern apartheid. The ahistorical timelessness in which Dilsey and Benjy – to name only two – exist has for far too long received the title 'redemptive'.[58] If the oppressed tolerate outrages past and present, and the threat of future outrages, then they have no choice but to 'endure' into eternity. Their 'redemption', by this measure, is eternal damnation. The sermon by Reverend Shegog may be a structural and even ethical highpoint in the novel, but its futility becomes clear as soon as Dilsey leaves the all-black church for the Compson household.[59] Shegog has, in the standard manner of the Afro-American gospel sermon, allowed blacks to speak freely *for themselves*, in the jazz-like counterpoint of call-and-response repetition.[60] He may even be aware of the ultimately futile exercise of liberty involved here, but wants to lift his listeners for the moment beyond order and class. A black Mississippi congregation in 1928 would certainly be in the 'hollows' of death, the 'pit' of social value, but Easter is the day of resurrection, a lifting up out of suffering. Shegog promises his flock that they will ultimately be lifted from the dead. In his self-portrait as Shegog, Faulkner forges the most delicately poised ambiguity of his literary career, precisely illustrating both the promise and peril of a racial fence-crossing that would have been a legal, if not a literary, misdemeanour in 1929. Later, he would canonize in his Nobel Prize acceptance speech 'the old verities and truths of the heart'.[61] As if we also needed our hands on his heart too, he would exalt the writer's 'privilege to help man endure by lifting his heart'.[62] But *The Sound and the Fury* delivers a different sermon – perhaps Faulkner had forgotten it twenty years later – even on Easter Sunday, the most angelic blacks have no choice but to walk from the church.[63] □

The studies of Sundquist and Snead were the most powerful contributions in the 1980s to a new approach to Faulkner's treatment of history and race, an approach that combined close attention to the language and structure of literary texts with a strong awareness of the political, social and psychological resonances of those texts. In the 1990s, that combination would be deployed in further analyses of Faulkner's treatment of race, and in analyses of other, related aspects of his fictions, most notably their representations of gender. Major examples of such analyses are provided in the last chapter of this Guide.

CHAPTER FIVE

Mothers, Signifyin(g) Monkeys, and Significant Eyes: *The Sound and the Fury* and *As I Lay Dying* in the 1990s

IN CHAPTER three of this Guide (p. 101), it was observed that a disciplined eclecticism characterised the best criticism of the 1990s. The previous decade had been different: intense partisan commitments to particular theoretical and political positions in literary and cultural studies had characterised the 1980s in the USA and the UK: it had been an era of angry young critics, even if some of their mentors, like Jacques Lacan, were elderly or extinct. It had seemed necessary to blast a way through entrenched attitudes that, it was charged, prevented sustained attention to pressing social and intellectual issues. But by the last decade of the twentieth century, the battle to restructure criticism had been won; and the wide range of perspectives that the 1980s had made available provided a rich repertoire of interpretative possibilities. Faulkner studies made full use of them. As well as pursuing and enlarging the exploration of the 'new' questions that the 1980s had put unavoidably on the agenda, they began to retable, in fresh contexts, 'old' questions that that decade seemed to have consigned irretrievably to the past. The final chapter of this Guide provides excellent examples of recent criticism that tackles both 'new' and 'old' questions, and sometimes brings them together.

Among a number of feminist studies that have appeared in the 1990s, such as Minrose C. Gwin's *The Feminine and Faulkner: Reading (Beyond) Sexual Difference* (1990) and Doreen Fowler's *Faulkner: The Return of the Repressed* (1997), perhaps the most significant is Deborah Clarke's *Robbing the Mother: Women in Faulkner* (1994). In *Robbing the Mother*, Clarke devotes a chapter to *The Sound and the Fury* and *As I Lay Dying*, arguing, as other critics had done before her, that the 'pairing' of the two novels in the 1946 Random House Modern Library edition, 'makes sense' – despite

Faulkner's own objection to it – because 'the two books have much in common beyond their narrative structures'.[1] But Clarke's sense of what the two novels have in common is not quite the same as that of previous critics: she sums up their similarities in the following way:

■ [B]oth books reverberate with the paradoxical power of women's bodily absence and presence, of women's silence and language. Both examine men's desperate attempts to deal with maternal absence, to use language as a replacement for the mother. Caddy and Addie, caught in a world which vanquishes women's bodies, nonetheless exert a powerful control over the literal and figurative, bodies and language, forcing brothers and sons to confront the fragility of their egos in the face of maternal power.[2] □

Like Faulkner himself, and critics such as André Bleikasten, Clarke focuses on the absence of Caddy in *The Sound and the Fury*, insofar as she is not given a monologue or section of her own: 'If Caddy is the empty center [of the novel], then Faulkner has robbed the novel of its mother by robbing the mother of her voice'.[3] Clarke develops the point in the following way:

■ [*The Sound and the Fury*] is not a novel about Caddy, despite Faulkner's claims, but about her brothers' responses to her, about how men deal with women and sexuality. In fact, Faulkner's almost obsessive insistence on Caddy's importance begins to sound defensive, an apology, perhaps, for essentially writing her out of the text. Caddy's linguistic absence from the novel undercuts her centrality in a text formed and sustained by voice. If she is his heart's darling, why does she not rate a section of the novel, the chance to tell her own story? But Faulkner goes further than just silencing Caddy; he ties her silence to her beauty, her femininity, and claims that 'Caddy was still to me too beautiful and too moving to reduce her to telling what was going on, that it would be more passionate to see her through somebody else's eyes'.[4] David Minter has suggested that Faulkner found 'indirection' a useful strategy 'for approaching forbidden scenes, uttering forbidden words, committing dangerous acts'.[5] Yet the 'forbidden words' and 'dangerous acts' appear not to be Caddy's but those of her brothers: Quentin's incestuous desires, Jason's criminality, and Benjy's groping for the language 'to say' which culminates in attempted rape. Indirection may approach male forbidden desires, but it does not approach Caddy except as the object of those desires.
    Particularly in Faulkner's work, however, silence does not necessarily confer marginality. Paul Lilly has called Caddy's silence 'a hallmark of the perfect language that Faulkner the artist knows can never be realized but which he knows he must keep on "working,

trying again" to reach'.[6] But why must it be women who speak the perfect silence instead of language, even imperfect language? Linda Wagner argues that, despite their full or partial silences, Caddy and her mother control the narrative:

> Linguistic theory would define the narrator of any fiction as the person whose speech act dominates the telling of the fiction, yet Caddy and Caroline Compson are in many ways essential narrators of the Compson story. So much of their language, so much of their verbal presence, emanates through the novel that they are clearly and vividly drawn. Rather than being given one section, they take the novel entire.[7]

They are indeed 'clearly and vividly drawn'. Yet the fact remains that they are drawn rather than draw-ers, constructed rather than constructor, while the Compson brothers draw not only themselves but also 'their' women.

Caddy's voice may never be restored, but the evidence of her physical substance remains. If her 'speech act' does not dominate the text, her creative act does. Caddy's presence makes itself known less through her voice than through her body and its literal replication. Her physical procreation essentially engenders the linguistic acts which form the novel, thereby making this text, in a sense, her child. Yet it is difficult to claim that she 'mothers' the novel when the process of mothering – and, particularly, Caddy's participation in that process – is hardly presented within the book as a triumphant creative experience. Her abandonment of her daughter to Jason and his malicious exploitation seriously undermines both her idealized status and her maternal position. While she serves as an admirable if temporary mother to Benjy, her treatment of Miss Quentin merits her no consideration as Mother of the Year. Faulkner has robbed the mother not just of her voice but her maternity. Because the brothers control the terms of the narrative, Caddy exists as sister rather than mother.

The problem, however, is that she serves as a mother as well, not just to Benjy but to all of her brothers, who find themselves confronted with problematic maternal ties to both their biological and symbolic mothers. Thus while their narratives, except for Jason's, lack the overt condemnation of Caddy which they all display towards Caroline (and even Jason saves his strongest complaints for Miss Quentin, displacing much of his resentment toward Caddy onto her daughter), they also reveal their unbreakable ties to Caddy, ties which deny them full control over their own identities. By his indirection, Faulkner has allowed Caddy to approach the position of all-powerful and all-encroaching mother rather than simply mother of Miss Quentin.

Doubly abandoned, first by Caroline and then by Caddy, the Compson men achieve a kind of revenge in fixing both, in allowing each woman to be defined only through the perspective of her son/brother.

They fail to score a significant victory, however, because just as each brother inscribes his vision of Caddy, he also finds himself defined through his own relation to her. Quentin is trapped by being the weaker older brother to a powerful sister, by his own attraction to her, and by his sexual innocence as opposed to her experience . . . . . . Jason struggles against his sense of being unimportant and unloved, the brother whom Caddy never valued. Benjy cannot perceive himself as anything other than connected to Caddy, as his entire life constitutes an elegy of her loss. As both a presence and absence, Caddy's maternity determines the fate of the Compson family.

The novel, in fact, is full of mothers; besides Caroline and Caddy, we also have Dilsey, Frony, and Damuddy [the Compson grandmother]. But Damuddy dies before we ever meet her, and Frony, Luster's mother, functions as a daughter rather than a mother. Dilsey, more a mammy than a mother, primarily mothers ungracious and unappreciative children she did not give birth to: the Compson children and Luster. Thus, there are at once too many and too few mothers in this novel. These replacements, substitutions, and reversals in the function of mothering all undermine Faulkner's professed admiration for Caddy by linking her most disturbingly to her own mother – and to the failure of mothering, which holds such a crucial position in this text.

The lack of adequate mothering, as so many scholars have noted, causes many of the problems within the Compson family. Quentin's often quoted remark, *'if I'd just had a mother so I could say Mother Mother'* (p. 171), lays the blame for his numerous problems squarely at Caroline Compson's feet, a reading many critics tend to uphold. Interestingly, Mr. Compson's alcoholic disregard for his family finds much more sympathetic treatment. Lack of adequate fathering is apparently not seen in as nefarious a light.[8] Even Thomas Sutpen [in *Absalom, Absalom!*], surely one of the worst fathers in literary history, is granted a Faustian grandeur which Caroline Compson certainly lacks. While Faulkner may overtly distance his 'heart's darling' from such a problematic function, enough symbolic connections remain to call her idealized position into question. If even Caddy fails to be an adequate mother, can there be any hope left in motherhood, or is the dungeon ['Mother herself'], as Quentin says (p. 172). The fact that we see remarkably little of Caddy once she becomes a mother – only a few glimpses from Jason, the most hostile of the narrators – suggests that Faulkner was chiefly concerned with Caddy prior to maternity, before she becomes wholly identified as female; as a child, not only does she lack sexual maturity but she genders herself as male: 'she never was a queen or a fairy she was always a king or a giant or a general' (p.172). In growing up she loses her childhood appeal and her sexual innocence as she moves towards femininity and motherhood . . . . . . As Minrose Gwin points out, Caddy is a 'text which speaks multiplicity, maternity, sexuality, and as such she retains not just one voice but many'.[9] The many voices of woman overwhelm the Compson brothers who find in their own lack of differentiation from the feminine the true threat of Caddy's transgression – we have looked on the female outlaw and she is us. The body of the mother/sister, the 'very site of the uncanny', according to [Madelon] Sprengnether,[10] [because it 'represents both home and not home, presence and absence, the promise of plenitude and the certainty of loss'[11]] denies masculine authority the power to order the world. The uncanny, a reminder of castration fears, quite literally fulfils its threat in this novel, as all three brothers are rendered impotent, unable to vanquish the spectral presence of a sister who represents home and not-home, self and not-self.[12] □

Clarke's analysis of the significance of Caddy is followed by an elaboration of an issue she has already raised in the above extract – how Mrs Compson is to be viewed:

■ [W]hat about the primary mother in the novel, Caroline Compson, the character everyone loves to hate?[13] How much responsibility does she bear for the disruptions within her family? A cold, selfish, complaining woman, she neglects all of her children, including her later favorite, Jason, who cries every night when he can no longer sleep with his grandmother. Her maternal absence is largely filled by Caddy, but Caddy has no maternal model, for her own mother has only indicated how to be a lady. She orders Caddy not to carry Benjy because it will ruin her back. '"All of our women have prided themselves on their carriage. Do you want to look like a washerwoman?"'. Caddy should not spoil – love – Benjy: '"Damuddy spoiled Jason that way and it took him two years to outgrow it"' (p.61). No wonder Jason cries himself to sleep when his grandmother dies. Finally, when her daughter emerges into womanhood, Caroline wears black and goes into mourning after she sees Caddy kissing a boy. For a woman to express sexual desire is for her to be denied status as lady, and thus, as living entity: 'I was taught that there is no half-way ground that a woman is either a lady or not' (pp.101–2). By accepting no halfway ground, Caroline Compson denies the grounding of motherhood itself, which is predicated upon an essential duality. Having challenged and defied maternity, it comes as no surprise to discover that she refuses to let her motherhood get in the way of her ladyhood. '"I'm a lady. You might not believe that from my offspring, but I am"' (p. 300).

After Caddy's transgression it is Caroline who judges her. It is Caroline who refuses to allow her to return home, and Caroline who will not permit her name to be spoken, thus reversing the strategy of her husband and son, who invent labels – virginity – in an attempt to control female sexuality. Mrs. Compson erases Caddy by refusing to name or label her; Caddy exists only through what she is not: a lady. If she is not a lady, she cannot be named. Names have great significance for Caroline Compson who insisted that Maury's name be changed to Benjamin when his mental disabilities became known. She strenuously objects to both 'Caddy' and 'Benjy' as names because '[n]icknames are vulgar. Only common people use them' (p. 61). Jason, she repeatedly states, is the only one of her children who is a 'real Bascomb'; the others are all Compson, that being the mark of their difference from her.

Caroline, the strongest proponent of the lady, who marries Caddy off in an attempt to prevent scandal, nonetheless resists the traditional expectations of how a married woman should behave: that she will take on her husband's name and define herself through him. Just as Rosa Coldfield will refuse to become an incubator for Sutpen sons, Caroline rejects the Compson identity. She may have married a Compson, but she has not become a Compson, insisting to the end that she is a lady and a Bascomb. While far from being a protofeminist, Mrs. Compson nevertheless undermines the patriarchal structure of marriage and motherhood somewhat differently, but no less significantly, than Caddy, who turns out to inherit more from her mother than the ability to procreate.

. . . Caroline Compson, having thoroughly internalized the cult of southern gentility, clings to . . . labels [and names] – emblems of masculine discourse – as a means of separating herself from her family. She puts great faith in the power of language; by changing her son's name she denies his association with her brother and thus erases any equation of the Bascombs with idiocy. And by refusing to allow her daughter's name to be spoken she denies Caddy's identity as both mother and daughter.

In this focus on the power of the name, the label, Caroline achieves the kind of power for which her sons seek in vain. Despite her repeated claims that she'll soon be dead, she outlives both husband and eldest son. While Quentin cannot live in a world where virginity is just a word and Benjy is castrated for 'trying to say', Caroline successfully 'masters' a language which imposes limits and boundaries, interestingly enough, the language of the Father. Critics have long castigated Mrs. Compson for being unmotherly, but maybe she simply plays the wrong parental role. She takes over the position of the father, redefining the Compson family as the Bascombs. She is left with Jason, a 'real' Bascomb, Benjy, whom she renamed, and young Quentin, nameless. If it is generally the father, as Bleikasten asserts, 'who names, places, marks',[14] Caroline Compson is a father par excellence. While Mr. Compson wallows in alcoholic verbiage, unable to impose order or even to oppose his wife's interdiction against speaking Caddy's name, Mrs. Compson is redefining her family and her world. If Quentin wants someone to say *'Mother Mother'* (p. 171) to, maybe he should turn to his father.[15] In this novel, mothers are, above all else, survivors, certainly a feature that would attract the artist/robber. One robs the mother because she will always be there, controlling both procreation and language.[16] □

Clarke then turns to the 'one other significant mother'[17] in *The Sound and the Fury* – Dilsey – a discussion in which feminist questions about the representation of women combine with questions about the representations of race:

■ Dilsey, identified by Sally Page as Faulkner's 'ideal woman',[18] by David Williams[19] and more recently Philip M. Weinstein[20] as a madonna, has long been hailed as the novel's savior, the only truly admirable character in the book. Her warmth and endurance have endeared her to generations of readers, and, apparently, to Faulkner himself. But Faulkner and his readers tend to overlook the problematic issue of race in deifying [making a god[dess] of] the stereotype of the black mammy. The suggestion that African American women make the best mothers – especially to white children – reflects not an idealization of the mother or the black woman but a cultural disdain for both. Mothers are only 'good' when socially powerless, when controlled by those they 'mother', when selflessly dedicated to selfish undeserving children. A close examination of Dilsey's maternal halo reveals the inadequacy of white cultural assessments of mothering when applied to African American women.

Whence comes this halo? Certainly Dilsey appears to feel more compassion for the Compson children than any of their biological parents. She cares for Benjy, defies Jason in giving Caddy a chance to see her daughter, and protects Miss Quentin from physical abuse. Yet she cannot function as a mother to these children, not because she didn't give birth to them but because she lacks selfhood and power in a white racist world. '"You damn old nigger"' (p. 184), says Miss Quentin after Dilsey saves her from a beating. In calling attention to her race, and thus to her cultural powerlessness, Miss Quentin denies Dilsey maternal control. While Dilsey stands up to Jason, who seems to live in some fear of her, she makes no attempt to defy Mrs. Compson's selfish and inconsiderate demands, dedicating her life to the people who oppress her. In fact, she favors her white employers above her own family, granting Luster no hearing or compassion in his monumental task of caring for Benjy. Her selflessness confers sainthood upon her in the eyes of her white creator and a large proportion of predominantly white readers. As Myra Jehlen points out, Dilsey's virtues 'recall the traditional Mammy virtues Faulkner extolled in his own Mammy'[21] . . .

. . . Dilsey's idealized status as a maddona/mammy denies her both subjectivity and sexuality, and thus robs her of the mother's pervasive power, her control over being and language. The descriptions of her body focus on its decay, not its feminine appeal or procreative potential. She has a 'collapsed face that gave the impression of the bones themselves being outside the flesh' (p.266). Dilsey's 'indomitable skeleton' (p.265) evokes only the body's framework, the mother's potential worn away by the oppressive demands of a racist culture.

The narrative strategy of the fourth section of the novel, sometimes called Dilsey's section, reconfirms her questionable status. If this is Dilsey's section, why does she not get a voice? If Caddy was too beautiful and too moving, is Dilsey too much of a madonna and not enough of a mother to speak? Thadious Davis suggests that the use of the third-person narrator here establishes 'the perspective of time. Faulkner creates a sense of the passing of an era, and within that perspective he presents the destruction of one family and the endurance of another'. Dilsey, Davis says, 'exists as a kind of sacred vessel, suggesting an experience that is both visionary and tragic'.[22] She may be a 'visionary and tragic' vessel, but she is not a maternal vessel. Her lack of direct voice highlights her symbolic rather than her bodily role. Not until *Light in August* does Faulkner make his first serious attempt to deal with black subjectivity. And mothers, above all else, are subjects in Faulkner's work. Dilsey, possibly more a wish-fulfillment than a real character, more symbolic than human, may endure, but as an idealized image, not as a source of being and not-being, of language and separation – not, in other words, as a mother.[23] □

When Clarke moves on to discuss *As I Lay Dying*, she reiterates her earlier point that both this novel and *The Sound and the Fury* deal with absent mothers, but then suggests that 'the absences have different causes and implications':

■ While [*The Sound and the Fury*] grows out of Caddy's maternity, *As I Lay Dying* is born out of Addie's death. A maternal corpse replaces maternal absence. Faulkner sets up two creative paradigms in the novel: mothering and speaking. What he does not do, however, is to set them in opposition to each other, with women as literal and men as figurative creators. After all, Addie's voice is strong enough to be heard through her coffin, and her son Darl achieves, at times, a kind of non-linguistic 'feminine' intuition.

The two dominant motifs in the book – corpse and voice – twist slightly the kind of dichotomy between the semiotic and the symbolic presented in [*The Sound and the Fury*], for by placing the mother's literal dead body rather than the mother's absence in the center of the text, Faulkner grants greater power to the physical, while at the same time erasing its boundaries as the decaying corpse disperses its odor and its influence throughout the novel. Then, after finally getting the mother into the ground, returning her to the earth, the Bundrens are still left with Dewey Dell, defeated in her attempts to end her pregnancy, and presented with a second Mrs. Bundren. The mother's body, ultimately, cannot be vanquished. Neither does that body, a speaking corpse, give up control over language, thus reducing even further the division between physical and linguistic power. In fact, language in the novel is strongly tied to maternity. Just as the Compson brothers find symbolic discourse an inadequate replacement for the mother, so the Bundrens struggle in vain to fill her place with words and symbols. The mother's body and the mother's voice are vividly present, as Faulkner constructs a tale where even killing the mother does not silence her.[24]

Warwick Wadlington, examining the role of voice in Faulknerian tragedy, argues that voice 'says No to death primordially: voice is the breath of life transformed through sound into communication, communion.'[25] Certainly voice serves as one of – if not the – most important empowering forces in Faulkner's work. In [*As I Lay Dying*] in particular, even the dead speak. Yet not only is that voice often disembodied, it is also often unspoken in a text which highlights the close connections between voice and silence. The 'dark voicelessness' Addie experiences 'in which the words are the deeds' (p. 162) transforms language into action, taking it out of the realm of the spoken voice and into a prediscursive semiotic sphere. Thus the blurred boundaries between voice and silence resemble the collapsing distinction between . . . paternal and maternal discourse, between body and language. Does voice also say no to maternity, the primordial reality which precedes language, or does it emanate from the mother's body?

[*As I Lay Dying*], even more than *The Sound and the Fury*, focuses on voice; created out of its many speakers, *As I Lay Dying* attests to the power of spoken language but also insists, through its title, on the centrality of the body. The mother may die, but her body remains. Voice, however, proves a bit more evanescent, for the book frequently documents the characters' reluctance to employ verbal discourse. Darl and Dewey Dell communicate without words; Addie realizes that 'words are no good' (p. 159); Vardaman finds he 'couldn't say it' (p. 59) when he understands that his mother is about to be placed in a coffin; Whitfield 'frame[s]' (p. 168) rather than speaks his confession. In order for voice to say no to death, one must use it as a vehicle for linguistic expression, a feat often left unaccomplished in this book.

But those who do place faith in language often find themselves deluded by their misguided beliefs in language's controlling power. Anse repeatedly announces, '"I give her my promised word"' (p. 112), to justify a journey which costs Jewel a horse, Cash a leg, and Darl his freedom. Cora worries about losing the cost of the eggs that went into the cakes, for it was on her 'say-so' that they bought the hens (p. 3). Her daughter Kate resents the lady who changes her mind about buying them, insisting '"She ought to taken those cakes when she same as gave you her word"' (p. 4). This comic undercutting of the power of the word reveals Faulkner's scepticism regarding language's ability to represent 'truth' and delineate human experience, reflecting his modernist agenda and tying him to another great modernist practitioner, [the poet] Robert Frost. Whitfield's attempt to 'frame' the words of his confession conjures up the final lines of Frost's 'Oven Bird': 'The question that he frames in all but words/Is what to make of a diminished thing'.[26]

To frame is not to speak, but to circumscribe, limit, and define a shape: in this novel, however, words, as Addie says, are 'just a shape to fill a lack' (p. 160). While filling and framing would seem to be antithetical operations, they do have a common element – both present language as a physical form, a characteristic, [Luce] Irigaray claims, of women's language. 'This "style", or "writing", of women . . . does not privilege sight; instead, it takes each figure back to its source, which is among other things *tactile*.'[27] By conceiving words as 'tactile', Faulkner ties language to the literal, to the body. Because words are cast *as* physical they cannot function as a replacement or substitution *for* the physical. Thus Faulkner's recognition of the limitations of language reflects the pervasive power of the mother both to enable and to inhibit symbolic discourse, to transform words into shapes and so to deny their purely symbolic nature.

When presented as abstract concepts, words, to Addie, only get in the way because they dangle 'like spiders . . . swinging and twisting and never touching' (p. 160), a mode which prevents true knowledge and intimacy. This can only be achieved through blood – when she whips her students and when she gives birth to Cash. Initially, she is exhilarated by the blood-letting of motherhood, believing that she has found an escape from symbolic discourse. Next to the experience of maternity, 'words dont ever fit even what they are trying to say at'. Her blissful union with Cash exists beyond language: 'Cash did not need to say it [love] to me nor I to him'. But her second pregnancy destroys her belief that motherhood's prediscursive communion heals the gap which words, 'never touching', inscribe. Having once been 'made whole again by the violation' (p. 160) of childbirth, an additional childbirth re-violates her. She now recognizes that motherhood is as great a trick as language: 'I realized that I had been tricked by words older than Anse or love' (p. 161) – the word *motherhood*, invented by men but referring to an experience which predates language, the presence of prediscursive reality.

Betrayed by both the figurative word and the literal experience, Addie finds no comfort in maternity once it becomes repetitious. Where the initial act liberates her, the repetition entraps her. She seems to recognize the problem inherent in the feminist privileging of the maternal metaphor. As Domna Stanton explains, while this paradigm does value the female experience, it also reinforces the essential Law of the Father.[28] The privileging of wombs over words still restricts women to their role as wombs. Once, for Addie, motherhood provides a haven from symbolic discourse; twice, however, forces her to realize, as Constance Pierce says, 'the power of what has been as persistent an enemy as language: her own biology and her inevitable place in the biological scheme of things'.[29] Despite her powerful control over the process of figurative thought, her body now defines her identity. She takes a final stand against maternal definition by returning to her own father, both symbolically in her realization that he 'had been right' (p. 161), and literally in her insistence on being buried next to him.

But if Addie thinks she has abjured mothering by realigning herself with her father and his belief that 'the reason for living is getting ready to stay dead' (p. 164), she is wrong. Her tie to her mother is even more compelling. Doreen Fowler points out, '[i]f Addie's father "planted" her, then Addie's mother is the land, in which the seed grows. But the mother herself is never named. She is the repressed referent, the origin that imbues all symbols with meaning, but is herself absent'.[30] This description could refer to the state which the Bundrens hope to impose on Addie: returned to the land, repressed, and, most of all, absent. But while Addie's mother may be the repressed unspoken referent, Addie herself is far more difficult to deny, at once mother and earth, present and absent. Not only does she live on as corpse rather than staying dead, but her maternal influence lives on in her children, further denying the finality of death. Thus though T. H. Adamowski has called Addie a 'woman with a penis',[31] her womb exerts a far more powerful force over her life and the lives of those around her.

Rather than becoming a phallic mother, Addie rebels against both the language of the father and that of the mother. Not only do words take on physical shapes, they take on the feminine of the vessel: 'I could see the word as a shape, a vessel'. Gendering words as feminine, Addie uses them to transform abstract concepts into physical reality, then collapses the reality back into the abstract concept: 'I would watch him [Anse] liquefy and flow into it like cold molasses flowing out of the darkness into the vessel, until the jar stood full and motionless: a significant shape profoundly without life' (p. 161). Words neither protect nor contain life; they, like the physical body, are subject to disintegration, as she repeats the names of her husband and sons 'until their names would die and solidify into a shape and then fade away'. Words, as either figurative names or literal shapes, cannot cohere to their referents. As Addie phrases it, 'I would think how words go straight up in a thin line, quick and harmless, and how terribly doing goes along the earth, clinging to it, so that after a while the two lines are too far apart for the same person to straddle from one to the other' (p. 162). Though she sets up an opposition between the figurative and literal, her analysis is not quite accurate, for these two forms of discourse do intersect within her own body. Both die, and both share the same shape: the word, 'a significant shape profoundly without life like an empty door frame' and the 'shape of my body where I used to be a virgin' (p. 161) are empty vessels. Neither words nor virgin bodies produce life.

That the mother's body literally subsumes life and language, collapses literal and figurative, is absolutely appropriate for a novel in which the mother is both figured and embodied as a corpse. Emblemizing the dissolution of both bodies and language, Addie's corpse stands beyond the control of either literal or symbolic discourse, presenting a formidable challenge to the family that must repudiate it. Thus while the Compson brothers attempt to fill the gap Caddy leaves behind with language, in As I Lay Dying, where words, 'profoundly without life' (p. 161), are too much a part of the mother's body to replace it, the Bundrens try to lessen the impact of Addie's death more through deeds and symbols. They must combine doing and language to deal with a body which has transcended both. Their struggles reflect the broader concerns of the novel which, says André Bleikasten, 'interrogates the relationship – or lack of relationship – between world and language'.[32] This problematic connection intensifies the dilemma of Addie's children, who attempt to use a language that is 'no good' (p. 161) in achieving their separation from a mother's body which is all too vividly present. The corpse, both origin and end, refuses to die. As Julia Kristeva explains in *Powers of Horror: An Essay on Abjection* (1982), 'the corpse, the most sickening of wastes, is a border that has encroached upon everything'.[33] □

As the above extracts show, Deborah Clarke offers a powerful rereading of *The Sound and the Fury* and *As I Lay Dying* from a feminist perspective, and also, in her discussion of the representation of Dilsey, touches on the question of race. Questions of race and gender in Faulkner have acquired further dimensions in the 1990s as his work has increasingly been brought into conjunction with the work of a fellow winner of the Nobel Prize for Literature – Toni Morrison, the celebrated African American woman writer whose master's thesis was on Faulkner and Virginia Woolf, and whose fiction, especially in her best-known novel, *Beloved* (1987), can seem both to echo and to revise Faulkner. In an essay published in the *Mississippi Quarterly* in 1996, William Dahill-Baue explores issues of 'Black English' and 'Standard English' in relation to Faulkner and Morrison. The essay had its origins in a moment of tension in the seminar room, when Dahill-Baue 'spoke of how', in *The Sound and the Fury*, 'Faulkner transforms Reverend Shegog's speech in his Easter sermon from "Standard English" to "Black English"'. A woman African American student objected to his use of these terms because she felt that he 'was denigrating Black English by placing it in hierarchical opposition to Standard English', and also that he 'was over-generalizing' since 'Black English' was not spoken by all African Americans and the English spoken by specific characters in a novel should not be defined 'according to racial identity'.[34] The controversy became public after an article about it was published in the *Burlington Free Press*. As Dahill-Baue points out, what was at issue in this debate were not 'abstract theoretical notions but rather highly politicized views that charge this (and every American) classroom with the contentious and unresolved issues of race'[35] – and it might be added that these views could also arise in British classrooms, or in any literature classroom where there is an ethnically various group of students. Dahill-Baue sets out in his essay, 'not to validate his perception'[36] over that of his woman African American student, but to explore 'whether and how [the] racial identity of [Faulkner and Morrison] affects and controls their representations of blackness'.[37] The extract that follows focuses on *The Sound and the Fury*; it is important to stress that this focus is dictated by the topic of this Guide and is not at all intended to imply a hierarchy akin to that of which Dahill-Baue's student complained, in which 'Morrison' is subordinate to 'Faulkner'.[38]

■ William Faulkner, according to his biographer Joseph Blotner, understood his lack of understanding of black consciousness:

> Even toward the end of his life, Faulkner would talk of the diffi-culty of understanding Negroes' thoughts and feelings. He seemed to feel that not only had they perforce developed a pattern of con-cealment from white people, but their modes of thought and

feeling were often different and therefore difficult for a white person to understand.[39]

This is not for lack of trying, however; in the opinion of Toni Morrison, Faulkner was 'the only [white] writer who took black people seriously. Which is not to say he was, or was not, a bigot'.[40] Morrison defends Faulkner's literary integrity, though she leaves open to question his personal and political integrity.

[James] Baldwin is not so forgiving; he finds Faulkner's personal, political, *and* literary integrity lacking in true conviction for substantial change in the political, social, and material situation of blacks in the American South before the Civil Rights movement.[41] Baldwin here summarily dismisses Faulkner's fiction as 'something very closely resembling a high and noble tragedy'.[42] While Faulkner's troping [turning] of classical Greek modes of tragedy onto a more contemporary political and social landscape may have served to marginalize certain issues of race, his texts advance other tropes [figures of speech] that complicate this formulation.

In *The Sound and the Fury*, Faulkner describes Reverend Shegog as a 'monkey' of 'insignificance', repeating both these terms three times in the span of [three pages. '[M]onkey' is used four times (pp. 293, 294, 295), 'insignificance' twice, (pp. 293, 294), and 'insignificant' twice (pp. 293, 294)]. Faulkner characterizes the preacher in racist terms, animalizing him based on racial features, and thus enforces Baldwin's view of him as a bigot not only in the political but also in the literary arena. A closer consideration of Faulkner's language suggests another, quite opposite possibility. The proximity of the two terms, 'monkey' and 'insignificance', suggests a characterization modeled on or playing off a nineteenth-century African-American folk hero, the Signifying Monkey.[43]

Henry Louis Gates, Jr., discusses the name of this figure after whom he titles one of his books:

> The ironic reversal of a received racist image of the black as simian-like, the Signifying Monkey, he who dwells at the margins of discourse, ever punning, ever troping, ever embodying the ambiguities of language, is our trope for repetition and revision, indeed our trope of chiasmus [reversal], repeating and reversing simultaneously as he does in one deft discursive act.[44]

The Signifying Monkey plays off racist definitions by imperceptibly shifting and reversing those linguistic markers and definitions through language itself, undermining the racist slur by turning it back in on itself and thereby gaining control over the power to define. Gates describes the African-American rhetorical device, from which the Signifying Monkey gains his strength, of 'Signification':

> The mastery of Signifyin(g) creates *homo rhetoricus Africanus* [African rhetorical man], allowing – through the manipulation of these classic black figures of Signification – the black person to move freely between two discursive universes. This is an excellent example of what I call linguistic masking, the verbal sign of the mask of blackness that demarcates the boundary between the white linguistic realm and the black, two domains that exist side by side in a homonymic relation signified by the very concept of Signification [homonymic is from the noun 'homonym', meaning a 'word of the same form as another but [a] different sense'].[45]

Faulkner, of course, introduces Reverend Shegog not as a Signifying Monkey, nor even as a significant monkey, but as a monkey who is insignificant. It is precisely Shegog's initial insignificance, his ability to conceal his power beneath the mask of his physical meekness, that establishes him as a trickster figure in his act of Signifyin(g). He commences his sermon in the 'white linguistic realm', an instance of 'linguistic masking', until, the reader later realizes, he slips skillfully and undetected into the black vernacular, or 'linguistic realm'. 'When the visitor rose to speak he sounded like a white man' (p. 293); the congregation, however, 'did not mark just when his intonation, his pronunciation, became negroid, they just sat swaying a little in their seats as the voice took them into itself' (p. 295).

Reverend Shegog's personal linguistic transformation becomes a communal event, transforming the entire congregation into a single unit in the act of transforming himself into a Christ-like figure:

> And the congregation seemed to watch with its own eyes while the voice consumed him, until he was nothing and they were nothing and there was not even a voice but instead their hearts were speaking to one another in chanting measures beyond the need for words, so that when he came to rest against the reading-desk, his *monkey* face lifted and his whole attitude that of a *serene, tortured crucifix* that transcended its shabbiness and *insignificance* and made it of no moment, a long moaning expulsion of breath rose from them, and a woman's single soprano: 'Yes, Jesus!' (p. 295; [Dahill-Baue's italics])

Reverend Shegog, as a Signifying Monkey, frames his speech as a means first of mimicking standard 'White English',[46] but then the Reverend undercuts the standard ('"I got the recollection and the blood of the Lamb!"' (p. 294)) by abandoning it in favor of the more comfortable black dialect ('"I got de ricklickshun en de blood of de Lamb!"' (p.295)) that draws his congregation into a communal space of identification where barriers between selves are broken down, and all are bound together by their common voice and suffering (pp.295–97). Reverend Shegog accomplishes what he couldn't with standard White English; he identifies the suffering of his congregation with that of Jesus, as he himself becomes God-like: '"Ef you be Jesus, lif up yo tree en walk! I hears de wailin of women en de evenin lamentations; I hears de weeping en de crying en de turnt-away face of God: dey done kilt Jesus; dey done kilt my Son!"' (pp.296–97). Reverend Shegog's language conflates the sufferings of Christ at the hands of the Romans with the sufferings of the African-American congregation at the hands of white society; in this instance, Faulkner converts to a black idiom as a means of subverting the idiom (as well as the historical actions) of the master.[47] Whether consciously or not, Faulkner represents Reverend Shegog as a Signifying Monkey and thereby utilizes Black English not as burlesque but as a demonstration of the transformative powers of language.

Another black character who practices the art of Signifyin(g) takes his title, as does the Reverend, from the church. The Deacon,[48] in part two of *The Sound and the Fury*, first appears speaking Standard English; '"glad to have chatted with you"' (p.95), he says to two Harvard freshm[e]n as Quentin approaches him. Quentin reflects:

> That was the Deacon, all over. Talk about your natural psychologists. They said he hadn't missed a train at the beginning of school in forty years, and that he could pick out a Southerner with one glance. He never missed, and once he had heard you speak, he could name your state. He had a regular uniform he met trains in, a sort of Uncle Tom's cabin outfit, patches and all.
> 'Yes, suh. Right dis way, young marster, hyer we is,' taking your bags. 'Hyer, boy, come hyer and git dese grips.' Whereupon a moving mountain of luggage would edge up, revealing a white boy of about fifteen, and the Deacon would hang another bag on him somehow and drive him off. 'Now, den, don't you drap hit. Yes, suh, young marster, jes give de old nigger yo room number, and hit'll be done got cold dar when you arrives.' (p.95)

Faulkner represents the Deacon the same way he does the Reverend, as a Signifying Monkey, except in a reversed dynamic: the Reverend role-plays as a speaker of Standard English before shifting his speech into the black (evangelistic) vernacular; here, the Deacon tricks the Southerners by playing the role of the slave, punctuating with his

Southern black dialect, complete with 'Marster' and 'Suh', until he reverses roles and 'completely subjugate[s]' them as his speech 'gradually move[s] northward' (p. 95) and blanches itself white as a Brooks Brothers shirt. At the same time, Faulkner reveals hidden behind a mound of luggage the Deacon's true identity as a master himself, with a teenage *white* boy as his slave, and the Southern Harvard freshmen soon enslaved to his capitalistic preyings on their Southern sense of place.

Mark W. Lencho, in writing about Faulkner's use of Black English, focuses his attention on dialect 'variability' in Faulkner's representations of different black characters' speech.[49] Lencho concludes that three main factors influence these dialect variations: positioning in the text indicating 'changing artistic intentions during the process of composition'; the 'functional load of a passage'; and the geographical origins of the speakers.[50]

A close consideration of these three theses proves disturbing. The first thesis suggests a developmental view, whereby Faulkner 'suddenly incorporate[d] more complete examples of black dialect' as the composition of the book progressed.[51] Lencho's comparison of the speech of Dilsey and Luster at the beginning as opposed to the end of the text supports this point well; Lencho does not draw a similar comparison between Reverend Shegog and the Deacon, except to suggest that they are both 'bidialectal', that is, they 'style-shift' from Northern to Southern black dialects. In equating the Reverend and the Deacon, Lencho does not take into consideration nor account for the over two-hundred pages that separate them; according to his theory, the Reverend's 'black dialect' should be more complex and realistic than the Deacon's, but a close reading does not bear this out. Lencho's first thesis, that Faulkner 'became increasingly concerned with verisimilitude in language as the story advanced',[52] seems to be contradicted by this example.

Lencho's second thesis determines variability depending on the 'functional load of a passage'. This stance assumes a monolithic interpretation of the text that doesn't allow for multifunctionality of passages depending on the perspective of the reading. For example, in interpreting literature, I often find myself gleaning great significance from a passage that seems otherwise insignificant. Lencho's theory would predetermine passages as having 'low function loads' or 'high function loads'; I find this kind of linguistic Calvinism suspect and of very little use in a literary criticism that attempts to remain open-minded to possibilities in the text. Finally, Lencho attributes the more complex characterizations of the Deacon and the Reverend to their geographic distance from the South, as if only Northern blacks, influenced by white speakers of Standard English, could speak in a variety of different modes; this seems like a type of regionalism at best, and at worst a type of racism.

Focusing on the Signifyin(g) of these two characters, the Reverend and the Deacon, reveals them to be complex, realistic individuals who resist stereotype and simplification in their transformative uses of language: both utilize various speech patterns in dialects in response to the moment. In Gates's terms, considering the linguistic realms of black and white, these two characters 'move freely between two discursive universes' in a way that reveals Faulkner's portrayal of them as true human beings and not merely signposts of racial difference.[53] □

Dahill-Baue's essay concludes that both 'Faulkner and Morrison invent language [which] reveals not so much the racial identity of the author but mostly the author's faith in the humanity and complexity and "sheer intelligence" (to quote Morrison) of black characters'.[54]

The vigorous concern with race, gender and history evident in much recent criticism has undoubtedly been powerfully productive, but it might seem to have displaced what could once have appeared to be a central topic for literary and cultural critics: art and the artist. It is therefore important to note the appearance in 1996 of a very stimulating book called *Faulkner and the Artist*: this gathers together papers delivered at the annual 'Faulkner and Yoknapatawpha' conference in 1993. As the Faulkner critic and scholar Donald M. Kartiganer concedes in his 'Introduction' to the volume, the topic announced by the title seems 'anachronistic, even quaint . . . the "art" of the writer, his power to render into a unique language and vision the world around him, has given way in current literary criticism to the power of the external world itself: the contextual forces of history and culture, of race, class, and gender, of prior uses of language from sources high and low'.[55] In one of the essays in the volume, Wesley Morris observes that 'we are now in an age called the postmodern' in which 'the artist as artist receives only marginal attention from literary theory'; indeed, 'postmodernism has erased the word "artist" from our critical language. The modernist concept of imagination, which suggested genius and was integral to our sense of what constituted artistry, has been thoroughly discredited over the past thirty years'. Morris contends that 'this is a serious problem for literary critics because the erasure of the artist has left a blank space in many of our critical texts'.[56] Certainly ideas of art and the artist mattered for Faulkner; and to explore them in relation to his work need not mean retreating from issues of history, culture, race, class and gender; indeed, our understanding of such issues may be enriched by engaging with questions of art.

As far as art and gender are concerned, this is vividly demonstrated in Candace Waid's contribution to *Faulkner and the Artist*, 'The Signifying Eye: Faulkner's Artists and the Engendering of Art'. Waid proposes that '[i]n his fiction Faulkner reveals a complex and often obsessive association between art and gender, especially when he enters into the realm of the visual arts: depicting the relation of the artist and the work of art, representing acts of artistic reproduction, and even incorporating graphic representation into his texts'.[57] The extract from Waid's essay that follows provides a fascinating exploration of the 'association' between art and gender in *The Sound and the Fury*, and also a concise but suggestive account of *As I Lay Dying*:

■ There is no recognizable artist figure in *The Sound and the Fury*, but one might argue that at least in retrospect Faulkner cast himself in the role of the artist. Indeed, in his accounts of the novel's origins, Faulkner seems to echo the gendered terms he had used to frame the idea of art and the making of art in his earlier fiction. Whereas the cuckolded husband of *Mosquitoes* takes *The Decameron* [1349–51 – a collection of 100 stories by the Italian writer and poet Giovanni Boccaccio (1313–75)] to bed with him every night, Faulkner in the introduction he drafted for the proposed 1933 edition of *The Sound and the Fury* reveals his own fantasies about the comforts of art. Describing sitting down to write the novel, Faulkner recalled thinking: 'Now I can write. Now I can make myself a vase like that which the old Roman kept at his bedside and wore the rim slowly away with kissing it.' As he compares the writing of his novel to the making of a vase and tells of his desire to 'make a beautiful and tragic little girl'[58] Faulkner clearly casts *The Sound and the Fury* in the role of the sexualized and idealized work of art described in the early works.

Like Gordon [the sculptor in *Mosquitoes*], Faulkner conceives of his art as a making of girls and like Benbow [the glass blower in *Sartoris*], whose art is also articulated through breath, Faulkner sees himself as a maker of vases. However, if Faulkner links himself to Horace Benbow and his creation of sisterly vases, the repeatedly crossed female thresholds of *The Sound and the Fury* represent a dramatic change from the earlier focus on the inviolable feminine form as providing the structure for the idealized work of art. Caddy Compson, the female figure whom Faulkner equates with the novel itself, is not finally just a virginal vase or a 'tragic . . . girl'; from the outset, she is (as the Appendix suggests) 'a frail doomed vessel'.[59] In *The Sound and the Fury*, Faulkner seems to realize that the work of art will never be chaste; he seems to know, to borrow a line from David Lodge, that words are 'never virgin: words come to the writer already violated by other men'.[60]

Endowing Quentin with his earlier artists' obsessions with chastity, [Faulkner] returns again and again in this novel to the moment of conception. *The Sound and the Fury* repeatedly recalls and re-enacts the juncture of male and female as a site of origins which is crucial to art; in this sexualized conjunction, words seem to be coded as masculine and linked with impotence, and pictures (or more precisely the pictorial) seem to be coded not just as feminine, but as gestures toward embodiment, efforts to picture the female body as an originary space. Relatively rare in Faulkner's work, these pictorial forms – the coffin [⬭] of *As I Lay Dying* (p. 80), the upside down delta [∇] of 'Delta Autumn',[61] and the eye ◉ of *The Sound and the Fury* (p. 311) – call attention to their author's interest in the visual arts; and, at the same time, each of these pictures serves as a graphic portrayal of a female container, a vessel associated with fecundity and generation. Even more suggestively, perhaps, these pictorial forms are linked by the fictions themselves to the shapes of instruments used to tell time.

The least obvious yet the most obsessively represented of these images is the eye of *The Sound and the Fury*; in this novel, the eye is not merely the window to the soul but also the displaced gateway of the female body: the site of lost virginity and the site of human origin. *The Sound and the Fury*, a book which returns again and again to the signifying eye, is obsessed with the moment of origin, the sexualized conjunction which is implicated in both the reproduction of offspring and the production of art. In this novel, Faulkner is obviously concerned with the virginity or chastity of his characters but like the artists of his earlier works, he is also concerned with questions about the chastity of art. In *The Sound and the Fury*, Faulkner seems to focus on the concept of purity as a lost ideal. Obsessed with the idea of loss, *The Sound and the Fury* turns repeatedly to the moment of conception, the site of a fertile breaking which marks a scene of origins. While these fertile conjunctions produce art and discover a potency in words, the male Compsons (the first three narrators of *The Sound and the Fury*) are faced with the threat of impotence as they find themselves caught in and taunted by the futility and sterility of words. Again and again, the Compson brothers tell stories in which they find themselves feminized by their experience of dangerous female thresholds. Benjy goes through the gate which he associates with his missing sister and he is literally dismembered as a result of his pursuit of a schoolgirl, castrated for his only effort at speech in the novel as he describes himself as 'trying to say' (p. 51). Associated with money robbed from women and pawing at his mother's empty pockets, Jason Compson seems to feed on telling and retelling his story of 'outrage' and 'impotence'. In contrast, Quentin repeatedly insists on his own sexual experience; however, this experience exists only in the form of words. As Donald Kartiganer argues, Quentin is driven by his desire 'to see words as the originator rather than the imitator of deeds . . . [insisting] that words have a substance more real than bodies'.[62] Entrapped in their own narratives, the Compson brothers find themselves defined by the impotence of words, particularly in relation to the potency of sexually active women (Caddy Compson, Miss Quentin, and Lorraine [Jason's prostitute girlfriend]) who threaten to embody life and death.

In *The Sound and the Fury*, Faulkner is not merely concerned with the virginity or chastity of his characters, as the artists of his earlier works are concerned with the chastity of art. The novel itself is generated to fill the vacuum left by a missing woman, the lost sister. André Bleikasten describes *The Sound and the Fury* and *As I Lay Dying* as 'novels *about* lack and loss' that themselves 'have sprung *out of* a deep sense of lack and loss – texts spun around a primal gap' (p. 101).[63] Caddy Compson, the figure who combines the sexual and maternal, is the absence around which Faulkner structures his entire novel. Speaking to students at the University of Virginia, Faulkner explained the novel's genesis: '[t]o me she was the beautiful one, she was my heart's darling. That's what I wrote the book about . . . to try to tell, try to draw the picture of Caddy'.[64] Gary Lee Stonum, commenting on Faulkner's return to the terms of 'his earlier, image-based art' to explain the 'gestation of the novel', notes that in this description 'Faulkner abandons a narrative term, "tell", for a pictorial one'.[65] This pictorial image of Faulkner's artistic enterprise in *The Sound and the Fury* is significant because Caddy Compson embodies the source of vision in the novel; and this image of her as a picture helps to locate Faulkner's inscription of himself as an artist in the text. If *The Sound and the Fury* does not explicitly portray an artist, it recapitulates Faulkner's representation of the conceiving of art and it stages Faulkner's own surprising and overdetermined entry into the graphic representation of the visual.

Indeed, Faulkner locates Caddy in what may be considered the primal scene of the novel. In this scene, she climbs the tree, exposing her muddy drawers, to look in through a window onto death. As she tries to understand what is going on, she sees a forbidden scene that reveals the death of Damuddy – a name that seems to join 'Daddy' and 'mother', as well as call attention to Caddy's suggestively stained underclothes. This association of soiled sexuality, death, and the witnessing of a forbidden sight might be enough to evoke a scene of origins in Faulkner's psychic landscape; but this is also recalled as a primal scene of literary conception, a glimpse into the origins of the novel itself. Faulkner claimed that this scene of Caddy looking in on death with muddied drawers was the originary germ of the novel . . . We can see in this scene of Caddy looking through a window at a scene not only an image of the novel's conception but also a frame through which we understand both the novel's concern with the visual and the significance of its focus on the eye.[66]

At a crucial moment in the career of the fainting and bleeding Compson brothers, having been threatened with a hatchet, and fearing that his head is bleeding where he has hit it, Jason sees a sign. Nearly blind, he is led to an 'empty platform' where 'grass grew rigidly in a plot bordered with rigid flowers' and he sees 'a sign in electric lights: Keep your 👁 on Mottson, the gap filled by a human eye with an electric pupil' (p. 311). As he represents a slogan of the New South (and alludes to the dollar bill), Faulkner actually reproduces the sign, breaking into the words of his text in what is for him an unprecedented way and filling 'the gap' with a pictorial eye. This sign of the visual is given a visual form which changes the way we read the words encoded in the sign. Like everything else in Faulkner, this overdetermined sign signifies too much. This sign instructs the viewer to '[k]eep your 👁 on Mottson', replacing a word with a picture. On one level we might see Faulkner indulging in the Joycean bilingual wordplay that appears elsewhere in the novel: as the word is eschewed for a picture, one might see French words and read the sign as warning: '[k]eep your 👁 on *Mot* son' – as if to say, 'Keep your eye on the word, son' . . . Or, still keeping our eye on French, we might read: '[k]eep your 👁 on Mot son' – 'Keep your eye on the word-sound, on the sound of the word that does not appear, "I"'. Whether one wants to hear this wordplay or not, this passage is crucial because it pictures the sound of a word (a word sound) and replaces a verbal sign with a pictorial symbol. It opens up a gap in the text and dramatizes a graphic illustration that stands in the place of a word.

To understand what it means for Faulkner to fill this gap with a picture rather than a word, we need to speculate on the meaning of the eye in *The Sound and the Fury*: the signifying eye which must also be understood as 'signifying nothing'. Obsessed with incest and driven by Oedipal tensions, the novel is particularly concerned with eyes. The placement of the sign of the eye 'in a plot bordered with rigid flowers' (p. 311) takes us back to the beginning of the book, to one of the novel's many bizarre scenes of sexual displacement and the first definition of Caddy's name (based on the sound of the word). Here, Benjy watches '[t]hrough . . . the curling flower spaces' (p. 1) to see men hitting balls with sticks and calling their 'caddies'. The wordplay is obvious as Benjy and Luster look for lost balls. When Luster asks the young woman at the branch, '"You all found any balls yet"', he is told '"Ain't you talking biggity. I bet you better not let your grandmammy hear you talking like that"' (p. 14). Later the word itself has become unnecessary as Benjy looks down at himself and Luster tells him simply, *'Looking for them ain't going to do no good. They're gone'* (p. 71). The inventory of castration symbols in Faulkner's novels is well known and I will not catalogue the one-handed men, one-armed straight jackets, one-handed clocks, or the biblical associations of the Ethiopian queen Candace with eunuchs;[67] but in this scene, which brings together the 'curling flower spaces' and men with sticks, we might well ask: does a Caddy look for balls because she has them or because she lacks them?

Preoccupied with castration, *The Sound and the Fury* also repeatedly returns to potential moments of generation and conception. Throughout the novel, the eye is linked to the mystery of women's sexuality and the question of what sort of ball Caddy might have . . . . . . the symbolic association between eyes and the female genitals . . . is . . . present throughout *The Sound and the Fury*. Both Mrs. Compson and Benjy sense irrevocable change as they look into Caddy Compson's eyes. Insisting that there is 'no half-way ground . . . a woman is either a lady or not', Caddie's [*sic*] mother concludes, 'I can look at her eyes and tell' (p. 102); and what might just be a cliché as it comes from her mouth is supported by her more insightful idiot son. Earlier when Benjy sees Caddy on the swing with Charlie (probably kissing because it is the sight of kissing which precipitates this memory), he takes her into the kitchen, where she washes her mouth out with soap. In a later related scene, the problem becomes more severe as it focuses on the eyes rather than just the mouth. As Benjy describes the scene, 'Caddy came to the door and stood there, looking at Father and Mother. Her eyes flew at me . . . Her eyes ran' (p. 66), and finally, '[h]er hand was against her mouth and I saw her eyes and I cried' (p. 67). Benjy drags her through the house again but according to Faulkner's morphology [study of the forms] of houses the kitchen is no longer appropriate; Caddy tries to enter her bedroom but Benjy pulls her toward the bathroom. In this displacement upward, Faulkner seems to have chosen to focus on the eyes as the site of the female genitals. Perhaps familiar with the vulgar nineteenth-century euphemism for sexual intercourse, 'to be poked in the blind eye', Faulkner builds as much on the fact that Caddy's formal name 'Candace' means 'the one eyed warrior queen' as he does on its allusion to the incandescence of 'white fire'. The broken eyes and balls of *The Sound and the Fury* (such as Quentin's bloody eye) are signs of feminization.

The eyes are of crucial importance in the scenes that Quentin recalls from the past in which he symbolically loses possession of the phallus in the form of a knife and a gun. In the scene of attempted suicide in which Quentin ultimately drops his knife, the narrative reads as an almost embarrassing lesson in sexual intercourse or masturbation: 'will you close your eyes/no like this you'll have to push it harder/touch your hand to it/but she didnt move her eyes were wide open'. Almost immediately Quentin recalls the primal scene of

Caddy seeing; but faced with her eyes, he instead remembers her muddy panties: 'Caddy do you remember how Dilsey fussed at you because your drawers were muddy' (p.151). A few lines earlier, he has asked out of nowhere: 'do you remember the day damuddy died when you sat down in the water in your drawers'. This query has followed another fertile conjunction of symbols put together in Quentin's mind as he announces 'I could see a rim of white under her irises I opened my knife' (p.150). Here, Quentin announces that he has dropped his knife after we learn that Caddy's 'muscles gathered' (p.151). In his related confrontation with Dalton Ames, Quentin refuses a gun that is presented to him 'butt first' (p.160) in what is understood to be the feminine position. In this seminal scene, in which smoke streams from the barrel of Ames's gun while cigarette smoke streams from his nose, Quentin refuses the gun and instead (in his words) 'passe[s] out like a girl' (p.161). Having given himself a bloody or broken eye, Quentin recalls 'looking at [Dalton Ames] through a piece of coloured glass' (p.160); in the relentless symbolism of *The Sound and the Fury*, this wound seems to confirm Quentin's feminization. Broken glass and bloody eyes appear in a dense conjunction of images which bring Quentin back to the present and memories of a more recent past. The pain from his punch in the eye brings him back to the feeling of his face 'cold and sort of dead, and my eye, and the cut place on my finger was smarting again' (p.162).

The word 'rim' is used twice by Quentin to describe the edges of Caddy's eyes. It first appears in Quentin's narrative in another representation of the sexual act which emphasizes the novel's obsession with dismemberment; he smashes the glass face of his watch, twists off its hands, and carefully removes the glass from the rim. (The symbolic associations between watching and eyes and eyes and watches are of course underlined repeatedly in the opening scenes of Quentin's narration.) Wrenching off the hands, he cuts his own hand and the cut finger leaves a bloody smear on what is later in this section called the 'eye of the clock' (p.119). The blood on the watch is suggestive here. Quentin is confused about blood in acts which involve males and females ('*Oh her blood or my blood Oh*' (p.133)) and he is particularly confused about castration and sexual difference. In an important juxtaposition of thoughts, as he tells Versh's story of a man who castrates himself, Quentin immediately thinks of the female body and is stumped: 'It's not not having them. It's never to have had them then I could say O That That's Chinese I don't know Chinese' (p.114). One of the rare occasions in the novel when the 'O' is rendered without an 'h', as in 'Oh', we might read the 'O' in this discussion of the female absence as a turn to the pictorial. (Faulkner already had used this form of the pictorial in *Mosquitoes* where he describes a woman's mouth as 'a small red O'.[68]) Whether one accepts this 'O' as a picture of absence – the zero, aught, or naught, what was referred to in common slang as 'the divine monosyllable' – when faced with the female and the source of generation, Quentin seems to find words to be inadequate, as if somehow from the wrong language. For Quentin, female difference is like Chinese: an unknown, exotic foreign language – perhaps not coincidentally made up of pictographs.

Caddy's ball, what is described in the Appendix as 'the minute fragile membrane of her maidenhead'[69] and 'a miniature replica of all the whole vast globy earth . . . poised on the nose of a trained seal',[70] is there to be broken; and although the loss or breaking of balls signals impotence in men, in Caddy Compson and other women like her it paradoxically marks the initiation of potency. When broken, Caddy's ball-like hymen establishes her potency as a sexual figure. If we accept that '[p]urity is a negative state' (p. 115), the loss of virginity is arguably a positive state, marking the possibility of generation, a beginning of being and of time. The awareness that time begins at conception causes Quentin repeatedly to wish to return to the moment before conception. Near the opening of his narrative, Quentin has fantasies of thwarting beginnings as he imagines himself as Dalton Ames's mother refusing to lie with her husband and preventing the birth of Caddy's seducer: '[i]f I could have been his mother lying with open body lifted laughing, holding his father with my hand refraining, seeing, watching him die before he lived' (p. 78). Quentin has equally desperate fantasies in which he tries to use language to become his own father so that he can act to preclude both his and Caddy's existence as individuals as well as characters in a book.[71]

Despite these imagined states, there is a fatalism in Quentin's understanding of generation. One meditation about this negative primal scene significantly focuses on a picture in a book. Quentin recalls a picture in one of his childhood books which shows two people trapped in a dungeon, a 'dark place into which a single weak ray of light came slanting upon two faces lifted out of the shadow'. To him, this seems to be a picture of his parents and the horror of generation. Caught in an obsessive cycle of rereading, Quentin recalls: 'I'd have to turn back to it until the dungeon was Mother herself she and Father upward into weak light holding hands and us lost somewhere below even them without even a ray of light'. Imagining himself and his siblings in the darkness below their parents, Quentin understands that his mother is the 'dungeon', the bodily room which will trap them into life. In an act which shows her potency, Caddy, who 'never was a queen or a fairy [but] always a king or a giant or a general', is said to declare that if she were a king she would *break that place open*'; and then we read: '[i]t was torn out, jagged out' (p. 172).

Paradoxically, this power to tear out the page which seems to picture generation and the inevitability of conception involves an act of 'breaking' and tearing which signals woman's potency and the crossed threshold of female sexuality.

Quentin's memory of a picture that has been torn out, this absent image of the 'dark place' (p. 172) of the mother, is another indication of Faulkner's deep associations between the work of art, the visual image, procreation and reproduction, and the female body. As the overdetermined image of the 'eye of the clock' (p. 119) suggests, these associations are also related to Faulkner's obsession with time . . . We might briefly recall . . . the picture of the coffin in *As I Lay Dying*, which critics have seen as a womb with the corpse upside down in the position for birth.[72] Like a caddy, a small box for holding things, this structure, ⬭, which is repeatedly called a 'box', functions as a container for the body of the mother, herself a vessel for so many children, as she returns to the earth. The coffin is said to be 'clock-shape[d]' (p. 80) but the picture tells us that this clock is not like an eye but rather like a grandfather clock, again framing the process of generation in patrilineal terms [that is, in terms of descent through the fathers].[73] Buried in the ground, the coffin is like the fecund, triangular wedge pictured in 'Delta Autumn' in *Go Down, Moses* to represent a ' ∇ -shaped section of earth'.[74] Yet this funnel-like figure (described as 'brooding' and 'impenetrable'), pointing downward in the shape of the mound of Venus, the triangle of fertility, is also the Greek letter delta turned on its head – a rather abstract but still evocatively pictorial depiction of the fertile flanks of the Mississippi Yazoo delta [as a geographical term, a 'delta' is a triangular alluvial tract – that is, a tract made up of a deposit of earth, sand, etc., left by a flood – at the mouth of a river enclosed or traversed by its diverging branches]. Like the top of an hour glass built up through the alluvial sands of time, this triangle of wilderness is becoming smaller as its tangled growth and earthen banks are being eroded by an encroaching civilization.

In *As I Lay Dying*, Faulkner also pictures a blank space, an actual gap between words. Addie Bundren speaks of Anse's 'name' – 'I could see the word as a shape, a vessel' – and 'a significant shape profoundly without life like an empty door frame', and she describes herself thinking: '[t]he shape of my body where I used to be a virgin is in the shape of a   ' (p. 161). Faulkner leaves a blank space on the page to represent the look of the place where Addie Bundren's virginity used to be. This absence is anticipated in *Flags in the Dust* in Horace Benbow's fantasy about the pinkness of unnamed female parts which leads to the single word 'unchaste' followed by a word-sized blank space and a question mark: 'Unchaste   ?'[75] For the writers in Faulkner's *Mosquitoes* and for Addie Bundren in *As I Lay Dying*, words are instruments of masculine desire, but Addie Bundren has learned to despise the words that from her husband's mouth are 'just a shape to fill a lack' (p. 160). Addie, who has experienced unmediated life as a 'dark voicelessness in which the words are the deeds', insists that 'the other words that are not deeds . . . are just the gaps in peoples' lacks' (pp. 162–63). Each of these pictorial images might be said to signify nothing; not only the actual gaps or blank spaces on the page but also the images that stand for an eye, a coffin, and the landscape. Like the eye that stands as a symbol of the sexual presence and absence at the center of the woman, these figures evoke female sexuality: both its terrifying embodiment of nothing and the transformative force of the female form. They represent the 'nothing' which in the slang of Shakespeare referred to the female genital and what comes from nothing. Faulkner seems to try obsessively to fill the gaps in these lacks with words; but sometimes, as if declaring himself an artist, he resorts to pictures that signify the absence of language and the tensions inherent in the artist's acts of creation.[76] □

Waid's return at the end of her essay to 'the tensions inherent in the artist's acts of creation' does not entail a reinstatement of a romantic or modernist exaltation of the (white male) creator. As her preceding arguments suggest, the work of art emerges out of a 'nothing' already marked by notions of gender – and also marked, as this chapter and the previous one have shown, by notions of race, by the multiple inscriptions of history. Artists make their own works of art, but not just as they please or in circumstances of their own choosing; they do so in the given and inherited conditions that confront them. And it is vital that criticism should investigate those given and inherited conditions, especially with a writer like Faulkner, in whose real and imagined worlds the traditions of the dead generations did indeed weigh like a nightmare on the minds of the living. But to acknowledge and analyse the determinations of the work of art is not necessarily to abolish the notion of the artist. Perhaps if Faulkner had not existed, it would have been necessary to invent him; but it is hard to imagine anyone inventing Faulkner except Faulkner himself. Who in the mid-1920s could have conceived that such a writer would emerge, that he would produce works like *The Sound and the Fury* and *As I Lay Dying*, texts that continue to astonish by constantly coming into being for their readers out of nothing, by performing their acts of creation before our eyes, in our ears, on our bodies, within and beyond our minds? Conceived in that time of crisis that the mid-twentieth-century academy tried to contain, for a while, under the comforting rubric of 'modernism', *The Sound and the Fury* and *As I Lay Dying* have continued to speak to readers and critics vividly, urgently and surprisingly, to pose, in the way that only novels can, questions that run all the

way from the meaning of the most minute textual details to the significance of the huge forces of history and the import of first and last things.
In today's world in transition, where the peculiar agonies and fitful joys
of Faulkner's 'postage stamp of native soil'[77] are echoed on a global scale,
the multiple voices of these two texts should resound more than ever
before; they are likely to prove essential reading on our rough journey
into the future.

NOTES

INTRODUCTION

1 Joseph Blotner, *Faulkner: A Biography*, 2 vols (New York: Random House, 1974; London: Chatto and Windus, 1974), vol. 1, pp. 210–11.

2 Joel Williamson, *William Faulkner and Southern History* (New York and Oxford: Oxford University Press, 1993), p. 36.

3 See Williamson (1993), pp. 22–29. For a fascinating account of the research that led Williamson to posit the possible (though, as he stresses, not definite) existence of the 'Old Colonel''s 'shadow family', see his essay 'A Historian Looks at Faulkner the Artist', in Donald M. Kartiganer and Ann J. Abadie, eds, *Faulkner and the Artist: Faulkner and Yoknapatawpha, 1993* (Jackson: University Press of Mississippi, 1996), pp. 3–21.

4 Williamson (1993), p. 55.

5 O. B. Emerson, *Faulkner's Early Literary Reputation in America*, Studies in Modern Literature series no. 30 (Ann Arbor, Michigan: UMI Research Press, 1984), p. viii.

6 Blotner (1974), vol. 1, p. 211.

7 Blotner (1974), vol. 1, p. 196.

8 Noel Polk, 'Introduction', in William Faulkner, *The Marionettes* (Charlottesville: University Press of Virginia for the Bibliographical Society of the University of Virginia, 1977), p. ix.

9 This is the date given in the 'Publisher's Note' (no page number) to William Faulkner, *'The Marble Faun' and 'A Green Bough'* (New York: Random House, no date).

10 James B. Meriwether, 'The Textual History of *The Sound and the Fury*', in Meriwether, ed., *The Merrill Studies in 'The Sound and the Fury'*, Charles E. Merrill studies series (Columbus, Ohio: Charles E. Merrill, 1970), p. 4. This essay is a revised version of Meriwether's 'Notes on the Textual History of *The Sound and the Fury*', *Papers of the Bibliographical Society of America*, 56 (Third Quarter, 1962), pp. 285–316.

11 Philip Cohen and Doreen Fowler, 'Faulkner's Introduction to *The Sound and the Fury*', *American Literature*, 62:2 (June 1990), p. 276. This includes the fullest printing of Faulkner's surviving manuscript and typescript drafts for the 1933 Introduction. Less full versions are James B. Meriwether, 'An Introduction to *The Sound and the Fury*', *Southern Review*, 8 (1972), pp. 705–10; 'An Introduction to *The Sound and the Fury*', *Mississippi Quarterly*, 26 (1973), pp. 156–61 – extract in Harold Bloom, ed., *Caddy Compson*, Major Literary Characters series (New York and Philadelphia: Chelsea House, 1990), pp. 5–6; 'Introduction to *The Sound and the Fury*, 1933', in André Bleikasten, ed., *William Faulkner's 'The Sound and the Fury': A Critical Casebook*, Garland Faulkner Casebooks series no. 1 (New York and London: Garland, 1982), pp. 7–14 – this is the fullest printing prior to Cohen and Fowler (1990).

12 Meriwether (1970), p. 5.

13 Blotner (1974), p. 583.

14 Meriwether (1970), p. 5.

15 John E. Bassett, ed., *William Faulkner: The Critical Heritage*, Critical Heritage series (London and Boston: Routledge and Kegan Paul, 1975), p. 5.

16 Meriwether (1970), p. 13.

17 The biographical note to UK Penguin paperback editions of Faulkner's work in the 1950s and 1960s reinforce the myth of the 'coal heaver'. The biographical note at the front of the Penguin Modern Classics edition of *As I Lay Dying* (Harmondsworth: Penguin, 1963) says: 'It was in 1929, the year of his marriage, that he took a job as a coal-heaver on night-work at the local power station and wrote *As I Lay Dying* (1930) between the hours of midnight and 4 a.m. during a space of six summer [*sic*] weeks'. The 'coal-heaver' (or 'coal heaver', without the hyphen) story is repeated in the Penguin editions of, for example, *Sanctuary* (1953), *The Unvanquished* (1955), *Go Down, Moses* (1960), *Light in August* (1960) and *Requiem for a Nun* (1960), and survives into the Penguin

1982 impression of *Absalom, Absalom!*

18 Blotner (1974), vol. 1, p. 634; Williamson (1993), vol. 1, p. 226.

19 Blotner (1974), vol. 1, p. 633; Williamson (1993), p. 227.

20 Blotner (1974), vol. 1, p. 641.

21 Blotner (1974), vol. 1, p. 642.

22 Blotner (1974), vol. 1, p. 667.

CHAPTER ONE

1 Evelyn Scott, *On William Faulkner's 'The Sound and the Fury'* (New York: Jonathan Cape and Harrison Smith, 1929; reprinted Norwood Editions (no place of publication given), 1977), no page number. Extract in Michael H. Cowan, ed., *Twentieth Century Interpretations of 'The Sound and the Fury'*, Twentieth Century Views series (Englewood Cliffs: Prentice-Hall, 1968), pp. 25–29; reprinted in Bassett (1975), pp. 76–81.

2 Ivor H. Evans, ed. and revised, *Brewer's Dictionary of Phrase and Fable*, Centenary Edition (London: Book Club Associates, 1977), p. 878.

3 William Blake, *Songs of Innocence and Experience: Showing the Two Contrary States of the Human Soul*, 1789, 1794, with an introduction and commentary by Sir Geoffrey Keynes (London: Oxford University Press, 1970), plate 42.

4 See 'The Little Mermaid', in Hans Christian Andersen, *Fairy Tales*, trans. Reginald Spink, Everyman's Library Children's Classics series (London: David Campbell, 1992), pp. 75–102.

5 Scott (1977), pp. 5–10.

6 Frances Lamont Robbins, 'Novels of the Week', *Outlook and Independent* (16 October 1929), p. 268.

7 Anon., 'Decayed Gentility', *New York Times Book Review* (10 November 1929), p. 28.

8 Basil Davenport, 'Tragic Frustration', *Saturday Review of Literature* (28 December 1929), p. 601.

9 Davenport (1929), p. 601.

10 Davenport (1929), p. 602.

11 Davenport (1929), p. 602.

12 *Classical Literary Criticism: Aristotle: 'On the Art of Poetry'; Horace: 'On the Art of Poetry'; Longinus: 'On the Sublime'*, trans. T. S. Dorsch, Penguin Classics series (Harmondsworth: Penguin, 1965), pp. 38–39.

13 Henry Nash Smith, 'Three Southern Novels', *Southwest Review*, 15 (Autumn 1929), pp. iii–iv. Reprinted in M. Thomas Inge, ed., *William Faulkner: The Contemporary Reviews*, The American Critical Archives series no. 5 (Cambridge: Cambridge University Press, 1995), pp. 33–34; Bassett (1975), pp. 85–87.

14 Harry Hansen, 'The First Reader', *The World* (9 October 1929), p. 16.

15 Hansen (1929), p. 16.

16 Lyle Saxon, 'A Family Breaks Up', *New York Herald Tribune Books* (13 October 1929), p. 3.

17 Clifton P. Fadiman, 'Hardly Worth While', *The Nation*, 130:3367 (15 January 1930), p. 74. Hereafter referenced as Fadiman (1930a). Extract in Inge (1995), pp. 38–39.

18 Scott (1977), p. 10.

19 Fadiman (1930a), pp. 74–75.

20 Henry James, 'Gustave Flaubert' (1902), in Morris Shapira, ed., *Selected Literary Criticism* (Harmondsworth: Penguin, 1968), p. 263.

21 See Inge (1995), pp. 40–41. Bassett (1975), p. 95, gives her third name as 'Wetherill' when he reprints part of her review of *As I Lay Dying*.

22 See Bassett (1975), p. 95, who says that the 'Literature and Less' column of the *Times-Picayune*, 'first John McClure and then Mrs[.] Baker, gave Faulkner substantial coverage during these years'. Bassett gives Mabel C. Simmons as the source of the description of Baker as 'a real southern literary lady of the old school', but provides no reference.

23 John McClure [Julia K. W[etherill] Baker], 'Literature and Less: A Page on Books of the [D]ay', *Times-Picayune* (29 June 1930), p. 23. Hereafter referenced as McClure [Baker] (1930a). Extract in Inge (1995), pp. 39–40.

24 McClure [Baker] (1930a), p. 23.

25 McClure [Baker] (1930a), p.23.

26 McClure [Baker] (1930a), p.23.

27 Walter L. Myers, 'Make-Beliefs', *Virginia Quarterly Review*, 6 (January 1930), p.138.

28 Myers (1930), pp.139–40.

29 Myers (1930), p.140.

30 Dudley Fitts, 'Two Aspects of Telemachus', *Hound and Horn*, 3 (April–June 1930), p.445. Reprinted (with omission of *The Sound and the Fury* quotation) in Bassett (1975), pp.87–89.

31 Fitts (1930), p.447.

32 Fitts (1930), p.445.

33 'Technic' is the term Stuart Gilbert uses in his landmark study, *James Joyce's 'Ulysses'*, first published in 1930, to denote the different dominant techniques, one for each section of the novel, which Joyce employs in *Ulysses*. See Gilbert, *James Joyce's 'Ulysses'* (Harmondsworth: Penguin, 1963), pp.37–39.

34 See Gilbert (1963), pp.328–44.

35 T.S. Eliot, *The Complete Poems and Plays* (London: Book Club Associates, 1977), p.72.

36 [*Editor's Note:*] Though Fitts praises the way in which Benjy is realised as a character, he does get Benjy's age wrong, calling him 'a man of thirty' (Fitts (1930), p.445) and thus losing the significance of the age that Faulkner gives him, 33 – the same age as Christ when he was crucified.

37 [*Fitts's Note:*] [Compare] *Ulysses* . . . '. . . and then I asked him with my eyes to ask again yes and then he asked me would I say yes to say yes my mountain flower and first I put my arms around him yes and drew him down to me so he could feel my breasts all perfume yes and his heart was going like mad and yes I said yes I will Yes.' [*Ulysses* [The 1922 text], Jeri Johnson, ed., World's Classics series (Oxford: Oxford University Press, 1993), p.732].

38 Fitts (1930), pp.445–47.

39 Fitts (1930), p.450.

40 Edward Crickmay, 'Recent Fiction', *Sunday Referee* (26 April 1931), p.9. Section on *The Sound and the Fury* reprinted in Bassett (1975), pp.90–91.

41 Crickmay (1931), p.9.

42 Frank Swinnerton, 'Writers Who Know Life', *The Evening News*, 15 May 1931, p.8. Section on *The Sound and the Fury* reprinted in Bassett (1975), pp.91–92.

43 Roland Barthes's 'Blind and Dumb Criticism', in his *Mythologies*, selected and trans. Annette Lavers (London: Paladin, 1973), p.34, contends that critics who proclaim 'their lack of understanding' do so because they believe themselves 'to have such sureness of intelligence that acknowledging an inability to understand calls into question the clarity of the author and not that of [their] own mind[s]'.

44 Swinnerton (1931), p.8.

45 Swinnerton (1931), p.8.

46 Anon., 'A Witch's Brew', *The New York Times Book Review* (19 October 1930), p.6. Reprinted in Bassett (1975), pp.93–94.

47 See Bassett (1975), pp.95–96 and Inge (1995), pp.47–48.

48 John McClure [Julia K. W[etherill] Baker], 'Literature and Less', *Times-Picayune* (26 October 1930), p.33. Hereafter referenced as McClure [Baker] (1930b). For McClure [Baker] (1930a) see note 23 above. Partly reprinted in Bassett (1975), pp.95–96, Inge (1995), pp.47–48.

49 McClure [Baker] (1930b), p.33.

50 McClure [Baker] (1930b), p.33.

51 Clifton P. Fadiman, 'Morbidity in Fiction', *The Nation*, 131:3409 (5 November 1930), pp.500, 501. Hereafter referenced as Fadiman (1930b). For Fadiman (1930a) see note 17 above.

52 'Jeffers, Robinson', in Ian Ousby, ed., *The Cambridge Guide to Literature in English* (Cambridge/London: Cambridge University Press and Hamlyn Publishing Group, 1988), pp.511–12.

53 Fadiman (1930b), p.500.

54 Fadiman (1930b), p.501.

55 Kenneth White, '*As I Lay Dying* by William Faulkner', *New Republic* (19 November 1930), p.27.

56 Basil Davenport, 'In the Mire', *Saturday Review of Literature* (22 November 1930), p.362.

57 John Donald Wade, 'The South in its

Fiction', *Virginia Quarterly Review,* 7 (1931), p.124.

58 Wade (1931), p.125.

59 Wade (1930), pp.125–26.

60 Gerald Gould, 'New Novels: Six Books in Search of a Theory', *The Observer* (Sunday 29 September 1935), p.6. Section on *As I Lay Dying* reprinted in Bassett (1975), pp.97–98. This reference to Gould (1935).

61 Edwin Muir, 'New Novels', *The Listener* (16 October 1935), p.681. Section on *As I Lay Dying* reprinted (with omission of quotation from the novel) in Bassett (1975), pp.99–100.

62 F.R. Leavis, 'Dostoevsky and Dickens', *Scrutiny: A Quarterly Review,* 2:1 (June 1933), pp.92–93. Extract in Robert Penn Warren, ed., *Faulkner: A Collection of Critical Essays,* Twentieth Century Views series (Englewood Cliffs, New Jersey: Prentice-Hall, 1966), pp.277–78. According to Raymond Williams, Leavis in later life was even more scathing about Faulkner. In 'Seeing a Man Running', a contribution to Denys Thompson, ed., *The Leavises: Recollections and Impressions* (Cambridge: Cambridge University Press (1984)), Williams recalls Leavis saying at a Cambridge committee meeting, with 'fierce pleasure in the argument but also . . . surprising conviction', '"Faulkner! . . . When the Americans moved in on Europe after the War, they had to have a great novelist. That's who they chose, Faulkner"'. (p.117). Interestingly, this view bears some resemblance to the case argued in Lawrence H. Schwarz's *Creating Faulkner's Reputation: The Politics of Modern Literary Criticism* (Knoxville: University of Tennessee Press, 1988).

63 Quoted in Frederick J. Hoffman and Olga W. Vickery, eds., *William Faulkner: Two Decades of Criticism* (East Lansing: Michigan State College Press, 1951, 1954), p.2, and Emerson (1984), p.73.

64 Quoted in Hoffman and Vickery (1954), p.2.

65 Quoted in Emerson (1984), p.80.

66 Quoted in Emerson (1984), p.98.

67 Warrren (1966), pp.279, 280.

68 Maurice Coindreau, 'France and the Contemporary American Novel', trans. Madeline Ashton, *Kansas City University Review,* 3:4 (1937), pp.273–79. Reprinted in Coindreau, *The Time of William Faulkner: A French View of Modern American Fiction,* George McMillan Reeves, ed. and chiefly trans. (Columbia, South Carolina: University of South Carolina Press, 1971), pp.3–13. This quotation, Coindreau (1971), p.9.

69 For a translation of Coindreau's 'Preface' to *The Sound and the Fury,* see Coindreau (1971), pp.41–50. Condensed version in Cowan (1968), pp.30–32.

70 Jean-Paul Sartre, '*Sartoris* par William Faulkner', in *Situations I* (Paris: Gallimard, 1947), pp.2–13. The essay is dated February 1938. Published in English as 'William Faulkner's *Sartoris*' in Sartre, *Literary and Philosophical Essays,* trans. Annette Michelson (London: Rider, 1955; Radius / Hutchinson, 1968), pp.73–78.

71 'À propos de *Le Bruit et Le Fureur*: La temporalité chez Faulkner' in Sartre (1947), pp.70–81. Published in English as 'On *The Sound and the Fury*: Time in the Work of Faulkner', Sartre (1968), pp.79–87. Reprinted in Warren (1966), pp.87–93. Also trans. Martine Darmon, with assistance from Frederick J. Hoffman and Olga W. Vickery, as 'Time in Faulkner: *The Sound and the Fury*' in Frederick J. Hoffman and Olga W. Vickery, ed., *William Faulkner: Three Decades of Criticism* (East Lansing: Michigan State University Press, 1960), pp.225–32.

72 Sartre (1947), p.72.

73 Hoffman and Vickery (1960), p.227. A footnote adds a 'translator's note' that 'the word *suspension* seemed the most suitable translation [of '*l'enfoncement'*] in view of the context' (p.227, asterisked note).

74 See Sartre (1947), pp.9–10 and Sartre (1955), p.75 – though Sartre speaks of 'Acts' ('Les Actes') in his essay

on *Sartoris*, rather than of 'events' ('les événements'): 'Faulkner does not speak of acts, never mentions them, and thus suggests that there is no naming them, that they are beyond language. He shows only their results . . . ' (Sartre (1955), p.75).

75 Sartre (1947), p.73.

76 [*Editor's Note:*] Sartre's original essay has 'Blaid' for 'Bland' (Sartre (1947), p.74); this is repeated in Sartre (1955), p.82, but altered to 'Bland' in Hoffman and Vickery (1960), p.228. [*Sartre's Note:*] Compare the dialogue with Bla[i]d inserted into the middle of the dialogue with Ames: 'did you ever have a sister' (p.160; [compare p.166]), etc., and the inextricable confusion of the two fights.

77 Sartre (1947), p.74.

78 *Harrap's Shorter Dictionary: English/French: French/English* (1996) renders 'casser la figure à q[uelqu'u]n' as 'to smash s[ome]b[ody]'s face in' (p.396).

79 Hoffman and Vickery (1960), p.228.

80 [*Editor's Note:*] the French word translated as 'monitor' here is 'censeur' (Sartre (1947), p.74). *Harrap's Shorter Dictionary* (1996), p.149, gives the meaning of 'censeur' as 'vice-principal' or 'deputy headmaster'. The translation in Hoffman and Vickery (1960), renders 'censeur' as 'principal' (p.228).

81 Sartre (1955), pp.79–83.

82 Sartre (1955), p.84.

83 Sartre (1955), p.85.

84 Sartre (1955), p.87.

85 John T. Matthews, '*The Sound and the Fury': Faulkner and the Lost Cause'*, Twayne's Masterwork Studies series no. 61 (Boston: Twayne, 1990), p.27. Despite his reservations, Matthews does also say that Sartre's essay 'brilliantly demonstrates how the past entirely overshadows the present in the novel'.

86 Henry J. Underwood, Jr, 'Sartre on *The Sound and the Fury*: Some Errors', *Modern Fiction Studies*, 12 (1996), p.478.

87 Conrad Aiken, 'William Faulkner: The Novel as Form', *Atlantic Monthly*, 144 (November 1939), p.654. Reprinted in Hoffman and Vickery (1954), pp.139–47; Hoffman and Vickery (1960), pp.135–42; Warren (1966), pp.46–52.

88 Aiken (1939), p.650.

89 Aiken (1939), p.652.

90 Aiken (1939), p.652.

91 Aiken (1939), pp.652–53.

92 *Concise Oxford Dictionary of Current English*, 7th edn (Oxford: Clarendon Press, 1982), p.1193.

93 Aiken (1939), p.653.

94 Aiken (1939), p.653.

95 Aiken (1939), p.653.

96 Aiken (1939), p.654.

97 George Marion O'Donnell, 'Faulkner's Mythology', *Kenyon Review* (Summer 1939), p.285. Reprinted in Hoffman and Vickery (1954), pp.49–62; Hoffman and Vickery (1960), pp.82–93; Warren (1966), pp.23–33; Linda Welshimer Wagner, ed., *William Faulkner: Four Decades of Criticism* (Michigan: Michigan State University Press, 1973), pp.83–93.

98 O'Donnell (1939), p.286.

99 William Faulkner, *Absalom, Absalom!* (Harmondsworth: Penguin, 1971), p.9.

100 O'Donnell (1939), p.288, note 1.

101 Faulkner (1971), p.6.

102 O'Donnell (1939), pp.288–89.

103 Anthony Thorlby, ed., *The Penguin Companion to Literature: Europe* (London: Allen Lane, The Penguin Press, 1969), p.39.

104 Elizabeth A. Livingstone, ed., *The Concise Oxford Dictionary of the Christian Church* (Oxford, London and New York: Oxford University Press, 1977), p.241.

105 O'Donnell (1939), pp.290–91.

106 Schwarz (1988), p.9.

107 Schwarz (1988), pp.21–25.

108 Malcolm Cowley, ed., *The Portable Faulkner* (New York: Viking Press, 1946. Revised and expanded edition: London: Penguin, 1977), p.viii. Cowley's original 'Introduction' reprinted in Hoffman and Vickery (1954), pp.82–101; Hoffman and Vickery (1960), pp.94–109; Warren (1966), pp.34–45.

109 Cowley (1977), p.x.

110 Cowley (1977), p.xi.

111 Cowley (1977), p. xv.

112 Cowley (1977), p. xvi.

113 Cowley (1977), p. xx.

114 *Brewer's Dictionary* (1977), p. 192.

115 Cowley (1977), pp. xx, xxi, xxii.

116 Cowley (1977), p. xxiv.

117 Cowley (1977), p. xxv.

118 Cowley (1977), p. xv. For 'Appendix: The Compsons', see Cowley (1977), pp. 704–21.

119 The term 'paratextual' is from Gérard Genette, whose book *Seuils* (Paris: Editions du Seuil, 1987), trans. Jane E. Lewin as *Paratexts: Thresholds of Interpretation*, Literature, Culture, Theory series no. 20 (Cambridge: Cambridge University Press, 1997), defines a paratext thus: '[the] text [of a literary work] is rarely presented in an unadorned state, unreinforced and unaccompanied by a certain number of verbal or other productions, such as an author's name, a title, a preface, illustrations . . . These accompanying productions, which vary in extent and appearance, constitute . . . the work's *paratext* . . . More than a boundary or a sealed border, the paratext is, rather, a *threshold* . . . an undefined zone between the inside and the outside' (Genette (1997), pp. 1–2). Genette does not mention the Compson Appendix in this book, though he does cite, as other paratextual examples, the title of *The Sound and the Fury* as an example of 'quotation-titles' (Genette (1997), p. 91). See also p. 157, where he classifies the title among those that allude to another text but are not accompanied by an epigraph elaborating the allusion. Genette mentions as well (p. 405) that Faulkner drew a map of Yoknapatawpha County for *The Portable Faulkner*. A detailed study of Faulkner in relation to 'paratexts' could be fascinating.

120 For further discussion of Faulkner's Appendix and *The Portable Faulkner*, see Schwarz (1988); Cheryl Lester, 'To Market, To Market: *The Portable Faulkner*', *Criticism: A Quarterly for Literature and the Arts*, 33 (Summer 1987), pp. 371–92; Thadious M. Davis,

'Reading Faulkner's Compson Appendix: History from the Margins', in Donald M. Kartiganer and Ann J. Abadie, ed., *Faulkner and Ideology: Faulkner and Yoknapatawpha, 1992* (Jackson: University Press of Mississippi, 1995), pp. 238–52.

121 Robert Penn Warren, 'William Faulkner', *New Republic* 115 (12 August 1946), pp. 176–80, (26 August 1946), pp. 234–37. Reprinted in Hoffman and Vickery (1954), pp. 82–101; Warren, *Selected Essays* (New York: Random House, 1958), pp. 59–79; Hoffman and Vickery (1960), pp. 109–24; Wagner (1973), pp. 94–109. Future Warren references to Wagner (1973).

122 Wagner (1973), p. 94.

123 In fact, Jason does not use the term 'kike'; according to the *Concordance* (p. 334 – see Bibliography for details), the term occurs only once in the novel, in Quentin's section, in the phrase 'Land of the kike home of the wop' (p. 124).

124 Wagner (1973), p. 97.

125 Wagner (1973), p. 104.

126 Wagner (1973), p. 106. For the quotation from the Compson genealogy, see Cowley (1977), p. 721.

127 Wagner (1973), pp. 104, 105.

128 Wagner (1973), p. 108.

129 Wagner (1973), p. 109.

130 Lawrence Edward Bowling, 'Faulkner: Technique of *The Sound and the Fury*', *Kenyon Review*, 10 (Autumn 1948), p. 552.

131 Cowley (1973), p. xxv.

132 Cowley (1973), p. xxv.

133 Cowley (1973), p. xv.

134 Bowling (1948), pp. 564–65.

CHAPTER TWO

1 Williamson (1993), p. 274.

2 Cowley (1977), p. 723.

3 Cowley (1977), p. 723.

4 Schwarz (1988), p. 6.

5 Irving Howe, *William Faulkner: A Critical Study.* (New York: Random House, 1952); second edn (1962); third edn, revised and expanded (Chicago and London: University of Chicago Press,

1975). Extract from 1962 edn in Cowan (1966), pp. 33–39. The references in this Guide to Howe (1975). This quotation, p. 3.

6 Quoted Howe (1975), p. 157.

7 Howe (1975), p. 157.

8 Howe (1975), p. 158.

9 Howe's implied definition of the function of Marlow in Conrad's stories is open to question; it is doubtful that Marlow always functions for Conrad as an 'external observer' who provides 'breadth and balance of judgement'. His role in 'Heart of Darkness' (1902), for example, seems much more complex; for discussions of this, see Nicolas Tredell ed., *Joseph Conrad: 'Heart of Darkness'*, Icon Critical Guides series (Cambridge: Icon Books, 1998). In fact, the idea of Marlow turning up in Yoknapatawpha County – perhaps to work as the captain of a river steamboat – and staying for a spell at the Compson residence is a fascinating one, possibly a theme for a post-modernist novel!

10 Howe (1975), pp. 158–61.

11 Howe (1975), pp. 161, 162.

12 [*Howe's Note:*] Pages 87–92 in the Modern Library Edition.

13 Howe (1975), pp. 162–66.

14 Howe (1975), p. 167.

15 Howe (1975), p. 174.

16 Howe (1975), pp. 176–77, 180–81, 182.

17 Howe (1975), pp. 190–91.

18 Olga W. Vickery, *The Novels of William Faulkner: A Critical Interpretation*, revised edn (Baton Rouge: Louisiana State University Press, 1959); revised edn (Baton Rouge: Louisiana State University Press, 1964), p. vi. Extract on *As I Lay Dying* from 1959 edn in Hoffman and Vickery (1960), pp. 232–47; extracts on *The Sound and the Fury* from 1964 edn in Cowan (1968), pp. 40–52 and Bloom (1990), pp. 11–13.

19 Vickery (1964), pp. 28–32.

20 Vickery (1964), pp. 50–53.

21 See James Baldwin's essay 'Faulkner and Desegregation', originally published in *Partisan Review* in 1956, and collected in Baldwin's *Nobody Knows My Name: More*

Notes of a Native Son (London: Michael Joseph, 1964). Urbanely, with restrained passion, Baldwin satirises the advice of 'the squire of Oxford' to 'go slow' in regard to desegregation in the South: 'it is, I suppose, impertinent to ask just what Negroes are supposed to do while the South works out what, in Faulkner's rhetoric, becomes something very closely resembling a high and noble tragedy' (p. 102). For a more sympathetic account of Faulkner's attitudes to race in the 1950s, which draws attention to the hostility he aroused among some white Southerners, see Williamson (1993), pp. 300–12. Williamson concludes that '[i]n race relations, Faulkner's confusion mirrored the confusion of the South as a whole over the centuries. At one time or another, he advocated every position that Southern whites had taken in that long and too often sad history' (pp. 311–12).

22 Cleanth Brooks, *William Faulkner: The Yoknapatawpha Country* (New Haven and London: Yale University Press, 1963), p. vii. Extract in Cowan (1968), p. 63–70.

23 Brooks (1963), p. viii.

24 William Shakespeare, *The Complete Works*, Stanley Wells, Gary Taylor, John Jowett, William Mongomery, eds. (Oxford: Oxford University Press, 1988), p. 651.

25 Brooks (1963), pp. 143–44.

26 Brooks (1963), pp. 336–37.

27 Brooks (1963), pp. 334.

28 Brooks (1963), pp. 341–42.

29 William Rose Benét, *The Reader's Encyclopedia*, 2nd edn (London: Book Club Associates, 1977), p. 800.

30 Brooks seems to assume that Luster is Dilsey's son rather than her grandson, the child of her daughter Frony and an unknown man. See Edmond L. Volpe, *A Reader's Guide to William Faulkner* (London: Thames and Hudson, 1964), p. 88. For a discussion of Dilsey's treatment of Luster, see Sandra D. Milroy, 'Dilsey: Faulkner's Black Mammy in *The Sound and the Fury*', *Negro Historical Bulletin*, 46:3 (1983), p. 71. Milroy calls Dilsey's treatment of Luster 'unduly

harsh' but suggests it may be because of a desire to toughen him for survival in a white-dominated society and because Dilsey 'so exhausts her patience and love with her white family that she has little left for her black family'.

31 Brooks (1963), pp. 342–44.

32 Brooks (1963), p. 348.

33 Frederick L. Gwynn and Joseph L. Blotner, eds., *Faulkner in the University: Class Conferences at the University of Virginia 1957–1958* (Charlottesville, Virginia: University of Virginia Press, 1959), p. 6. Extracts in Cowan (1968), pp. 18–24; Bleikasten (1982), pp. 21–29; Bloom (1990), pp. 9–11.

34 Gwynn and Blotner (1959), p. 1.

35 Robert A. Jeliffe, ed., *Faulkner at Nagano* (Tokyo: Kenyusha Press, 1956), p. 72.

36 Michael Millgate, *The Achievement of William Faulkner* (London: Constable, 1966), pp. 95–98.

37 Millgate (1966), p. 104.

38 Millgate (1966), p. 314, note 1.

39 Millgate (1966), p. 86.

40 Millgate (1966), p. 87.

41 Shakespeare (1988), p. 760.

42 Cohen and Fowler (1990), p. 275.

43 Millgate (1966), pp. 104, 105, 106–8.

CHAPTER THREE

1 André Bleikasten, *Faulkner's 'As I Lay Dying'*, revised and enlarged edition, trans. Roger Little with the collaboration of the author (Bloomington and London: Indiana University Press, 1973), p. vii.

2 See André Bleikasten, *The Ink of Melancholy: Faulkner's Novels from 'The Sound and the Fury' to 'Light in August'* (Bloomington and Indianapolis: Indiana University Press, 1990), p. xiv. This book incorporates later versions of Bleikasten's studies of *The Sound and the Fury* and *As I Lay Dying*.

3 Henry James, *The Art of the Novel: Critical Prefaces* (New York: Charles Scribner's sons, 1934), p. 110.

4 [*Editor's Note:*] This note is from Bleikasten (1973), p. 153, note 4.

5 R.P. Blackmur, 'Introduction', in James (1934), pp. xviii–xix.

6 Bleikasten (1973), pp. 46–50.

7 [*Bleikasten's Note:*] [Compare] Henry James (*Notes on Novelists*): 'To lift our subject out of the sphere of anecdote and place it in the sphere of drama . . . we supply it with a large lucid reflector, which we find only . . . in that mind and soul concerned in the business that have at once the highest sensibility and the highest capacity, or that are . . . most admirably agitated'. Quoted by Wayne C. Booth in *The Rhetoric of Fiction* (Chicago: University of Chicago Press, 1961), p. 270.

8 [*Bleikasten's Note:*] The distinction between *history* and *discourse* – *récit* and *discours* in the original – is taken from Emile Benveniste. See [Benveniste's] *Problems in General Linguistics*, trans. Mary Elizabeth Meek (Coral Gables, Florida: University of Miami Press, 1971), pp. 205–17.

9 [*Bleikasten's Note:*] As Wayne C. Booth puts it, Faulkner's method in *As I Lay Dying* is 'omniscience with teeth in it' [(Booth (1961)], p. 161).

10 Bleikasten (1973), pp. 56–64.

11 From Gwynn and Blotner (1959), p. 77. Quoted as epigraph to André Bleikasten, *The Most Splendid Failure: Faulkner's 'The Sound and the Fury'* (Bloomington and London: Indiana University Press, 1976). Extract from Bleikasten (1976) in Bloom (1990), pp. 73–83.

12 Bleikasten (1976), p. x.

13 Bleikasten (1976), p. 53.

14 [*Bleikasten's Note:*] The importance of this image and of the scene it heralds is confirmed by a study of the manuscript. Originally section 2 started thus: 'One minute she was standing there. The next Benjy was yelling and pulling at her. They went down the hall to the bathroom and stopped there, Caddy backed against the door . . . '. This page of the manuscript is reproduced in James B. Meriwether, *The Literary Career of William Faulkner: A Bibliographical Study*

(Princeton: Princeton University Library, 1961), illustration 11.

15 [*Bleikasten's Note:*] See also p.70: 'Her hair was like fire, and little points of fire were in her eyes'.

16 [*Bleikasten's Note:*] The reversible metaphor *girl = tree* can be traced back to Faulkner's earliest work; in *The Marble Faun* poplars are compared to 'slender girls'; girls are likened to trees in *Marionettes*, his early play, as well as in *Soldiers' Pay* and *Mosquitoes*.

17 [*Bleikasten's Note:*] A similar ritual cleansing occurs in 'There Was a Queen'. See Faulkner, *Collected Stories* (New York: Random House, 1950), p.741.

18 Jean-Paul Sartre, *Baudelaire* (Paris: Gallimard, 1947), p.201. [Bleikasten's translation].

19 Chris Baldick, *The Concise Oxford Dictionary of Literary Terms* (Oxford and New York: Oxford University Press, 1991), p.221.

20 [*Bleikasten's Note:*] The phrase is from Harry Modean Campbell and Ruel E. Foster, *William Faulkner: A Critical Appraisal* (Norman: University of Oklahoma Press, 1951), p.54.

21 Paul Claudel, *La Ville*, 2nd edn (Paris: Mercure de France, 1920), p.307 [Bleikasten's translation].

22 [*Bleikasten's Note:*] For a full discussion of Caddy in psychological and moral terms see Catherine B. Baum, '"The Beautiful One": Caddy Compson as Heroine of *The Sound and the Fury*', *Modern Fiction Studies*, 13 (Spring 1967), pp.33–44; [extract in Bloom (1990), pp.39–49. See also] Eileen Gregory, 'Caddy Compson's World', [Meriwether (1970)], pp.89–101.

23 Arthur Rimbaud, *Complete Works, Selected Letters*, trans. Wallace Fowlie (Chicago and London: University of Chicago Press, 1966), p.187.

24 Henry James, *Notes and Reviews* (Cambridge, Massachusetts: Dunster House, 1921), p.226.

25 Bleikasten (1976), pp.53, 57–66.

26 John E. Bassett, *Faulkner in the Eighties: An Annotated Critical Bibliography*, Scarecrow Author Bibliographies series no. 88 (Metuchen, New Jersey and London: Scarecrow Press, 1991), p.2.

27 John T. Irwin, *Doubling and Incest/Repetition and Revenge: A Speculative Reading of Faulkner* (Baltimore and London: Johns Hopkins University Press, 1975; second expanded edn, 1996), p.25. Extract from first edn in Bloom (1988), pp.9–22; Bloom (1990), pp.59–67. Quotations in this Guide from first edn.

28 [*Editor's Note:*] See Pausanius, *Guide to Greece*: vol. 1: *Central Greece*, trans. Peter Levi (Harmondsworth: Penguin, 1979), p.376: 'Narkissos [Narcissus] had a twin sister; they were exactly the same to look at with just the same hair-style and the same clothes, and they even used to go hunting together. Narkissos was in love with his sister, and when she died he used to visit the spring; he knew what he saw was his own reflection, but even so he found some relief in telling himself it was his sister's image'.

29 Otto Rank, *Das Inzest-Motiv in Dichtung und Sage* (Leipzig and Vienna: Franz Deuticke, 1912), pp.443–65.

30 Lucy Menzies, *The Saints in Italy* (London: [Irwin gives no publisher], 1924), pp.153–54. Irwin (1975), pp.35–36, 37, 38–39, 41–47, 48–49, 51–53.

31 Irwin (1975), pp.53–55.

CHAPTER FOUR

1 For analyses of key aspects of this transformation, see Nicolas Tredell, *The Critical Decade: Culture in Crisis* (Manchester: Carcanet, 1993); for extensive interviews with some of its leading figures, such as Terry Eagleton and Sir Frank Kermode, see Nicolas Tredell, *Conversations with Critics* (Manchester: Carcanet, 1994).

2 For a discussion and key examples of Dickens criticism as applied to one novel in the 1980s, see Nicolas Tredell, ed., *Charles Dickens: 'Great Expectations'*, Icon Critical Guides series (Cambridge: Icon Books, 1998), pp.121–43.

3 See Donald M. Kartiganer, *The Fragile*

Thread: The Meaning of Form in Faulkner's Novels (Amherst: University of Massachusetts Press, 1979), p. xv, where he says: 'My intention is not to deconstruct [Faulkner's] novels – they perform this act admirably themselves'. Extract in Bloom (1988), pp. 23–38.

4 For a discussion of Achebe's attack on Conrad, a substantial extract from it, and a comparison of its two versions, see Nicolas Tredell, ed., *Joseph Conrad's 'Heart of Darkness'*, Icon Critical Guides series (Cambridge: Icon Books, 1998), especially pp. 71–86 and p. 168, note 10.

5 Eric J. Sundquist, *Faulkner: The House Divided* (Baltimore and London: Johns Hopkins University Press, 1983), p. ix. Extract in Bloom (1988), pp. 117–45.

6 Sundquist (1983), p. xi.

7 Sundquist (1983), p. 8.

8 Sundquist (1983), p. 9.

9 Cowley (1977), p. 710.

10 Joel Williamson, *New People: Miscegenation and Mulattoes in the United States* (New York: The Free Press, 1980), p. 95.

11 Cowley (1977), pp. 709–10; Faulkner, *Requiem for a Nun* (New York: Vintage-Random, 1975), p. 199.

12 Sundquist (1983), pp. 21–23, 24–25.

13 Sundquist (1983), p. 28.

14 Sundquist (1983), p. 29.

15 Sundquist (1983) has 'logically disengaged for the corporeal self' (p. 30), but the version of this chapter published in 1984 has 'logically disengaged from', which seems more appropriate. See William E. Cain, ed., *Philosophical Approaches to Literature: New Essays on Nineteenth- and Twentieth-Century Literature* (Lewisburg: Bucknell University Press; London and Toronto: Associated University Presses, 1984), p. 167.

16 John K. Simon, 'The Scene and Imagery of Metamorphosis in *As I Lay Dying*', *Criticism*, 7:1 (Winter 1965), p. 14.

17 [*Sundquist's Note:*] André Bleikasten suggests an interesting approach to the fish analogy by noting that 'it is perhaps not going too far to consider it also as a regressive image of the child. Is a fetus not physiologically a fish in its mother's womb?' If so, 'the image should then be read as an expression of prenatal nostalgia, an emblem of the primal union of child and mother Vardaman is unconsciously yearning for' [Bleikasten (1973), p. 97)]. This seems perfectly plausible, though there is no reason to insist that the wish for union is wholly unconscious: on the contrary, the desire to be reunited with Addie, whether as pre- or post-natal mother, is what so much of the book's rhetorical power depends on.

18 Hoffman and Vickery (1960), p. 82.

19 Bleikasten (1973), p. 39.

20 Sundquist (1983), pp. 29–32, 35–40.

21 For vivid accounts of Snead, see the 'Forewords' by Colin MacCabe and Cornel West in Snead's posthumously published *White Screens: Black Images: Hollywood from the Dark Side*, MacCabe and West, eds. (New York and London: Routledge, 1994), pp. vii–xx.

22 James A. Snead, *Figures of Division: William Faulkner's Major Novels* (New York and London: Methuen, 1986), p. x.

23 Snead (1986), p. xii.

24 *Brewer's Dictionary* (1977), p. 588.

25 Snead (1986), pp. xiii–xiv.

26 Ovid, *Metamorphoses* (Harmondsworth: Penguin, 1970), trans. Mary M. Innes, p. 29.

27 [*Snead's Note:*] John T. Matthews, *The Play of Faulkner's Language* (Ithaca: Cornell University Press, 1982), especially the chapter entitled 'The Discovery of Loss in *The Sound and the Fury*' [extract in Bloom (1988), pp. 79–102], and Gail L. Mortimer, *Faulkner's Rhetoric of Loss* (Austin: University of Texas, 1983) [extracts in Bloom (1988), pp. 103–15; Bloom (1990), pp. 37–38], 'Introduction', both expand upon Faulkner's theme of 'loss' and absence, both of which his central characters refuse to acknowledge.

28 [*Snead's Note:*] See Ferdinand de Saussure, *Course in General Linguistics*, trans. Wade Baskin (New York: McGraw-Hill, 1966), pp. 111–34.

29 [*Snead's Note:*] See Roman Jakobson, 'Two Aspects of Language and Two Types

of Aphasic Disturbances', in *Selected Writings*, vol. 2: *Word and Language* (The Hague: Mouton, 1971), p. 251.

30 Howe (1975), p. 160.

31 Brooks (1963), p. 326.

32 Shakespeare (1988), p. 997.

33 [*Snead's Footnote:*] Arthur Geffen notes that the day after Quentin's suicide, June 3, is Jefferson Davis's birthday and a Confederate holiday. The day after the last section of the novel, April 9, is also the anniversary of the surrender [of the Confederate Army] at Appomattox. See 'Profane Time, Sacred Time, and Confederate Time in *The Sound and the Fury*', *Studies in American Fiction*, 2, pp. 175–97.

34 [*Snead's Note:*] See particularly in this regard Maurice Blanchot, 'Literature and the Right to Death', in *The Gaze of Orpheus and Other Literary Essays*, preface by Geoffrey Hartman, trans. Lydia Davis (Barrytown, NY: Station Hill Press, 1981), pp. 21–62. See also Roland Barthes, 'The Death of the Author', in *Image/Music/Text*, trans. Stephen Heath (London: Fontana, 1977), pp. 142–48.

35 Cowley (1977), p. 719.

36 Cowley (1977), p. 718.

37 [*Snead's Note:*] May Cameron Brown, 'The Language of Chaos: Quentin Compson in *The Sound and the Fury*', *American Literature*, 51:4 (January 1980), p. 544, notes this oscillation, citing 'an unusual blend of order and chaos in Quentin's section'.

38 [*Snead's Note:*] See [Irwin (1975)]. Irwin's elegant and 'speculative' argument reads Quentin's dilemma as a futile 'revenge' against the past which would suppress all memory of time, desire, and difference, missing in large part the racial and gender implications of Quentin's behavior. According to Irwin, Quentin takes 'revenge' against the repetitious self-encloses and incestuous pairings within the current and ancestral family line by reproducing them in his own, hermetic [wholly enclosed, totally sealed] terms. But the taboo against such merging reintroduces the differentiations of society into Quentin's conception. Each object of Quentin's desire reacquaints him with loss and impurity, even as he had hoped to banish these hindrances. Irwin suggests that Southern racial and sexual politics work by exploiting without resolving these tensions between 'purity/endogamy [marriage within the tribe]/incest' on the one hand and 'miscegenation/exogamy [marriage outside the tribe]/intermarriage' on the other.

39 [*Snead's Note:*] Brooks [(1963), p. 326] thinks that Jason feels 'victimized', but Howe [(1975), p. 171] is closer in noticing 'the numerous references to money that wind through the Jason section' . . . But they have less to do with money itself than with an entire monetary approach that treats others as exchange objects.

40 [*Editor's Note:*] For 'That Evening Sun', see William Faulkner, *Faulkner's County: Tales of Yoknapatawpha County* (London: Chatto and Windus, 1955), pp. 339–55.

41 Cowley (1977), p. 716.

42 Cowley (1977), p. 720.

43 [*Snead's Note:*] Hyatt H. Waggoner, *William Faulkner: From Jefferson to the World* (Kentucky: University of Kentucky Press, 1959), p. 58 [extract in Cowan (1968), pp. 97–101]; [Millgate (1966)], p. 99; Brooks [(1963)], p. 325. For standard plot reconstructions, see George R. Stewart and Joseph M. Backus, 'Each in its Ordered Place: Structure and Narrative in "Benjy's Section" of *The Sound and the Fury*', *American Literature*, 29 (January 1958), pp. 440–56, and [Volpe (1964)], pp. 353–77.

44 Millgate (1966), p. 101.

45 Arthur F. Kinney, *Faulkner's Narrative Poetics: Style as Vision* (Amherst: University of Massachusetts Press, 1978), p. 154.

46 Waggoner (1959), p. 55.

47 Matthews (1982), p. 106.

48 Reed (1973), p. 82.

49 Walter J. Slatoff, *Quest for Failure: A Study of William Faulkner* (Westport, Connecticut: Greenwood Press, 1972), p. 155. Extract from 1960 edn in Cowan (1968), pp. 93–96.

50 [*Snead's Note:*] *As I Lay Dying* . . .

repeats this originally Homeric inter-relationship between the *bothros*, or 'hollow', and black 'otherness', 'death', but also transcendence.

51 [*Editor's Note:*] See Homer, *The Odyssey*, trans. E.V. Rieu (Harmondsworth: Penguin, 1946), pp. 171–88, 'The Book of the Dead'. 'Thus she [the ship] brought us to the deep-flowing River of Ocean and the frontiers of the world' (p. 171).

52 Kinney (1978), p. xv.

53 Howe (1975), p. 214.

54 [*Snead's Note:*] Faulkner wrote to Malcolm Cowley: 'It is my ambition to be, as a private individual, abolished and voided from history, leaving it markless, no refuse save the printed books': letter dated 11 February 1949, in William Faulkner, *Selected Letters of William Faulkner*, Joseph Blotner, ed. (New York: Random House, 1977), p. 285. In his next novel [*As I Lay Dying*] Faulkner will conceive of the narrative voice as Blanchot's 'neuter'.

55 Bleikasten (1976), p. 205.

56 Bleikasten (1976), pp. 196, 197, 199.

57 [*Snead's Note:*] Myra Jehlen is one of the few Faulkner critics who notices the particularly *un*satisfactory 'salvation' of the Dilsey section, which 'is really no more redemptive than any other section'. For her, *The Sound and the Fury* also implies that 'there is no way out of history and time but in death': Myra Jehlen, *Class and Character in Faulkner's South* (New York: Columbia University Press, 1976), p. 44.

58 [*Snead's Note:*] To one critic, Benjy, for instance, seems 'an essentially timeless mind which contains thirty years of time': Richard P. Adams, *Faulkner: Myth and Motion* (Princeton: Princeton University Press, 1968), p. 239. For another, Benjy's 'moment *is* eternal, always present, forever recallable': Waggoner [(1959)], p. 57. Benjy seems superior to the others on the basis of this quality, and this critical mishandling has been applied to black characters as well. For many, Shegog's 'rhetoric . . . succeeds partly because it . . .

enables him to telescope time': Adams [(1968)], p. 227. Incredibly – but typically – one even encounters the sentiment that 'to Dilsey, neither the past nor the future nor the present is oppressive, because to her they are all aspects of eternity, and her ultimate commitment is to eternity': Brooks [(1963)], p. 330. More blatantly, Douglas Messerli says, 'Dilsey transcends time while Quentin seeks time's extinction . . . Nowhere in the later novels, except perhaps in *A Fable* (1954), does a character transcend time and space in the way in which Dilsey does': 'The Problem of Time in *The Sound and the Fury*: A Critical Reassessment and Reinterpretation', *The Southern Literary Journal*, 6:2 (1974), pp. 23, 34. [Extract in Bloom (1990), pp. 33–38.]

59 [*Snead's Note:*] Kinney (1978), p. 158 suggests that 'the power of Shegog's Word – in a novel so concerned with the power of words – does not finally convert anyone previously unconverted. Everyone and everything return to what they were before'. Millgate (1966), p. 102, is equally unmoved: 'the sense of human communion rapidly dissolves as [the blacks] move into the world of "white folks"'.

60 [*Snead's Note:*] Helen Swink has speculated on the possible influences of black oral narratives upon Faulkner's general written style in 'William Faulkner: The Novelist as Oral Narrator', *The Georgia Review*, 26 (1971), p. 188.

61 Cowley (1977), pp. 723–24.

62 Cowley (1977), p. 724.

63 Snead (1986), pp. 20–24, 25–30, 31–39.

CHAPTER FIVE

1 Deborah Clarke, *Robbing the Mother: Women in Faulkner* (Jackson: University Press of Mississippi, 1994), p. 19.

2 Clarke (1994), p. 19.

3 Clarke (1994), p. 20.

4 Gwynn and Blotner (1959), p. 1.

5 Minter (1980), p. 103.

6 Paul R. Lilly, Jr, 'Caddy and Addie: Speakers of Faulkner's Impeccable

Language', *Journal of Narrative Technique*, 3 (1973), p. 174.

7 Linda W. Wagner, 'Language and Act: Caddy Compson', *Southern Literary Journal Review*, 14 (1982), p. 61. Reprinted in Bloom (1990), pp. 108–18.

8 [*Clarke's Note*:] David Minter, one of the exceptions, points to a failure of both parents and links that failure to Faulkner's mixed emotions towards his own parents, especially his supportive but domineering mother. He asserts that Faulkner's sympathy lies with children in both this novel and *As I Lay Dying* [David L. Minter, *Faulkner: His Life and Work* (Baltimore: Johns Hopkins University Press, 1980)], p. 97. [Extract in Bloom (1990), pp. 33–38]. For condemnations of Mrs Compson see [Brooks (1963)], pp. 333–34; Mark Spilka, 'Quentin Compson's Universal Grief', *Contemporary Fiction*, 11 (1970), p. 456; Jackson J. Benson, 'Quentin Compson: Self-Portrait of a Young Artist's Emotions', *Twentieth Century Literature*, 17 (1971), pp. 143–59; Elizabeth Kerr, 'The Women of Yoknapatawpha', *University of Mississippi Studies in English*, 15 (1978), p. 94. Brooks offers one of the more sympathetic treatments of Mr Compson. While Mrs Compson has been the subject of fewer diatribes in recent criticism, in general the critical tendency seems to be to judge her while analyzing her husband, thus implicitly granting him a more privileged position.

9 Minrose C. Gwin, *The Feminine and Faulkner: Reading (Beyond) Sexual Difference* (Knoxville: University of Tennessee Press, 1990), p. 46.

10 Madelon Sprengnether, *The Spectral Mother: Freud, Feminism, and Psychoanalysis* (Ithaca: Cornell University Press, 1986), p. 232.

11 Sprengnether (1986), p. 232. Quoted Clarke (1994), p. 14.

12 Clarke (1994), pp. 20–23, 30.

13 [*Clarke's Note*:] Philip [M.] Weinstein also discusses Caroline Compson in a fine essay, '"If I Could Say Mother"', which I first saw after this chapter was written. While we come to many of the same conclusions, he focuses more on her failure and lack of power. [*Editor's Note*:] See Weinstein, '"If I Could Say Mother": Construing the Unsayable about Faulknerian Maternity', in Lothar Hönnighausen, ed., *Faulkner's Discourse: An International Symposium* (Tubingen: Max Niemeyer Verlag, 1989), pp. 3–15.

14 André Bleikasten, '*Light in August*: The Closed Society and Its Subjects', in Michael Millgate, ed., *New Essays on 'Light in August'*, The American Novel Series (Cambridge: Cambridge University Press, 1987), p. 87.

15 [*Clarke's Note*:] Weinstein [(1989), p. 5] also makes this point.

16 Clarke (1994), pp. 30–32.

17 Clarke (1994), p. 32.

18 Sally R. Page, *Faulkner's Women: Characterization and Meaning* (Deland: Everett/Edwards, 1972), p. 70.

19 David Williams, *Faulkner's Women: The Myth and the Muse* (Montreal: McGill-Queens University Press, 1977), p. 11.

20 Weinstein (1989), p. 7.

21 Jehlen (1976), p. 76.

22 Thadious M. Davis, *Faulkner's 'Negro': Art and the Southern Context*, Southern Literary Studies series (Baton Rouge: Louisiana State University Press, 1983), p. 106. Extract in Bloom (1988), pp. 69–78.

23 Clarke (1994), pp. 32–34.

24 [*Clarke's Note*:] Doreen Fowler's excellent article, 'Matricide and the Mother's Revenge' ['Matricide and the Mother's Revenge: *As I Lay Dying*', *Faulkner Journal: Special Issue on Faulkner and Feminisms*, 4 (Fall 1988/Spring 1989), pp. 113–25], appeared while I was revising this chapter after presenting it at the California State Symposium on American Literature in May 1989. Fowler and I have independently reached many similar conclusions and employed similar methodology, relying on feminist revisions of Lacanian models and Margaret Homans's treatment of the literal and figurative. But Fowler's treatment focuses more on the Lacanian move from the Imaginary to the Symbolic, while I emphasize creativity as

an interplay between the physical and the linguistic. [*Editor's Note:*] See Doreen Fowler's book *Faulkner: The Return of the Repressed* (Charlottesville and London: University Press of Virginia, 1997).

25 Warwick Wadlington, *Reading Faulknerian Tragedy* (Ithaca: Cornell University Press, 1987), p.105.

26 Robert Frost, *Complete Poems* (London: Cape, 1957), p.144.

27 Luce Irigaray, *The Sex Which is Not One*, trans. Catherine Porter (Ithaca: Cornell University Press, 1985), p.79.

28 See Domna C. Stanton, 'Difference on Trial: A Critique of the Maternal Metaphor in Cixous, Irigaray, and Kristeva', in Nancy Miller, ed., *The Poetics of Gender* (New York: Columbia University Press, 1986).

29 Constance Pierce, 'Being, Knowing, and Saying in the "Addie" Section of Faulkner's *As I Lay Dying*', *Twentieth Century Literature: A Scholarly and Literary Journal*, 26 (1980), p.297.

30 Fowler (1988/89), p.116.

31 T.H. Adamowski, 'Meet Mrs Bundren: *As I Lay Dying* – Gentility, Tact, and Psychoanalysis', *University of Toronto Quarterly*, 49 (Spring 1980), p.225.

32 Bleikasten (1990), p.40.

33 Julia Kristeva, *Powers of Horror: An Essay on Abjection*, trans. Leon S. Roudiez (New York: Columbia University Press, 1982) , p.3; Clarke (1994), pp.35–40.

34 William Dahill-Baue, 'Insignificant Monkeys: Preaching Black English in Faulkner's *The Sound and the Fury* and Morrison's *The Bluest Eye* and *Beloved*', *Mississippi Quarterly*, 3 (Summer 1996), p.457.

35 Dahill-Baue (1996), pp.458–59.

36 Dahill-Baue (1996), p.459.

37 Dahill-Baue, (1996), p.460.

38 Morrison's *Beloved* has already been the subject of an Icon Critical Guide. See Carl Plasa, ed., *Toni Morrison: 'Beloved'*, Icon Critical Guides series (Cambridge: Icon Books, 1997); Columbia Critical Guides series (New York: Columbia University Press, 1998).

39 Blotner (1974), vol. 2, pp.1038–39.

40 Claudia Dreifus, 'Chloe Wofford Talks About Toni Morrison', *The New York Times Magazine* (11 September 1994), p.73.

41 [*Dahill-Baue's Note:*] Baldwin suggests, in his scathing critique 'Faulkner and Desegregation', that Faulkner indeed understands the grim realities of the situation of blacks in the South just prior to the Civil Rights movement, but that he masks it with statements such as 'go slow', which Justice Thurgood Marshall reportedly interpreted as meaning 'don't go'. According to Baldwin, 'the time Faulkner asks for does not exist – and he is not the only Southerner who knows it. There is never time in the future in which we will work out our salvation. The challenge is in the moment, the time is always now'. [Baldwin (1964), pp.101, 107.]

42 Baldwin (1964), p.102.

43 [*Dahill-Baue's Note:*] The search for authorial intent has been proven futile by the New Critics, and both Foucault and Barthes have sounded the death knell of the author-function; in this instance, the text itself suggests this correlation, whether or not Faulkner intended it. The question is not whether Faulkner himself was racist, but rather the question is whether his fiction advanced racist characterizations or, on the other hand, resisted and problematized them.

44 Henry Louis Gates, Jr, *The Signifying Monkey: A Theory of African-American Literary Criticism* (New York: Oxford University Press, 1988), p.52.

45 Gates (1988), pp.75–76.

46 [*Dahill-Baue's Note:*] I use this term after Geneva Smitherman, who puns on its exclusivity by abbreviating it 'WE' while playing on the 'non-standard' usage of the verb 'to be' of Black English, abbreviating it 'BE'. Smitherman combines these two abbreviations in a neat act of signifyin(g) the 'White English'/'Black English' controversy: 'WE BE'. Geneva Smitherman, '"God Don't Never Change": Black English from a Black Perspective', *College English*, 34 (1973), p.828.

47 [*Dahill-Baue's Note*:] For support and extension of this argument, see James M. Mellard, 'Faulkner's *Commedia*: Synecdoche and Anagogic Symbolism in *The Sound and the Fury*', *Journal of English and Germanic Philology*, 83 (1984), pp. 534–46. Mellard takes up where I leave off, examining the 'impact upon central characters' of Reverend Shegog's sermon: 'Dilsey stands to the novel's characters as Christ stands to humanity, for it is she whose life fleshes out – in all its ambiguity – the redemptive message of the Reverend Shegog' (pp. 541, 546).

48 [*Dahill-Baue's Note*:] 'Someone spread the story years ago . . . that he was a graduate of the divinity school' [*The Sound and the Fury*, p. 96].

49 Mark W. Lencho, 'Dialect Variation in *The Sound and the Fury*: A Study of Faulkner's Use of Black English', *Mississippi Quarterly*, 41 (Summer 1988), p. 406.

50 Lencho (1988), p. 406, 408.

51 Lencho (1988), p. 410.

52 Lencho (1988), p. 410.

53 Dahill-Baue (1996), pp. 464–69.

54 Dahill-Blaue (1996), p. 473. [*Dahill-Baue's Note*:] Quoted in [James Baldwin, 'If Black English Isn't a Language, Then Tell Me, What Is?', in Gilbert H. Muller, ed., *Major Modern Essayists* (Englewood Cliffs, New Jersey: Prentice-Hall, 1991), p.] 189.

55 Kartiganer and Abadie (1996), p. ix.

56 Kartiganer and Abadie (1996), p. 141.

57 Kartiganer and Abadie (1996), p. 208.

58 William Faulkner, *The Sound and the Fury*, David Minter, ed., Norton Critical Edition, 2nd edn (New York: Norton, 1987), pp. 227, 228.

59 Cowley (1977), p. 710.

60 [*Waid's Note*:] [Lodge's words are cited] by Susan Gubar in 'The Blank Page', *Writing and Sexual Difference*, Elizabeth Abel, ed. (Chicago: University of Chicago Press, 1982), p. 77.

61 William Faulkner, in *Go Down, Moses* (Harmondsworth: Penguin, 1960), p. 259.

62 Kartiganer (1979), p. 13.

63 [*Waid's Note*:] [Bleikasten (1976)],

p. 53. For an important discussion of the significance of Caddy and the role of loss in the novel, see John T. Matthews, *The Play of Faulkner's Language* (Ithaca: Cornell University Press, 1982), pp. 17–23, 91–114. [Extract in Bloom (1988), pp. 79–102.]

64 Gwynn and Blotner (1959), p. 6.

65 Gary Lee Stonum, *Faulkner's Career: An Internal History* (Ithaca: Cornell University Press, 1979), p. 76. Extract in Bloom (1988), pp. 39–56.

66 [*Waid's Note*:] André Bleikasten links this scene to the '"primal fantasies" postulated by psychoanalysis'. Noting the emphasis on looking, he associates the scene with Freud's description of the male fear of castration upon discovering the difference of the female genitals. He reads this image as 'the emblem of a dual revelation: the simultaneous discovery of the difference between the sexes and of death' (Bleikasten (1976), pp. 54, 55. Michel Gresset comments on 'the exorbitant privilege the eye and the act of looking enjoy in Faulkner's novels' and the significance of 'the impotent Popeye's exopthalmia [bulging eyes]'. He argues that 'Freud went as far as to say that an organ, the eye for instance, could assume "as the consequence of an exaggerated erogenous zone, the conduct peculiar to the genital organ"'. In his understanding of the erotic potential of the eye, Gresset focuses on the idea of the penetrating gaze and writes about what he calls 'The Optical Rape' in *Sanctuary* (Gresset, *Fascination: Faulkner's Fiction 1919–1936* (Durham: Duke University Press, 1989), pp. 177, 157–211). See also Sigmund Freud, *Three Contributions to the Theory of Sex*, trans. A.A. Brill (New York: The Nervous and Mental Disease Publishing Co., 1925), pp. 23–24.

67 [*Editor's Note*:] For 'the associations of the Ethiopian queen Candace with eunuchs', see Irwin (1975), pp. 51–52, and the Acts of the Apostles 8: 26–40.

68 William Faulkner, *Mosquitoes* (New York: Boni and Liveright, 1927), p. 197.

69 Cowley (1977), pp.709–10.

70 Cowley (1977), p.710.

71 [*Waid's Note*:] John [T.] Irwin describes this process in terms of Quentin's desire to gain control of the narrative. He also discusses the idea of taking revenge by supplanting the father as the narrative authority and through the telling of the tale. [Irwin (1975), pp.82–135].

72 [*Waid's Note*:] See [Bleikasten (1973), p. 120]. Doreen Fowler writes: 'It is motherhood – symbolized by Addie's reversed, head-to-foot position in the coffin like a fetus in the mother's womb, a position imposed by '"them durn women"' (pp.82, 83) – that disturbs the balance' (Fowler (1988/1989), p.118).

73 [*Editor's Note*:] For other discussions of the pictorial aspects of *As I Lay Dying*, see Watson G. Branch, 'Darl Bundren's "Cubistic" Vision', *Texas Studies in Language and Literature*, 19 (Spring 1977), pp.42–59; reprinted in Dianne L. Cox, ed., *William Faulkner's 'As I Lay Dying': A Critical Casebook*, Garland Faulkner Casebooks series, vol. 4 (New York and London: Garland, 1985), pp.111–29; John Tucker, 'William Faulkner's *As I Lay Dying*: Working Out the Cubistic Bugs', *Texas Studies in Language and Literature* (Winter 1984), 26:4, pp.388–404.

74 Faulkner (1960), p.259.

75 William Faulkner, *Flags in the Dust* (New York: Random House, 1974), p.173. [*Editor's Note*:] As Waid has already observed (p.247, note 6), '*Flags in the Dust* was the original manuscript which in a cut and edited form appeared as *Sartoris*'.

76 Kartiganer and Abadie (1996), pp.235–47.

77 Meriwether and Millgate (1968), p.255.

SELECT BIBLIOGRAPHY

Works of William Faulkner
Novels
Details of first US and UK editions of all Faulkner's novels, and of recent US and UK editions of *The Sound and the Fury* and *As I Lay Dying*, are given below.

Soldiers' Pay. New York: Boni and Liveright, 1926. London: Chatto and Windus, 1930.

Mosquitoes. New York: Boni and Liveright, 1927. London: Chatto and Windus, 1964.

Sartoris. New York: Harcourt, Brace, 1929. London: Chatto and Windus, 1932.

The Sound and the Fury. New York: Cape and Smith, 1929. London: Chatto and Windus, 1931. Corrected edn: New York: Random House, 1984. US paperback edn: New York: Vintage, 1990. Norton Critical Edition, 2nd edn, David Minter, ed.: New York: Norton, 1994. UK paperback edn: London: Vintage, 1995.

As I Lay Dying. New York: Cape and Smith, 1932. London: Chatto and Windus, 1935. Corrected edn: New York: Random House, 1987. US paperback edn: New York: Vintage, 1990. UK paperback edn: London: Vintage, 1996.

Sanctuary. New York: Cape and Smith, 1931. London: Chatto and Windus, 1935.

Light in August. New York: Smith and Haas, 1932. London: Chatto and Windus, 1933.

Pylon. New York: Smith and Haas, 1935. London: Chatto and Windus, 1935.

Absalom, Absalom! New York: Random House, 1936. London: Chatto and Windus, 1937.

The Unvanquished. New York: Random House, 1938. London: Chatto and Windus, 1938.

The Wild Palms. New York: Random House, 1939. London: Chatto and Windus, 1939.

The Hamlet. New York: Random House, 1940. London: Chatto and Windus, 1940.

Intruder in the Dust. New York: Random House, 1948. London: Chatto and Windus, 1949.

Requiem for a Nun. New York: Random House, 1951. London: Chatto and Windus, 1953.

A Fable. New York: Random House, 1954. London: Chatto and Windus, 1955.

The Town. New York: Random House, 1957. London: Chatto and Windus, 1958.

The Mansion. New York: Random House, 1959. London: Chatto and Windus, 1961.

The Reivers. New York: Random House, 1962. London: Chatto and Windus, 1962.

Flags in the Dust. Douglas Day, ed. Uncut version of *Sartoris* (1929). New York: Random House, 1973.

Stories

These 13. New York: Cape and Smith, 1931. London: Chatto and Windus, 1933.

Doctor Martino and Other Stories. New York: Smith and Haas, 1934.

Go Down, Moses and Other Stories. New York: Random House, 1942. London: Chatto and Windus, 1942.

Knight's Gambit. New York: Random House, 1949. London: Chatto and Windus, 1951.

Collected Stories of William Faulkner. New York: Random House, 1950. London: Chatto and Windus, 1951.

Big Woods. New York: Random House, 1955.

Poems

The Marble Faun. Boston: The Four Seas Co., 1924.

A Green Bough. New York: Smith and Haas, 1932.

The Marble Faun and A Green Bough. New York: Random House, no date.

Play

The Marionettes, with an Introduction and Textual Apparatus by Noel Polk. Charlottesville: University Press of Virginia for The Bibliographical Society of the University of Virginia, 1977.

Letters

Blotner, Joseph L, ed. *Selected Letters of William Faulkner*. New York: Random House, 1977.

Interviews, conferences

Gwynn, Frederick L. and Blotner, Joseph L., eds. *Faulkner in the University: Class Conferences at the University of Virginia 1957–1958*. Charlottesville, Virginia: University of Virginia Press, 1959. Extracts in Cowan (1968), pp.18–24; Bleikasten (1982), pp.21–29; Bloom (1990), pp.9–11.

Jeliffe, Robert A., ed. *Faulkner at Nagano*. Tokyo: Kenyusha Press, 1956.

Meriwether, James B. and Millgate, Michael, eds. *Lion in the Garden: Interviews with William Faulkner, 1926–1962*. New York: Random House, 1968.

Concordance

Capps, Jack L., ed. '*As I Lay Dying*': *A Concordance to the Novel*. Faulkner Concordances series no 1. Ann Arbor, Michigan: Faulkner Concordance Advisory Board with the support of the Faculty Development and Research Fund, US Military Academy, 1977.

Polk, Noel and Privratsky, Kenneth L., eds. *'The Sound and the Fury': A Concordance to the Novel.* 2 vols. Faulkner Concordances series no. 5. Ann Arbor, Michigan: Faulkner Concordance Advisory Board with the support of the Faculty Development and Research Fund, US Military Academy, 1980.

Biographies

Blotner, Joseph. *Faulkner: A Biography.* 2 vols. New York: Random House, 1974. London: Chatto and Windus, 1974.

Faulkner, John. *My Brother Bill: An Affectionate Reminiscence.* London: Gollancz, 1964.

Karl, Frederick R. *William Faulkner: American Writer.* London and Boston: Faber and Faber, 1989.

Williamson, Joel. *William Faulkner and Southern History.* New York and Oxford: Oxford University Press, 1993.

Bibliographies

Bassett, John E. 'William Faulkner's *The Sound and the Fury*: An Annotated Checklist of Criticism'. *Resources for American Literary Study*, vol. 1 (1971), pp. 217–46.

—— *William Faulkner: An Annotated Checklist of Criticism.* New York: Lewis, 1972.

—— *Faulkner: An Annotated Checklist of Recent Criticism.* Kent: Kent State University Press, 1983.

—— *Faulkner in the Eighties: An Annotated Critical Bibliography*, Scarecrow Author Bibliographies series no. 88. Metuchen, New Jersey and London: Scarecrow Press, 1991.

Meriwether, James B. *The Literary Career of William Faulkner: A Bibliographical Study.* Princeton: Princeton University Press, 1961.

The Modern Language Association (MLA) database is an invaluable guide to more recent Faulkner criticism, though it should not be regarded as comprehensive. It can be accessed through many university and college computer systems.

Journals

The Faulkner Journal. Began Fall 1985. Usually twice yearly.

Faulkner Newsletter. Began 1980. Quarterly.

Faulkner Studies (published in Japan). Began 1991. Usually twice yearly.

Mississippi Quarterly. Summer issues, from 1971.

William Faulkner: Materials, Studies, and Criticism (published in Japan). Began 1978.

Studies of Faulkner's critical reputation

Emerson, O.B. *Faulkner's Early Literary Reputation in America.* Studies in Modern Literature, no. 30. Ann Arbor, Michigan: UMI Research Press, 1984.

Schwarz, Lawrence H. *Creating Faulkner's Reputation: The Politics of Modern Literary Criticism*. Knoxville: University of Tennessee Press, 1988.

General critical studies of Faulkner
Books
Adams, Richard P. *Faulkner: Myth and Motion*. Princeton: Princeton University Press, 1968.

Bleikasten, André. *The Ink of Melancholy: Faulkner's Novels from 'The Sound and the Fury' to 'Light in August'*. Bloomington: Indiana University Press, 1990.

Brooks, Cleanth. *William Faulkner: The Yoknapatawpha Country*. New Haven and London: Yale University Press, 1963. Extract on *The Sound and the Fury* in Cowan (1968), pp.63–70.

—— *William Faulkner: First Encounters*. New Haven: Yale University Press, 1983. Extract in Bloom (1990), pp.119–29.

Campbell, Harry Modean and Foster, Ruel E. *William Faulkner: A Critical Appraisal*. Norman: University of Oklahoma Press, 1951.

Clarke, Deborah. *Robbing the Mother: Women in Faulkner*. Jackson: University Press of Mississippi, 1994.

Coindreau, Maurice. *The Time of William Faulkner: A French View of Modern American Fiction*. George McMillan Reeves, ed. and chiefly trans. Columbia, South Carolina: University of South Carolina Press, 1971.

Davis, Thadious M. *Faulkner's 'Negro': Art and the Southern Context*. Southern Literary Studies series. Baton Rouge: Louisiana State University Press, 1983. Extract in Bloom (1988), pp.69–78.

Fowler, Doreen. *Faulkner: The Return of the Repressed*. Charlottesville and London: University Press of Virginia, 1997.

Gresset, Michel. *Fascination: Faulkner's Fiction, 1919–1936*. Adapted from the French by Thomas West. Durham: Duke University Press, 1989.

Gwin, Minrose C. *The Feminine and Faulkner: Reading (Beyond) Sexual Difference*. Knoxville: University of Tennessee Press, 1990.

Howe, Irving. *William Faulkner: A Critical Study*. New York: Random House, 1952. Second edn, 1962. Third edn, revised and expanded: Chicago and London: University of Chicago Press, 1975. Extract from second edn on *The Sound and the Fury* in Cowan (1968), pp.33–39.

Jehlen, Myra. *Class and Character in Faulkner's South*. New York: Columbia University Press, 1976.

Kartiganer, Donald M. *The Fragile Thread: The Meaning of Form in Faulkner's Novels*. Amherst: University of Massachusetts Press, 1979. Extract in Bloom (1988), pp.23–38.

Kinney, Arthur F. *Faulkner's Narrative Poetics: Style as Vision*. Amherst: University of Massachusetts Press, 1978.

Matthews, John T. *The Play of Faulkner's Language*. Ithaca: Cornell University Press, 1982. Extract in Bloom (1988), pp.79–102.

Millgate, Michael. *The Achievement of William Faulkner*. London: Constable, 1966.

Minter, David. *William Faulkner: His Life and Work*. Baltimore: Johns Hopkins University Press, 1980. Extract in Bloom (1990), pp.33–38.

Mortimer, Gail L. *Faulkner's Rhetoric of Loss: A Study in Perception and Meaning.* Austin: University of Texas, 1983. Extract in Bloom (1988), pp. 103–15; Bloom (1990), pp. 37–38.

Page, Sally R. *Faulkner's Women: Characterization and Meaning.* Deland: Everett/Edwards, 1972.

Reed, Joseph W., Jr. *Faulkner's Narrative.* New Haven: Yale University Press, 1973.

Slatoff, Walter J. *Quest for Failure: A Study of William Faulkner.* Westport, Connecticut: Greenwood Press, 1972. Extract from 1960 edn in Cowan (1968), pp. 93–96.

Snead, James A. *Figures of Division: William Faulkner's Major Novels.* New York and London: Methuen, 1986.

Stonum, Gary Lee. *Faulkner's Career: An Internal Literary History.* Ithaca: Cornell University Press, 1979. Extract in Bloom (1988), pp. 39–56.

Sundquist, Eric J. *Faulkner: The House Divided.* Baltimore and London: Johns Hopkins University Press, 1983. Extract in Bloom (1988), pp. 117–45.

Vickery, Olga W. *The Novels of William Faulkner: A Critical Interpretation.* Baton Rouge: Louisiana State University Press, 1959. Revised edn: Baton Rouge: Louisiana State University Press, 1964. Extract on *As I Lay Dying* from 1959 edn in Hoffman and Vickery (1960), pp. 232–47; extract on *The Sound and the Fury* from 1964 edn in Cowan (1968), pp. 40–52 and Bloom (1990), pp. 11–13.

Volpe, Edmond L. *A Reader's Guide to William Faulkner.* London: Thames and Hudson, 1964. Chronology of Scenes and Guide to Scene Shifts in Sections 1 and 2 of *The Sound and the Fury* reprinted and adapted in Cowan (1968), pp. 103–8.

Wadlington, Warwick. *Reading Faulknerian Tragedy.* Ithaca: Cornell University Press, 1987.

Waggoner, Hyatt H. *William Faulkner: From Jefferson to the World.* Kentucky: University of Kentucky Press, 1959. Extract in Cowan (1968), pp. 97–101.

Williams, David. *Faulkner's Women: The Myth and the Muse.* Montreal: McGill-Queens University Press, 1977.

Essay/review collections

Bassett, John, ed. *William Faulkner: The Critical Heritage.* Critical Heritage series. London and Boston: Routledge and Kegan Paul, 1975.

Hoffman, Frederick J. and Vickery, Olga W., eds. *William Faulkner: Two Decades of Criticism.* East Lansing: Michigan State College Press, 1951, 1954.

Hoffman, Frederick J. and Vickery, Olga W. *William Faulkner: Three Decades of Criticism.* East Lansing: Michigan State University Press, 1960.

Hönnighausen, Lothar, ed. *Faulkner's Discourse: An International Symposium.* Tubingen: Max Niemeyer Verlag, 1989.

Inge, M. Thomas, ed. *William Faulkner: The Contemporary Reviews.* American Critical Archives series no. 5. Cambridge: Cambridge University Press, 1995.

Kartiganer, Donald M. and Abadie, Ann J., eds. *Faulkner and Ideology: Faulkner and Yoknapatawpha, 1992*. Jackson: University Press of Mississippi, 1995.

Kartiganer, Donald M. and Abadie, Ann J., eds. *Faulkner and the Artist: Faulkner and Yoknapatawpha, 1993*. Jackson: University Press of Mississippi, 1996.

Wagner, Linda Welshimer, ed. *William Faulkner: Four Decades of Criticism*. East Lansing: Michigan State University Press, 1973.

Warren, Robert Penn, ed. *Faulkner: A Collection of Critical Essays*, Twentieth Century Views series. Englewood Cliffs, New Jersey: Prentice-Hall, 1966.

Weinstein, Philip W., ed. *The Cambridge Companion to William Faulkner*. Cambridge Companions to Literature series. Cambridge: Cambridge University Press, 1995.

Essays

Aiken, Conrad. 'William Faulkner: The Novel as Form'. *Atlantic Monthly*, 144 (1939), pp. 650–54. Reprinted in Hoffman and Vickery (1954), pp. 139–47; Hoffman and Vickery (1960), pp. 135–42; Warren (1966), pp. 46–52.

Baldwin, James. 'Faulkner and Desegregation', in *Nobody Knows My Name: More Notes of a Native Son*. London: Michael Joseph, 1964, pp. 101–7.

Coindreau, Maurice. 'France and the Contemporary American Novel'. Trans. Madeline Ashton. *Kansas City University Review*, 3:4 (1937), pp. 273–79. Reprinted in Coindreau (1971), pp. 3–13.

Cowley, Malcolm. 'William Faulkner's Human Comedy'. *New York Times Book Review* (29 October 1944), p. 4.

—— 'William Faulkner Revisited'. *Saturday Review of Literature*, 28 (14 April 1945), pp. 13–16.

—— 'William Faulkner's Legend of the South'. *Sewanee Review*, 53 (July 1945), pp. 343–61. Reprinted in Allen Tate, ed., *A Southern Vanguard*. New York: Prentice-Hall, 1947, pp. 13–27.

—— 'Introduction'. *The Portable Faulkner*. New York: Viking, 1946, pp. 1–24. Revised and expanded edn: London: Penguin, 1977, pp. vii–xxxiii. Original 'Introduction' reprinted in Hoffman and Vickery (1954), pp. 82–101; Hoffman and Vickery (1960), pp. 94–109; Warren (1966), pp. 34–45.

—— 'An Introduction to William Faulkner' in John Aldridge, ed. *Critiques and Essays on Modern Fiction 1920–1951. Representing the Achievement of Modern American and British Critics*. New York: Ronald Press, 1952, pp. 427–46.

Davis, Thadious M. 'Reading Faulkner's Compson Appendix: History from the Margins', in Kartiganer and Abadie (1995), pp. 238–52.

Geismar, Maxwell. 'William Faulkner: The Negro and the Female'. *Writers in Crisis*. Boston: Houghton Mifflin, 1942, pp. 143–83. Extracts on Faulkner in Warren (1966), pp. 278–81.

Kerr, Elizabeth. 'The Women of Yoknapatawpha'. *University of Mississippi Studies in English*, 15 (1978), pp. 83–100.

Leavis, F.R. 'Dostoevsky and Dickens'. *Scrutiny: A Quarterly Review*, 2:1 (June 1933), pp. 91–93. Extracts on Faulkner reprinted in Warren (1966), pp. 277–78.

Lester, Cheryl. 'To Market, To Market: *The Portable Faulkner*'. *Criticism: A Quarterly for Literature and the Arts*, 33 (Summer 1987), pp. 371–92.

O'Donnell, George Marion. 'Faulkner's Mythology'. *Kenyon Review* (Summer 1939), pp. 285–99. Reprinted in Hoffman and Vickery (1954), pp. 49–62; Hoffman and Vickery (1960), pp. 82–93; Warren (1966), pp. 23–33; Wagner (1973), pp. 83–93.

Swink, Helen. 'William Faulkner: The Novelist as Oral Narrator', *Georgia Review*, 26 (Summer 1972), pp. 183–209.

Waid, Candace. 'The Signifying Eye: Faulkner's Artists and the Engendering of Art' in Kartiganer and Abadie (1996), pp. 208–49.

Warren, Robert Penn. 'William Faulkner'. *New Republic*, 115 (12 August 1946), pp. 176–80. Reprinted in Hoffman and Vickery (1954), pp. 82–101; Warren, *Selected Essays*. New York: Random House, 1958; Hoffman and Vickery (1960), pp. 109–24; Wagner (1973), pp. 94–109.

Weinstein, Philip M. '"If I Could Say Mother": Construing the Unsayable about Faulknerian Maternity', in Hönnighausen (1989), pp. 3–15.

Williamson, Joel. 'A Historian Looks at Faulkner the Artist', in Kartiganer and Abadie (1996), pp. 3–21.

Studies of *The Sound and the Fury*
Books

Bleikasten, André. *The Most Splendid Failure: Faulkner's 'The Sound and the Fury'*. Bloomington and London: Indiana University Press, 1976. Extract in Bloom (1990), pp. 73–83.

Irwin, John T. *Doubling and Incest/Repetition and Revenge: A Speculative Reading of Faulkner*. Baltimore and London: Johns Hopkins University Press, 1975. Second expanded edn, 1996. Also discusses *Absalom, Absalom!* Extract from first edn in Bloom (1988), pp. 9–22; Bloom (1990), pp. 59–67.

Matthews, John T. *'The Sound and the Fury': Faulkner and the Lost Cause*. Twayne's Masterwork Studies series no. 61. Boston: Twayne, 1990.

Pamphlet

Scott, Evelyn. *On William Faulkner's 'The Sound and the Fury'*. New York: Cape and Smith, 1929. Reprinted Norwood Editions (no place of publication given), 1977. Extract in Cowan (1968), pp. 25–29; reprinted in Bassett (1975), pp. 76–81.

Essay/review collections

Bloom, Harold, ed. *William Faulkner's 'The Sound and the Fury'*. Modern Critical Interpretations series. New York and New Haven, Philadelphia: Chelsea House, 1988.

Bloom, Harold, ed. *Caddy Compson*. Major Literary Characters series. New York and Philadelphia: Chelsea House, 1990.

Cowan, Michael H., ed. *Twentieth Century Interpretations of 'The Sound and the Fury'*. Englewood Cliffs, New Jersey: Prentice-Hall, 1968.

Hahn, Stephen and Kinney, Arthur F. *Approaches to Teaching Faulkner's 'The Sound and the Fury'*. Approaches to Teaching World Literature series. New York: The Modern Language Association of America, 1996.

Meriwether, James B., ed. *The Merrill Studies in 'The Sound and the Fury'*. Charles E. Merrill Studies series. Columbus, Ohio: Charles E. Merrill, 1970.

Polk, Noel, ed. *New Essays on 'The Sound and the Fury'*. The American Novel series. Cambridge: Cambridge University Press, 1993.

Essays

Baum, Catherine B. '"The Beautiful One": Caddy Compson as Heroine of *The Sound and the Fury'*, *Modern Fiction Studies*, 13 (Spring 1967), pp. 33–44. Reprinted in Bloom (1990), pp. 39–49.

Benson, Jackson J. 'Quentin Compson: Self-Portrait of a Young Artist's Emotions'. *Twentieth Century Literature*, 17 (1971), pp. 143–59.

Bowling, Lawrence Edward. 'Faulkner: Technique of *The Sound and the Fury'*. *Kenyon Review*, 10 (Autumn 1948), pp. 552–66.

Brown, May Cameron. 'The Language of Chaos: Quentin Compson in *The Sound and the Fury'*, *American Literature*, 51:4 (January 1980), pp. 544–53.

Cohen, Philip and Fowler, Doreen. 'Faulkner's Introduction to *The Sound and the Fury'*, *American Literature*, 62:2 (June 1990), pp. 262–83. This is the fullest version of the surviving manuscript and typescript drafts of Faulkner's Introduction for the proposed 1933 Modern Library edition of *The Sound and the Fury*, which was never published. Less full versions are in James B. Meriwether, 'An Introduction to *The Sound and the Fury'*, *Southern Review*, 8 (1972), pp. 705–10; Meriwether, 'An Introduction to *The Sound and the Fury'*, *Mississippi Quarterly*, 26 (1973), pp. 156–61; 'Introduction to *The Sound and the Fury*, 1933' in Bleikasten (1982), pp. 7–14. The material in Bleikasten is the fullest prior to Cohen and Fowler (1990).

Geffen, Arthur. 'Profane Time, Sacred Time, and Confederate Time' in *The Sound and the Fury'*, *Studies in American Fiction*, 2, pp. 175–97.

Lencho, Mark W. 'Dialect Variation in *The Sound and the Fury*: A Study of Faulkner's Use of Black English'. *Mississippi Quarterly*, 41 (Summer 1988), pp. 403–19.

Lester, Cheryl. 'Racial Awareness and Arrested Development: *The Sound and the Fury* and the Great Migration (1915–1928)'. Weinstein (1995), pp. 123–45.

Mellard, James M. 'Faulkner's *Commedia:* Synecdoche and Anagogic Symbolism in *The Sound and the Fury'*. *Journal of English and Germanic Philology*, 83 (1984), pp. 534–46.

Meriwether, James B. 'Notes on the Textual History of *The Sound and the Fury'*. *Papers of the Bibliographical Society of America*, 56 (Third Quarter, 1962), pp. 285–316. Revised version in Meriwether (1970), pp. 1–32.

Messerli, Douglas. 'The Problem of Time in *The Sound and the Fury*: A Critical Reassessment and Reinterpretation', *The Southern Literary*

Journal, 6:2 (Spring 1974), pp. 37–41. Extract in Bloom (1990), pp. 22–25.

Milroy, Sandra M. 'Dilsey: Faulkner's Black Mammy in *The Sound and the Fury*', *Negro Historical Bulletin*, 46:3 (1983), pp. 70–71.

Sartre, Jean-Paul. 'À propos de *Le Bruit et Le Fureur:* La temporalité chez Faulkner' in Sartre, *Situations I*. Paris: Gallimard, 1947, pp. 70–81. Trans. Annette Michelson as 'On *The Sound and the Fury*: Time in the Work of Faulkner' in Sartre, *Literary and Philosophical Essays*. London: Radius/Hutchinson, 1955; 1968; trans. Martine Darmon, with assistance from Frederick J. Hoffman and Olga W. Vickery in Hoffman and Vickery (1960), pp. 225–32. Michelson translation in Warren (1966), pp. 87–93.

Spilka, Mark. 'Quentin Compson's Universal Grief'. *Contemporary Fiction*, 11 (1970), pp. 451–69.

Stewart, George R., and Backus, Joseph M. 'Each in its Ordered Place: Structure and Narrative in "Benjy's Section" of *The Sound and the Fury*'. *American Literature*, 29 (January 1958), pp. 440–56.

Underwood, Henry J., Jr. 'Sartre on *The Sound and the Fury*: Some Errors'. *Modern Fiction Studies*, 12 (1996), pp. 477–79.

Wagner, Linda W. 'Language and Act: Caddy Compson'. *Southern Literary Journal*, 14:2 (Spring 1982), pp. 49–61. Reprinted in Bloom (1990), pp. 108–18.

Reviews

Anon. 'Decayed Gentility'. *The New York Times Book Review* (10 November 1929), p. 28. Reprinted in Bassett (1975), p. 93.

Crickmay, Edward. 'Recent Fiction'. *Sunday Referee* (26 April 1931), p. 9. Section on *The Sound and the Fury* reprinted in Bassett (1975), pp. 90–91.

Davenport, Basil. 'Tragic Frustration'. *Saturday Review of Literature* (28 December 1929), pp. 601–2.

Fadiman, Clifton P. 'Hardly Worth While'. *The Nation*, 130: 3367 (15 January 1930), pp. 74–75. Extract in Inge (1995), pp. 38–39.

Fitts, Dudley. 'Two Aspects of Telemachus'. *Hound and Horn*, 3 (April–June 1930), pp. 445–50. Reprinted (with omission of *Sound and Fury* quotation) in Bassett (1975), pp. 87–89.

Hansen, Harry. 'The First Reader'. [New York] *World* (9 October 1929), p. 16.

McClure, John [Baker, Julia K. W[etherill]]. 'Literature and Less: A Page on Books of the [D]ay', [New Orleans] *Times-Picayune* (29 June 1930), p. 23. Extract in Inge (1995), pp. 39–40.

Myers, Walter L. 'Make-Beliefs'. *Virginia Quarterly Review*, 6 (January 1930), pp. 139–48 (pp. 139–41 focus on *The Sound and the Fury*).

Robbins, Frances Lamont. 'Novels of the Week'. *Outlook and Independent* (16 October 1929), p. 268.

Saxon, Lyle. 'A Family Breaks Up'. *New York Herald Tribune Books* (13 October 1929), p. 3.

Smith, Henry Nash. 'Three Southern Novels'. *Southwest Review*, 15 (Autumn 1929), pp. iii–iv. Reprinted in Inge (1995), pp. 33–34; Bassett (1975), pp. 85–87.

Swinnerton, Frank. 'Writers Who Know Life', *The Evening News* (15 May

1931), p.8. Section on *The Sound and The Fury* reprinted in Bassett (1975), pp.91–92.

Studies of *As I Lay Dying*
Book
Bleikasten, André. *Faulkner's 'As I Lay Dying'*. Revised and enlarged edn. Trans. Roger Little with the collaboration of the author. Bloomington and London: Indiana University Press, 1973.

Essay/review collection
Cox, Dianne L., ed. William Faulkner's *'As I Lay Dying': A Critical Casebook*. Garland Faulkner Casebooks series vol. 3. New York and London: Garland, 1985.

Essays
Adamowski, T.H. 'Meet Mrs Bundren: *As I Lay Dying* – Gentility, Tact, and Psychoanalysis'. *University of Toronto Quarterly*, 49 (Spring 1980), pp.205–27.

Bedient, Calvin. 'Pride and Nakedness in *As I Lay Dying*'. *Modern Language Quarterly*, 29:1 (March 1968), pp.61–76. Reprinted in Cox (1985), pp.95–110.

Branch, Watson G. 'Darl Bundren's 'Cubistic' Vision'. *Texas Studies in Language and Literature*, 19 (Spring 1977), pp.42–59. Reprinted in Cox (1985), pp.111–29.

Fowler, Doreen. 'Matricide and the Mother's Revenge: *As I Lay Dying*', *Faulkner Journal*, 4:1–2 (Fall 1988/Spring 1989), pp.113–25.

Pierce, Constance. 'Being, Knowing, and Saying in the "Addie" Section of Faulkner's *As I Lay Dying*', *Twentieth Century Literature: A Scholarly and Critical Journal*, 26 (1980), pp.294–305.

Ross, Stephen M. '"Voice" in Narrative Texts: The Example of *As I Lay Dying*', *PMLA*, 94:2 (March 1979), pp.300–10.

Simon, John K. 'The Scene and Imagery of Metamorphosis in *As I Lay Dying*'. *Criticism* 7:1 (Winter 1965), pp.1–22.

Tucker, John. 'William Faulkner's *As I Lay Dying*: Working Out the Cubistic Bugs'. *Texas Studies in Language and Literature*, 26:4 (Winter 1984), pp.388–404.

Reviews
Anon. 'A Witch's Brew'. *The New York Times Book Review* (19 October 1930), p.6. Reprinted in Bassett (1975), pp.93–94.

Davenport, Basil. 'In the Mire'. *Saturday Review of Literature* (22 November 1930), p.362.

Fadiman, Clifton P. 'Morbidity in Fiction'. *The Nation*, 131:3409 (5 November 1930), pp.500–1.

Gould, Gerald. 'New Novels: Six Books in Search of a Theory', *The Observer* (Sunday 29 September 1935), p.6. Section on *As I Lay Dying* reprinted in Bassett (1975), pp.97–98.

McClure, John [Baker, Julia K. Wetherill]. 'Literature and Less'. *The Times-*

Picayune (26 October 1930), p. 33. Partly reprinted in Bassett (1975), pp. 95–96 and in Inge (1995), pp. 47–48.

Muir, Edwin. 'New Novels', *The Listener* (16 October 1935), p. 681. Section on *As I Lay Dying* reprinted (with omission of quotation from the novel) in Bassett (1975), pp. 99–100.

Wade, John Donald. 'The South in its Fiction'. *Virginia Quarterly Review*, 7 (1931), pp. 124–29 (pp. 125–26 focus on *As I Lay Dying*).

White, Kenneth. '*As I Lay Dying* by William Faulkner'. *New Republic* (19 November 1930), p. 27.

Essays on *The Sound and the Fury* and *As I Lay Dying*

Campbell, Harry M. 'Experiment and Achievement: *As I Lay Dying* and *The Sound and the Fury*'. *Sewanee Review*, 51 (Spring 1943), pp. 305–20.

Collins, Carvel. 'The Pairing of *The Sound and the Fury* and *As I Lay Dying*'. *Princeton University Library Chronicle*, 18 (Spring 1957), pp. 114–23.

Lilly, Paul R., Jr. 'Caddy and Addie: Speakers of Faulkner's Impeccable Language'. *Journal of Narrative Technique*, 3 (1973), pp. 170–80.

Essays and books on Faulkner and Toni Morrison

Dahill-Baue, William. 'Insignificant Monkeys: Preaching Black English in Faulkner's *The Sound and the Fury* and Morrison's *The Bluest Eye* and *Beloved*'. *Mississippi Quarterly*, 3 (Summer 1996), pp. 457–73.

Kolmerten, Carol A., Ross, Stephen M., Wittenberg, Judith Bryant, eds. *Unflinching Gaze: Morrison and Faulkner Re-Envisioned* (Jackson: University Press of Mississippi, 1997).

Faulkner and film

Faulkner worked on a number of occasions as a Hollywood scriptwriter and his MGM scripts have been published as *Faulkner's MGM Screenplays*, Bruce F. Kawin, ed. (Knoxville: University of Tennessee Press, 1982). Several of his novels have been adapted into films – for example, *Pylon* (1935) became *The Tarnished Angels* (1957), directed by Douglas Sirk. A film of *The Sound and the Fury* was made in 1959, directed by Martin Ritt, with Jack Warden as Benjy, Yul Brunner as Jason and Joanne Woodward as Miss Quentin. *Halliwell's 1997 Film and Video Guide* (1996) quotes Stanley Kauffman's judgement on this film – '[a] fourth carbon copy of Chekhov in Dixie' (p. 698) – and Hahn and Kinney (1996) remark that '[t]he film significantly reinterprets the characters and the story line of the novel without providing insight into Faulkner's narrative' (p. 22). They recommend the following books for those interested in Faulkner and film:

Harrington, Evans and Abadie, Ann J., eds. *Faulkner, Modernism and Film: Faulkner and Yoknapatawpha, 1978*. Jackson: University Press of Mississippi, 1979.

Kawin, Bruce F. *Faulkner and Film*. New York: Ungar, 1977.

Phillips, Gene D., S.J. *Fiction, Film and Faulkner: The Art of Adaptation*. Knoxville: University of Tennessee Press, 1988.

ACKNOWLEDGEMENTS

The editor and publisher wish to thank the following for their permission to reprint copyright material: Norwood Editions (for material from *On William Faulkner's 'The Sound and the Fury'*); Hutchinson (for material from 'On *The Sound and the Fury*: Time in the Work of Faulkner'); Penguin (for material from *The Portable Faulkner*); Michigan State University Press (for material from *William Faulkner: Four Decades of Criticism*); University of Chicago Press (for material from *William Faulkner: A Critical Study*); Louisiana State University Press (for material from *The Novels of William Faulkner: A Critical Interpretation*); Yale University Press (for material from *William Faulkner: The Yoknapatawpha Country*); Constable (for material from *The Achievement of William Faulkner*); Indiana University Press (for material from *Faulkner's 'As I Lay Dying'* and *The Most Splendid Failure: Faulkner's 'The Sound and the Fury'*); Johns Hopkins University Press (for material from *Doubling and Incest/Repetition and Revenge: A Speculative Reading of Faulkner* and *Faulkner: The House Divided*); Methuen (for material from *Figures of Division: William Faulkner's Major Novels*); University Press of Mississippi (for material from *Robbing the Mother: Women in Faulkner* and *Faulkner and the Artist: Faulkner and Yoknapatawpha, 1993*); *Mississippi Quarterly* (for material from 'Insignificant Monkeys: Preaching Black English in Faulkner's *The Sound and the Fury* and Morrison's *The Bluest Eye* and *Beloved*').

There are instances where we have been unable to trace or contact copyright holders before our printing deadline. If notified, the publisher will be pleased to acknowledge the use of copyright material.

The editor is most grateful to his wife, Angela Tredell, and to her colleagues in East Sussex Library Services, especially Carol Russell and Shirley Race, for their speed and efficiency in obtaining copies of the many books and essays consulted in the preparation of this Guide.

Nicolas Tredell teaches American and English literature, art history, and cultural and film studies for Sussex University. He has contributed widely to journals in the UK and the USA, and his recent books include *Uncancelled Challenge: The Work of Raymond Williams*, *The Critical Decade: Culture in Crisis*, *Conversations with Critics*, *Caute's Confrontations: The Novels of David Caute*, and the Icon Critical Guides to *The Great Gatsby*, *Great Expectations* and 'Heart of Darkness'. He is currently preparing a Critical Guide to the fiction of Martin Amis, to be published in Spring 2000.

INDEX

Note: Abbreviations used in the index are: *ALD* for *As I Lay Dying*; WF for William Faulkner; *SF* for *The Sound and the Fury*. Books are listed under the names of their authors, except for *As I Lay Dying* and *The Sound and the Fury*, which are entered under their titles.